"Gaku Iwai tactfully achieves his aim of th
interpretation of a clichéd remark that Law
multilayered and overdetermined' by aptly p
political Zeitgeist. He is particularly succes
wartime writings, showing how intimatel
the atmosphere of the age by closely exam
tory book, *Movements in European Histo*
Lawrence's exquisite encapsulation of the
makes his works a profound testimony of m

—**Masas**
Kyot

"This new book by Gaku Iwai is a great
scholarship worldwide from which both sch
It discusses in detail a central aspect of La
motiv of British Culture in the early 20th ce
conflicts within social classes and the profou
overcoming British society at that time. Wi
of Lawrence's works, spanning from the
to *Lady Chatterley's Lover* and taking int
Movements in European History, Gaku Iv
conflicting aspect in Lawrence's aesthetic
forces and perspectives within his oeuvre,
writer appealing to the new generations."

—**S**

D. H. Lawrence and Ambivalence in the Age of Modernity

D. H. Lawrence is renowned for his scathing criticism of the ruling class, industrialisation of the country and wartime patriotism. However, his texts bear the imprint of contemporary dominant ideologies and discourses of the period. Comparing Lawrence's texts to various major and minor contemporary novels, journal articles, political pamphlets and history books, this book aims to demonstrate that Lawrence's texts are ambivalent: his texts harbour the dynamism of conflicting power struggles between the subversive and the reactionary. For example, in some apparently apolitical texts such as *The White Peacock* and *Movements in European History*, reactionary ideologies and wartime propaganda are embedded. Some texts like *Lady Chatterley's Lover* are intended to be a radical critique of the period wherein it was composed, but they also bear discernible traces of the contemporary frame of reference that they intend to subvert. Focusing on Lawrence's stories and novels set in the mining countryside and the works composed under the impact of the First World War, this book establishes that Lawrence's texts in fact consist of multiple layers that are often in conflict with each other, serving as a testimony to the age of modernity.

Gaku Iwai is Professor of English at Konan University in Kobe, Japan. He is a co-editor and co-translator of the Japanese version of the *Collected Letters of D. H. Lawrence*, and the former chief editor of *Japan D. H. Lawrence Studies*. He has published numerous articles on D. H. Lawrence, J. M. Barrie, J. G. Ballard and Margaret Atwood, among others. He is also a co-author of several books on Lawrence and twentieth-century British writers, including *D. H. Lawrence, Technology, and Modernity* (Bloomsbury Academic, 2019).

Routledge Studies in Twentieth-Century Literature

Strategies of Ambiguity
Edited by Matthias Bauer and Angelika Zirker

The Literary Role of History in the Fiction of J. R. R. Tolkien
Nicholas Birns

Valencian Folktales, Volume 2
Enric Valor
Edited and Translated by Paul Scott Derrick and Maria-Lluïsa Gea-Valor

Queer Kinship in Sarah Schulman's AIDS Novels
Jarosław Milewski

Durée as Einstein-In-The-Heart
Mary Butts and Virginia Woolf
Candice Lee Kent

A Study of Owen Barfield's Poetry, Drama, and Fiction
Rider on Pegasus
Jeffrey Hipolito

George Orwell and Communist Poland
Émigré, Official and Clandestine Receptions
Krystyna Wieszczek

D. H. Lawrence and Ambivalence in the Age of Modernity
Rereading Midlands Novels and Wartime Writings in Social and Political Contexts
Gaku Iwai

For more information about this series, please visit: www.routledge.com/Routledge-Studies-in-Twentieth-Century-Literature/book-series/RSTLC

D. H. Lawrence and Ambivalence in the Age of Modernity

Rereading Midlands Novels and Wartime Writings in Social and Political Contexts

Gaku Iwai

Routledge
Taylor & Francis Group
NEW YORK AND LONDON

First published 2024
by Routledge
605 Third Avenue, New York, NY 10158

and by Routledge
4 Park Square, Milton Park, Abingdon, Oxon, OX14 4RN

Routledge is an imprint of the Taylor & Francis Group, an informa business

ISBN: 9781032675664 (hbk)
ISBN: 9781032675688 (pbk)
ISBN: 9781032675671 (ebk)

DOI: 10.4324/9781032675671

Typeset in Sabon
by Newgen Publishing UK

To Saori

Contents

Figures

Acknowledgements

I would like to thank the following editors and a publisher for granting me permission to draw on my essays. I thank Eunyoung Oh, president of the D. H. Lawrence Society of Korea, for permission to draw on "Degeneration, Aestheticism and Empire: Middle-Class Ideology in *The White Peacock*" in *D. H. Lawrence Studies*, vol. 12, no. 2, 2004, pp. 15–38. Parts of Chapter 2 were originally published as "Bestwood and the Morels under Evolution: Parallelism of Evolution in *Sons and Lovers*" in *Doshisha Literature*, vol. 45, 2002, pp. 41–57 and I am grateful to the editors for permission to reproduce it. I thank Ginette Katz-Roy, editor of *Études Lawrenciennes*, for permission to draw on "Wartime Ideology in 'The Thimble': A Comparative Study of Popular Wartime Romance and the Anti-romance of D. H. Lawrence", vol. 46, 2015 and "Did Lawrence Like or Hate the Germans? Wartime Discourse on War and Peace in *Movements in European History*", vol. 47, 2016. I thank Bloomsbury Academic for permission to draw on "To Produce, or Not to Produce, That is the Question: Technology, Democracy, and War in *Women in Love*" in Indrek Männiste (ed.), *D. H. Lawrence, Technology, and Modernity*, 2019, pp. 85–99.

I am also grateful for the generosity of copyright holders who granted me permission to publish images in their possession for no charge: The National Archives of the UK for "Young colliers and Eastwood Market cheapjacks. June 1913"; Harry Ransom Center, The University of Texas at Austin for "Landscape with shepherd, sheep, trees" by D. H. Lawrence.

Extracts from the *Cambridge Edition of The Letters and Works of D. H. Lawrence* © Cambridge University Press 1979–2018 and "Landscape with shepherd, sheep, trees" by D. H. Lawrence are reproduced by permission of Paper Lion Ltd, the Estate of Frieda Lawrence Ravagli and Cambridge University Press.

Finally, but most importantly, I am deeply grateful to the Lawrence scholars in Japan and around the world. Without their invaluable advice, constructive criticism and unwavering friendship, I would not have been able to accomplish this project. I would like to express special gratitude to the late Peter Preston, whose generous support and encouragement to a young student from Japan has eventually come to fruition in this book.

Abbreviations

Works of D. H. Lawrence

EME *England, My England and Other Stories*. Edited by Bruce Steele, Cambridge UP, 1990.
FLC *The First and Second Lady Chatterley Novels*. Edited by Dieter Mehl and Christa Jansohn, Cambridge UP, 1999.
"Fox" "The Fox." *A D. H. Lawrence Miscellany*. Edited by Harry T. Moore, Southern Illinois UP, 1959, pp. 28–48.
LCL *Lady Chatterley's Lover and A Propos of "Lady Chatterley's Lover."* Edited by Michael Squires, Cambridge UP, 1993.
LEA *Late Essays and Articles*. Edited by James T. Boulton, Cambridge UP, 2004.
MEH *Movements in European History*. Edited by Philip Crumpton, Cambridge UP, 1989.
Plays *The Plays*. Edited by Hans-Wilhelm Schwarze and John Worthen, Cambridge UP, 1999.
PM *Paul Morel*. Edited by Helen Baron, Cambridge UP, 2003.
PO *The Prussian Officer and Other Stories*. Edited by John Worthen, Cambridge UP, 1983.
Poems *The Poems*. Edited by Christopher Pollnitz, Cambridge UP, 2013–18. 3 vols.
R *The Rainbow*. Edited by Mark Kinkead-Weekes, Cambridge UP, 1989.
RDP *Reflections on the Death of a Porcupine and Other Essays*. Edited by Michael Herbert, Cambridge UP, 1988.
SCAL *Studies in Classic American Literature*. Edited by Ezra Greenspan, Lindeth Vasey, and John Worthen, Cambridge UP, 2003.
SL *Sons and Lovers*. Edited by Helen Baron and Carl Baron, Cambridge UP, 1992.
STH *Study of Thomas Hardy and Other Essays*. Edited by Bruce Steele, Cambridge UP, 1985.

VicG The Vicar's Garden and Other Stories. Edited by N. H. Reeve, Cambridge UP, 2009.

WL Women in Love. Edited by David Farmer, Lindeth Vasey, and John Worthen, Cambridge UP, 1987.

WP The White Peacock. Edited by Andrew Robertson, Cambridge UP, 1983.

1L The Letters of D. H. Lawrence: Volume I: September 1901–May 1913. Edited by James T. Boulton, Cambridge UP, 1979.

2L The Letters of D. H. Lawrence: Volume II: June 1913–October 1916. Edited by George J. Zytaruk and James T. Boulton, Cambridge UP, 1981.

3L The Letters of D. H. Lawrence: Volume III: October 1916–June 1921. Edited by James T. Boulton and Andrew Robertson, Cambridge UP, 1984.

Other Works

BR Report of the Committee on Alleged German Outrages Appointed by His Britannic Majesty's Government and Presided over by the Right Hon. Viscount Bryce. HMSO, 1915.

EY John Worthen, *D. H. Lawrence: The Early Years 1885–1912*. Cambridge UP, 1991.

Gibbon 1 Edward Gibbon. *The Decline and Fall of the Roman Empire*. 1776. Edited by Oliphant Smeaton, vol. 1, Dent, 1910.

Gibbon 3 Edward Gibbon. *The Decline and Fall of the Roman Empire*. 1781. Edited by Oliphant Smeaton, vol. 3, Dent, 1910.

KK Berta Ruck, *Khaki and Kisses*. Hutchinson, 1915.

TE Mark Kinkead-Weekes, *D. H. Lawrence: Triumph to Exile 1912–1922*. Cambridge UP, 1996.

Introduction

> So that I myself could never go back into the working class, to the blindness, the obtuseness, the prejudice, the mass-emotions. But neither can I adapt myself to the middle-class, to sacrifice the old, deep blood-affinity between myself and my fellows.
>
> D. H. Lawrence, "Which Class I Belong To"

In one of his late essays, "Which Class I Belong To", D. H. Lawrence expresses his ambivalence towards both the working and middle classes. While he was a miner's son, Lawrence was elevated to intellectual society as a notable yet often controversial literary figure. Lawrence authored many literary works—from his first novel, *The White Peacock*, to his last, *Lady Chatterley's Lover*—set in his birthplace, a provincial Nottingham district. In his writings, he portrayed the bucolic lives of local farmers, miners, their families and gamekeepers, who became involved, or came into conflict, with middle- and upper-class characters including clergymen, their daughters, industrial managers and owners of country manors. As implied by the above-quoted passage, his texts reveal his complex feelings towards these two classes between which he believed there was "the indefinable gulf" (*LEA* 37): his inborn sympathy with, and unconquerable aversion to, the working class; likewise, his lifelong hostility to, and secret longing for, the middle class. For example, Paul Morel, the protagonist of *Sons and Lovers*, cannot form emotional ties with his father and abhors miners' working-class lifestyle. However, he forms a curious, close friendship with Baxter Dawes, who is a mirror image of his own father. Lawrence's mother was actually of the working class, but in the autobiographical novel, Mrs Morel is elevated to the middle class.[1] Paul holds a deep affection for his mother, who inculcates a middle-class sense of values in her son. Despite this, he tells her, "I don't want to belong to the well-to-do middle class. I like my common people best. I belong to the common people" (*SL* 298). Eventually, by his own hand, Paul hastens his middle-class mother's death,

DOI: 10.4324/9781032675671-1

not his father's, in opposition to the Oedipus complex theory, by which this novel has often been interpreted.[2]

Around the First World War, Lawrence's criticisms against the bourgeoisie became particularly noticeable. From then on, he persistently attacked them for the rest of his life. In his letters, essays and novels, he denounced middle-class attitudes and views, the bourgeois society that suppressed human emotions and the industrial civilisation built upon the materialist principles embraced by the middle classes. As a result, Lawrence is notorious for his unique and subversive texts. His fourth novel, *The Rainbow*, was banned on a charge of obscenity. His last novel, *Lady Chatterley's Lover*, led to the infamous trial, to mention just a few examples.

Nonetheless, I would argue that Lawrence's texts are also influenced by reactionary discourses, which were often created and dispersed by the ruling class at the turn of the century and in the early twentieth century. On the one hand, Lawrence's texts criticise the middle-class characters, industrialisation of the country and wartime patriotism. On the other hand, his texts are inscribed with dominant ideologies and discourses of the period—for example, social Darwinism that represented the middle-class views of the world, middle-class fear of the working class or wartime ideologies that helped justify the cause of the nation. Consequently, Lawrence's texts are ambivalent; they comprise plural elements and consist of multiple layers that are often in conflict with each other, unlike monologic texts that serve as mere propaganda and shallow media for the authors' messages.

Attempts to distil Lawrence's messages from his texts and decipher his fiction solely from the perspective of its authorial philosophy would reduce his creations to monologic texts. In doing so, we would fail to grasp their complexity and slight the historical contexts within which they were produced. Lawrence's shrewd remarks on modern civilisation or on how we lead our lives have fascinated (or repulsed) so many readers that critiques of him have tended towards monologic interpretations. However, several recent Lawrence studies have attempted to reveal the fact that the contemporary discourses infiltrated into Lawrence's texts. Studies ranging from Roger Ebbatson's *Lawrence and the Nature Tradition: A Theme in English Fiction 1859–1914* (1980) to David Game's *D. H. Lawrence's Australia: Anxiety at the Edge of Empire* (2015) have explored how evolutionary ideas are embedded in Lawrence's writings. I share a particular interest with Game who remarks that "[m]uch of Lawrence's *oeuvre* … register[s] contemporary anxieties about moral and social degeneration and about race and empire, which arose after the emergence of Darwinism, Social Darwinism and the intense industrialisation of the mid to late nineteenth century".[3] Andrew Harrison reveals in *D. H. Lawrence and Italian*

Futurism: A Study of Influence (2003) that Lawrence's writings, particularly from the last draft of *The Rainbow* to *Studies in Classic American Literature*, incorporate elements of Italian Futurism, contributing to the development of Lawrence's distinctive style and his thematic concerns. The First World War is an indispensable theme for Lawrence because he was one of the writers most dramatically affected by the war. Carl Krockel explores the magnitude of the impact of the Great War through its historical, cultural and ideological contexts in *D. H. Lawrence and Germany: The Politics of Influence* (2007) and *War Trauma and English Modernism: T. S. Eliot and D. H. Lawrence* (2011). More recently, Andrew F. Humphries focuses on the literal and metaphorical uses of transport in Lawrence's works in *D. H. Lawrence, Transport and Cultural Transition: "A Great Sense of Journeying"* (2017). He examines how Lawrence portrayed the interactions between the evolution of transport vehicles and pivotal questions related to human development in a period of social and technological turmoil.

My indebtedness to these studies is acknowledged in the chapters that follow. On the basis of these recent scholarship, my aim in this book is to divulge textual ambivalence in Lawrence's writings. I clarify my intentions by advantageously referencing two predecessors in Lawrence's criticism, Graham Holderness and Anne Fernihough. These critics revealed the ideological conflicts inherent in Lawrence's works. Holderness demonstrated that Lawrence's novels vacillate between the realist and mythological styles: the former approach dramatises human experience within a specific social and historical context and the latter aesthetic transforms a real historical society into a satisfying myth. Holderness further indicated that the pastoral world of Lawrence's creation was a myth designed to function as an ideological apparatus through which social contradictions were harmonised, dissolved or evaded. Fernihough demonstrated how the ambivalent concept of the organic functioned in Lawrence's writings as both reactionary and subversive. On the one hand, the idea of *völkisch* organicism, an ideology prevailing in Germany in the 1910s and 1920s, accorded Lawrence with a vocabulary set and imagery that would later associate him with fascism. On the other hand, another concept of the organic that rejected the mimetic, or logocentric, model of language helped Lawrence fashion the art theory ("aesthetics") that works of art could produce conflicting and pluralistic meanings. Fernihough argued that Lawrence's aesthetics celebrated difference and polyvalence and could thus contradict his authoritarian philosophy and subvert his own texts. Lawrence's art criticism could hence act as an antidote to the authoritarian politics he expressed, for example, in his leadership novels.

The readings of Lawrence's texts by the aforementioned critics and my construals do not necessarily converge at certain points, and there may be several issues that remain to be disputed in their studies. For example, Holderness' rather naïve contention that a work of art should embody "a wholeness of experience" and achieve "a complex but cohesive totality" (Holderness 156, 153) sounds Lukácian but is also reminiscent of the Romantic humanist tradition and somewhat approximates what he rather pejoratively called "[b]ourgeois critical practice" (11). In addition, he asserted Lawrence's "uncompromising and unremitting hatred of and opposition to the war" (193) and thus disregarded Lawrence's hidden fascination for the destructive impulse and his affirmation of war. Jeff Wallace also noted Fernihough's rather incautious categorisation of scientific discourse and technology as a phenomenon constructed through the mimetic model of language, which could risk positioning Lawrence in opposition to science, like the Leavisite humanist approach.[4]

Nonetheless, the examinations performed by Holderness and Fernihough divulged significant facets of Lawrence's texts. They demonstrated that works of art represent ideological constructs distinct from their author's intentions and proved that Lawrence's texts were no exception. These two critics revealed that Lawrence's texts encompassed internal ideological conflicts that I label "ambivalence". Holderness disclosed that the working class writer's works were not as radical and subversive as were thought and that Lawrence's texts contained numerous reactionary elements. Likewise, Fernihough argued that the writer's political doctrines could be counteracted by an implicit pluralism that invalidated rigid dualities and hierarchies.

I supplement these readings in the current study by repositioning Lawrence's texts into social and political contexts at the turn of the century and in the early twentieth century and thereby demonstrate that they are ambivalent, multilayered and overdetermined. Lawrence's texts frequently and ostensibly criticise the middle classes or the ongoing war; yet, they often simultaneously embrace bourgeois values or wartime propaganda. Contemporary conservative discourses infiltrate Lawrence's texts despite his severe denigration of certain tenets. Consequently, Lawrence's texts often harbour the dynamism of conflicting power struggles between the subversive and the reactionary.

Those who seized power and control in the age of modernity began to ruthlessly exploit people at home, at work and overseas. The development of industrial technology and capitalism enabled the mass manipulation of the working classes by the ruling classes. Simultaneously, the period from the turn of the century to the first few decades of the twentieth century witnessed the decline of bourgeois hegemony and the rise of the working classes, along with the diminishing sway of the British Empire. In Britain, the coal mining industry exemplified the extensive exploitation of people and their enslavement by mechanical technology. Several miners were mobilised in coal mining districts; the industry was mechanised, and the first few decades of the twentieth century witnessed the most intense conflicts between mine owners and mine workers. This misuse of the masses culminated in the First World War in which millions of young people and intensive mass technology were mustered on the battlefields. A gulf was subsequently created between sexes, generations and combatants versus non-combatants after the armistice. The emergence of a disabled working class of soldiers further threatened the governing stratum. Thus, the coal mining industry and the First World War epitomised social conflict in British society during the first few decades of the twentieth century. Therefore, this study focuses on Lawrence's stories and novels set in the mining countryside and the works he composed under the impact of the First World War.

In Chapter 1, I will analyse how *The White Peacock* endorses or opposes the middle-class narrator's perspective. The novel centres on the characters' love and friendship in a pastoral life within a local province, and it has often been read as an apolitical novel. The text, however, both implicitly and explicitly declares its preference for values favoured by the middle class, whose ideology formed political discourse at that time. Yet the text refuses to be simple propaganda and at times discloses the deception inherent in bourgeois ideology and exposes the actual situation of the rural district hidden under embellished visions.

Chapter 2 analyses *Sons and Lovers* and argues that the narrative structure of this text is pervaded by the dominant thought supported and propounded by middle-class intellectuals at the turn of the century—social Darwinism. Together with Arthur Schopenhauer's idea on procreation, Herbert Spencer's theory of social evolution penetrates the narrative. Spencer's influence has been highlighted by several critics in terms of common terminologies and references, but it permeates the text even more profoundly. This chapter demonstrates that procreation and evolution dominate the overall frame of its narrative.

The Rainbow has been conceived as a prequel to *Women in Love* and is often considered to mark a new phase in Lawrence's composition. Few would deny this fact, but this view seems to have allowed critics to disregard its connection with the previous novel. In Chapter 3, I argue that the basic framework of the narrative found in *Sons and Lovers* also dominates *The Rainbow*. The latter novel is again structured by procreation and evolution, the Lawrentian variation of Spencerian theory.

In Chapters 4 and 5, Lawrence's history textbook, *Movements in European History*, is discussed at length. This textbook, simple in prose for adolescents, has often been considered a mere potboiler. Therefore, it has been dedicated a relatively small place in the literature on Lawrence. *Movements in European History* is, however, a significant text to help decipher Lawrence's other wartime texts as it offers a good example of how contemporary discourses, and the author's responses to them, are inextricably entwined. In Chapter 4, I will summarise the historical context of the First World War and its influence on Lawrence and other British writers. First, I will examine how Lawrence's harsh condemnations of the war in his letters are intermingled with wartime discourses and national ideologies. I will also explore the historical context wherein several British writers composed their history books—Rudyard Kipling and C. R. L. Fletcher's *A School History of England* (1911), G. K. Chesterton's *A Short History of England* (1917) and H. G. Wells' *The Outline of History* (1920), in addition to Lawrence's *Movements*.

In Chapter 5, I will focus on the three chapters in *Movements in European History*—"The Germans", "The Huns" and "The Unification of Germany". I will compare these chapters with history books mentioned above primarily in terms of the anti-German discourse during the First World War. I will also juxtapose Lawrence's text with his sourcebooks, such as Edward Gibbon's *The Decline and Fall of the Roman Empire* (1776–88) and A. J. Grant's *A History of Europe* (1913). These analyses will reveal that within Lawrence's history book are inscribed traces of the controversial issues and anxieties that swirled throughout wartime Britain.

The next novel, *Women in Love*, is set in the early twentieth century, but the First World War is absent from the text and no war erupts in it. Despite this fact, contemporary wartime ideological discourse runs throughout *Women in Love*. The Great War had a considerable impact on the author and British society, and Lawrence's texts after the mid-1910s cannot be fully interpreted without reference to wartime ideologies. Chapter 6 challenges the conventional views of this novel—Birkin being a mouthpiece of the author, and Gerald representing destruction and the negative aspects in terms of Lawrentian philosophy—by analysing the text in terms of contemporary discourse on democracy, new liberalism and Germanophobia.

Chapter 7 examines several of Lawrence's wartime short stories. Lawrence's short stories have been analysed mainly in terms of their artistic achievements or in relation to the development of the author's philosophical ideas. His wartime stories are, however, deeply influenced by the huge impact of the Great War and should be analysed in the historical context of the war. In the first section, I analyse "The Thimble", which was composed during the first phase of the war in 1915. This short story is compared with a contemporary melodrama "The Infant-in Arms" by a popular writer Berta Ruck. The analysis will show that while Lawrence's story was composed as a severe satire on the romances that were immensely popular during wartime, it simultaneously embraces the wartime ideology that these popular romances espoused. In the second section, I examine Lawrence's poems composed in 1915, "New Heaven and Earth" and "Eloi, Eloi, Lama Sabachthani", along with the 1915 version of "England, My England". Like "The Thimble", these works explore themes of war and resurrection, albeit in a distinct manner. Reading these works as complementary texts elucidates the similarities and differences in the visions of resurrection portrayed in Lawrence's texts.

In the next section of Chapter 7, Lawrence's short stories composed during the last phase of the war, "The Blind Man" and "Tickets Please", are analysed to prove how deeply the condition and atmosphere of Britain around the armistice is inscribed in these ambivalent texts. Many of his wartime stories show a similar pattern: an outsider sets foot in a community and helplessly struggles to foster communion and intimacy, but he/she remains alienated as an intruder. This plot discloses the dark side of British society, which is overshadowed by a brave and belligerent nationalism. The analysis will reveal that while Lawrence's texts at the late-war period show traces of national ideologies, they simultaneously subvert contemporary wartime discourse.

Chapter 8 diachronically investigates the transition of the ruling-class perception of the working class that permeates Lawrence's texts, from the pre-war phase to the last. Plots of "Daughters of the Vicar", "Hadrian" and *Lady Chatterley's Lover* display the same pattern, where a working-class man disrupts the lives of a secluded governing-class family in a mining community. These works are ostensibly a critique of an outdated and inflexible upper- and middle-class society. However, the analysis will reveal that the first two stories are imbued with bourgeois anxiety for the working-class revolt. Moreover, while the former story reassures a bourgeois readership, the latter is more deeply inscribed with the middle-class fear of the working class. *Lady Chatterley's Lover* has also often been read as Lawrence's condemnation of the ruling class and admiration of the working-class gamekeeper. The last novel is, however, not so simplistic and rather dismantles such a dualist reading. By analysing the novel's class representations, the contemporary discourse on Englishness and the novel's hidden affinity with Lawrence's wartime play *Touch and Go*, I will discuss how and the degree to which *Lady Chatterley's Lover* integrates dominant contemporary discourses within itself. The period from the late Victorian era to the first few decades of the twentieth century witnessed the decline of the bourgeois hegemony and rise of the working class. This chapter demonstrates that Lawrence's texts record the transition of middle-class views concerning the rising lower classes.

Annihilating Borders: Nature, Human Beings, Machinery in "Odour of Chrysanthemums"

To conclude the introductory section, I would like to analyse "Odour of Chrysanthemums" as it presents some crucial points that would be discussed in the later chapters of this study. "Odour of Chrysanthemums" is set in the mining countryside and depicts an evening in the life of a local family. The narrative begins with the portrayal of those who inhabit and occupy the place—nature, human beings and machinery. The opening scene encompasses the three essential elements of the story. The first of these features concerns the relationship between nature and civilisation. These two facets are usually regarded as opposites; however, they do not necessarily contrast in this instance. Second, the narrative discloses the exploitation of nature by human beings, resulting in the advancement of mechanisation. Third, the story reveals the mode of human existence in the mining community caught in the process of shifting from anonymity to individuality. These three themes are symbolically presented in the initial tableau and are developed in the ensuing segments. I will focus on these three facets to examine the peculiar coexistence of nature, human beings and machinery in "Odour of Chrysanthemums".

The story begins with a "woman" with a basket "trapped" (*PO* 181) between the locomotive and the hedge. This scene apparently implies the relationship between nature, human beings and machines and elicits the typical interpretation of this text. Nature and civilisation are deemed opposites and human beings are immobile, captured between the two opposing forces.[5] In actuality, however, the boundaries between nature and civilisation are not so definite. For example, a hedge is planted for personal use by human beings and the locomotive is both constructed and operated by men.

Nature, human beings and machines do not exist separately in this story; instead, they are intimately intertwined. Julian Moynahan regards the pond and the pit-bank as counterparts that respectively represent nature and civilisation, but as Holderness indicates, the pond denotes a pit-pond that straddles both nature and civilisation.[6] Also, natural creatures are domesticated by people and become dependent on human beings: for instance, the fowls return to "the tarred fowl-house" (181) as their nest. The locomotive symbolises the threat of mechanical civilisation, appearing with clanking noise and menacing speed. Nevertheless, machines are not necessarily represented as external evils that have befallen humanity. The locomotive is fuelled by coals, a mineral unearthed by people, and is operated by human hands. That the protagonist Elizabeth's father is a locomotive engineer is not a mere coincidence; the connection indicates that machines are not aliens imposed from outside. Conversely, it may be deemed that their seeds have been sown in nature considering that coal is formed from the remains of animals and plants and that the mineral contributes to the emergence and development of machinery. The boundaries between nature and civilisation thus remain elusive in the text: the world depicted in this story cannot be apprehended through such reductive dualism.

The opening scene furthermore indicates human existence in a countryside centred principally around the activity of coal mining. Here, human lives are defined by the extraction of coal. In other words, human survival is based on the exploitation of nature, as is also implied by the hedge and the fowl-house. This motif reappears after the opening scene in which the panoramic perspective narrows to focus on Elizabeth's cottage. The narrative minutely depicts the garden plants and the surrounding flora: a large, bony vine, wintry primroses, twiggy apple trees, winter-crack trees, ragged cabbages and dishevelled pink chrysanthemums. Trees, flowers and vegetables are planted, grown or cherished by human beings. People create gardens, which may be contemplated as nature domesticated and made artificial, signifying the exploitation and monopoly of nature by human beings.

Elizabeth appears from the fowl-house, a symbol of the human manipulation of animals, after the above depiction of the human-engineered plant life. This theme of the exploitation of nature recurs in the next scene and is more obviously presented as mother and the son walk to their home. Elizabeth calls her son John, who sits by a brook, and goes back home with him. John tears chrysanthemum petals and drops them along the path. His mother chides him for the act, but not because he spoils nature. Her reproof emanates from an aesthetic point of view: "Don't do that—it *does* look nasty" (182; emphasis in original). She then breaks off a twig with some flowers and pushes it into her apron band. This spray is later placed in a vase in her home. The story's eponymic flower alludes to the human possession of nature in this description.

The narrative also illustrates human relations in the mining community, disclosing its process of metamorphosis into a town. Part I of the story portrays people rather anonymously: their obscurity is indicated by the introductory labelling of the protagonist merely as "a woman". The characters—the heroine as well as the miners and the Bates household—are presented as unindividual beings, as if they were not known by proper names. The miners are portrayed collectively as faceless, unindividual beings like "the miners, in grey sombre groups" (183) and "the dreary flow of men" (184). Their indiscriminate collectivity reveals the deprivation of their mode of being; they exist simply as a collective designated as the "miners" and not as individuals.

Such human existence is not unique to this story. It often appears in Lawrence's portrayals of mining countryside. The unindividuated miners of this story remind us of the ones in Wiggiston, owned by Ursula's uncle Tom in *The Rainbow*, or the anonymous, uncanny miners seen by Connie in Tevershall in *Lady Chatterley's Lover*. Tom argues that in Wiggiston, the miners are not individual beings; they merely discharge their roles in the mines or at home, forming an anonymous identity:

> Her husband was John Smith, loader. We reckoned him as a loader, he reckoned himself as a loader, and so she knew he represented his job. … One man or another, it doesn't matter all the world.
>
> (*R* 323)

The miners exist merely as the executors of their jobs and remain impersonal and interchangeable.

It is not only the miners who are deprived of their individuality in the first half of "Odour of Chrysanthemums"; the anonymity of their existence also pervades their homes. The mine and the home parallel each other in this text, as is indicated when Elizabeth calls her house "this dirty hole" (*PO* 187) as she waits for her husband to return home. The mine and the home are both dirty, gloomy and enclosed spaces; the wives who wait for their husbands are hemmed in within the walls of their homes just as much as the miners digging coal are trapped in underground tunnels.

The mother and the children of the Bates household are presented as characters who do exist but who remain strangely obscured. Elizabeth cannot spot her son in the dark when she comes out of the fowl-house and calls to him. The blurring of identities is even more clearly illustrated in the section that describes Elizabeth and the children beginning their tea after waiting for the father to return home. John is "almost hidden in shadow, only his movement seemed visible" (184), but he is not the only one who cannot be seen. None can see the faces of the others:

> John, at the end of the table near the door, was almost lost in the darkness. Their faces were hidden from each other. …
>
> Soon the room was busy in the darkness with the crisp sound of crunching.
>
> (185)

The text often deprives the members of the Bates family of their names as well as their faces. They are rarely addressed by their names and are generally referenced through common nouns such as "the mother", "the son" or "the boy". In the abovementioned tea scene in front of the fireplace, they are both faceless and nameless, dispossessed of any individuality, just as the miners (and, in fact, Elizabeth's father remains unnamed in the entire story). Their existence is instead defined by the roles they discharge within the family: the parents, children, wife or husband:

> The girl crouched against the fender slowly moving a thick piece of bread before the fire. The lad … sat watching her. …
>
> "I do think it's beautiful to look in the fire," said the child.
>
> "Do you?" said her mother. "Why?"
>
> "It's so red, and full of little caves—and it feels so nice, and you can fair smell it."
>
> "It'll want mending directly," replied her mother.
>
> (185)

Hence, human relationships are formed in this story through the network of family relations. The characters face others not as individuals with certain personalities but as faceless unindividuals who fill the relational slots of a parent, child or wife within a family network to which they have no choice but to be attached. Elizabeth's father thinks of remarrying because "Well, what's a man to do? It's no sort of life for a man of my years, to sit at my own hearth like a stranger" (183). It is not that her father desires to marry a particular person; rather he wants to fill a vacancy in the family network, an empty place that can easily be occupied by another person.

Such an attitude is not unique to the old locomotive driver; it is shared by his daughter. When Elizabeth hears that her husband may have been involved in an accident, her first thought concerns whether she can live on the pension she would receive:

> If he was killed—would she be able to manage on the little pension and what she could earn?—she counted up rapidly. … She turned to consider the children. … They were her business.
>
> (192)

Presumably, she uses the word "business" to allude to her duty as a mother. The term "husband" can hence be replaced by money as well as another male.

Such human relationships are also reminiscent of the Wiggiston scene in *The Rainbow*. Tom explains to Ursula that a woman who loses her husband to an accident in Wiggiston soon remarries another man. Whom she marries is of little importance; her partner must play the roles of "husband" and "miner": "But that's how they are. She'll be getting married again directly. One man or another—it doesn't matter very much. They're all colliers" (*R* 323). Both *The Rainbow* and "Odour of Chrysanthemums" depict similar human relationships characteristic of Lawrentian mining countries. Their characters are identified only by the roles they play in the societal or familial unit. People are entwined and dispersed within networks of social relations in which human relationships are established only through their functions as miners, husbands, wives and children. People exist masked in their roles, disconnected from the plane of immanence, or the field of individuality.

This absence of individuality pervades the mining villages and is symbolically associated with coal fires. Colliery flares occur through the spontaneous combustion of scattered pit refuse: "The pit-bank loomed up beyond the pond, flames like red sores licking its ashy sides ..." (*PO* 181). Dim flames burn fireplaces at the miners' home: "The kitchen was small and full of firelight; red coals piled glowing up the chimney mouth" (184). As evinced in the tea scene, the coal fire can only dimly illuminate obscure figures and does not reveal faces. Coal fires burn in mines and homes, and both places are conducive to anonymous human relations.

Such interpersonal connections nevertheless start transfiguring when the mother turns on the oil lamp, whose artificial light encourages the individualisation of the characters. Unlike the coal fire, which lights obscurely, the oil lamp shines to reveal faces. Elizabeth can now see her children's expressions as well as the hands of the clock: "She looked at the children. Their eyes and their parted lips were wondering. The mother sat rocking in silence for some time. Then she looked at the clock" (187). The room is no longer shrouded by hanging shadows and the narrative starts using proper names. The light of oil lamps bestows names to characters, erasing anonymity. The protagonist is increasingly called "Elizabeth" and "Elizabeth Bates" in the second half of the story. The light of the oil lamps starts to dominate homes instead of coal fires, and oil lamps begin to illuminate the whole mining town.

Coal fire is superseded by the oil lamp, indicating a civilisational phase of transition. Coal flames symbolically shape the anonymous human relationships in the mining village. However, the more coals are dug up, the more the village undergoes a metamorphosis. Work becomes mechanised and locomotives begin connecting one pit to another as the mining industry develops. Oil lamps begin to be used at home and the street lamps light the roads. The mining village transforms into a town. Within the homes, the light of oil lamps accords proper names to every member of the family. This correlation between civilisation and individuality is indicated at the beginning of the story, where the locomotive is given the distinctive marker "Number 4", unlike the human beings who appear only anonymously. While the text depicts the anonymous relationships kindled by coal fires in a mining village, it simultaneously signifies the transitioning of a mining village into a town.

"Odour of Chrysanthemums" concludes as Elizabeth realises the falsity of her relationship with her husband when she sees and touches his corpse after it is brought home by some miners. The dead Walter is peaceful, beautiful, pristine and pure, but also elicits a degree of fear and respect. She then immediately recognises the hollowness of her association with Walter: she has seen him not as an individual physical being but merely as the "husband" in her familial network. She also perceives that the terms such as "husband", "wife" and "children" do not really connect physical beings: "She was a mother—but how awful she knew it now to have been a wife. And he, dead now, how awful he must have felt it to be a husband" (198). Touching Walter's corpse, Elizabeth finally comprehends the existence of a physical being as an other. In front of her is neither a "husband" nor an individual named Walter Bates. It is a physical being as an other that is sacred and that no one can violate. It is salient to note the circumstances that enlighten this realisation in her: her moment of epiphany occurs not by the fire of the fireplace, nor by the oil lamp light that promotes individualisation. It happens under the tiny flame of a candle. Her moment of insight is markedly contrasted with the fact that the doctor's medical and scientific diagnosis of Walter's asphyxiation occurs in a "lamp cabin" (193). Elizabeth would perhaps have not attained her awakening by the coal flames of the fireplace or the shining light of the oil lamp.

One of the carriers knocks off a vase of chrysanthemums when Walter's corpse is brought into the house, and the broken vase and the flowers scatter on the floor. Elizabeth explains to her children: "It was chrysanthemums when I married him, and chrysanthemums when you were born, and the first time they ever brought him home drunk he'd got brown chrysanthemums in his button-hole" (186). The eponymous flower is hence symbolically associated with the construction of the anonymous network of family relations. The broken vase and scattered chrysanthemums foreshadow her realisation of the falsity of her human connections with her family. The chrysanthemums epitomise these fallacies.

Walter's corpse was accidentally buried but evinces certain qualities that are curiously incompatible with death when it is brought to his home. Walter's dead body looks pristine. It exhibits no bruises and retains warmth because it was cocooned in the coal mine. To Elizabeth, it represents a sacred body in the naïve dignity of death; to his mother, it seems the radiant body of a newborn. The corpse extracted from the underground mine is rejuvenated and vital; it appears as a body resurrected with some energy from the womb of the earth.[7] Here, life is not opposed to death; the miner's death is not an acceptance of defeat or the demise of life at the last stage of a person's life cycle.

The ambivalence that Walter's dead body symbolises invalidates the dualism of life and death. Walter's corpse is inanimate but is filled with energy. It is exactly like coal, which is an ambivalent substance. It is necessary for the development of mechanical civilisation but it originates from the remains of living organisms that were once full of life. It is a dead nature but nurtured in the womb of the earth and servile to man's industry and enlivens machinery. Coal is thus intrinsically ambivalent: a representative of dead carcasses that preserves vitality; a natural mineral that promotes mechanisation.

The dualist viewpoint is thus dissolved through the entire text of the story. The mining town is indeed growing and progressing. Its advancement is symbolically associated with the transitioning of its illumination from coal fires to lamplights and the transfiguration of human existence from anonymity to individuality. As elucidated by this discussion of the beginning of the story, mechanisation is not represented as the threat of an alien invasion against innocent nature. Rather, the seeds of civilisation are always-already contained within nature. Lawrence's text presents the relationship between nature and civilisation as complicated and ambiguous. Dualist schemata are invalidated throughout "Odour of Chrysanthemums", from its introductory exposition to its ending scene with Walter's corpse. The text reveals the impossibility and futility of attempting to reductively impose dualist notions of nature and civilisation, living creatures and machinery, or life and death on Lawrence's texts.

"Odour of Chrysanthemums" encapsulates many features that appear and are developed in Lawrence's other works: the theme of a mining village transitioning to a town in tandem with the shift from candle-light to oil lamps and gas lights; the depiction of anonymous and individual modes of being; subversion of dualism; and, above all, the textual ambivalence symbolised by coal that permeates Lawrence's texts. In the chapters that follow, I shall delve into his texts to demonstrate their ambivalence by placing them in appropriate social and political contexts.

That Lawrence's texts encompass multiple and often conflicting layers rather than a single monologic plane does not signify a lack of unity or an impoverished literary quality. Literary texts denote domains where resistance, conflicts or endorsements are inscribed through textual production. Such texts occasionally become verbose and disclose more than the author desires to express; at other times, they lapse into silence. Lawrence knew this fact too well; hence, his famous dictum—"Never trust the artist. Trust the tale. The proper function of a critic is to save the tale from the artist who created it" (*SCAL* 14). This study does not deem the author's voice as authoritative; rather, it is regarded as one of the competing voices heard in the texts. The textual ambivalence of Lawrence's *oeuvre* serves as a testimony to the age of modernity and it is revealed by positioning the texts into their contemporary social and political milieu and by detecting the reverberations of history within them.

Notes

1 John Worthen, in his celebrated biography, argues that Mrs Morel "is truly middle-class. ... [I]t became an established fact in the early 1930s that the writer D. H. Lawrence had had a working-class father and a middle-class mother. In actuality, both families were working-class ..." (*EY* 26).
2 Since the publication of the first full-length psychoanalytic study in 1916 by the American psychoanalyst Alfred Kuttner, *Sons and Lovers* has been recognised as a typical example of an Oedipal text. Daniel A. Weiss, for example, analyses the novel and argues that his "study is guided by the conviction that the Oedipal situation, as Freud describes it, prevails in the novel. ... *Sons and Lovers* (and Lawrence is clear enough on this point) is about the Oedipus complex" (Weiss 16). More recently, for instance, Margaret Storch interprets the text in terms of Melanie Klein's theory of the infantile defence mechanism. See Storch 97–130.
3 Game 2. Game offers a full account of the influence of Darwinism on Lawrence's intellectual development and regenerative vision, providing a comprehensive critical history of Lawrence and (Social) Darwinism. See Game 9–64.
4 See Wallace, *Posthuman* 32. In his groundbreaking study, *D. H. Lawrence, Science and the Posthuman* (2005), Wallace examines how Lawrence encountered and reacted to the science of his time as an ideological phenomenon through texts written by Charles Darwin, Herbert Spencer, Ernst Haeckel, T. H. Huxley and William James. In this book, Wallace succinctly elucidates the theoretical contexts of the concept of the posthuman and delivers a detailed analysis of the validity of applying this concept to Lawrence's texts.
5 Julian Moynahan, for example, views the duality between nature and civilisation:

> The principle of composition here is simple contrast. ... We see colt against locomotive engine, jolting wagons against flying birds, pit bank against pond. ... These arrayed contrasts between machinery and a natural setting. ... A woman stands motionless, trapped between track and hedge. ... She disappears immediately from the story but the anomaly of this human entrapment remains and becomes the central, moving motive of the story.
> (Moynahan 182)

6 Holderness quotes the passage deleted before publication to argue that "This deleted passage makes no attempt to distinguish clearly and absolutely between 'organic' and 'mechanical', 'natural' and 'human', but insists instead that in this industrialised community, nature, industry and human beings inhabit the same dimension—one world" (132). Referring to "Odour of Chrysanthemums", *The Rainbow* and *Women in Love* in his posthumanist reading, Wallace also argues against the dualistic reading of Lawrence's texts: "Technology and nature are not locked into pure, hypostatized difference: rather, the human seems to be the locus within which technology can *become* nature, through habituation" (Wallace, *Posthuman* 35). Wallace is critical of the traditional Lawrence

criticisms that have been based on the humanist tradition of the simplified dichotomies such as human and anti-human, human and machine, instinct and reason. He claims, for example, that *Women in Love* "presents a fluidity of boundaries between definitions of organic and inorganic life in such a way as to suggest that it might finally be anthropocentrism, the privileging of the human itself, that is at the heart of the industrial problem. Animals people the novel almost as much as humans, and both are consistently described in vocabularies of material force—electricity, mechanism" (*Science and Technology* 238). See also *Posthuman* 11–33.

7 The 1911 version, customarily labelled Version 3, concludes with a sentence: "Ah, he was so beautiful for the re-issuing into the next life" (*VicG* 121).

1 Degeneration, Aestheticism and Empire

Middle-Class Ideology and *The White Peacock*

> In some early chapter in this heap I compared all our present colour and abundance to October foliage before the frosts nip down the leaves. ... It may be I see decay all about me because I am, in a sense, decay. ... I, too, have a sort of hope, but it is a remote hope, a hope that finds no promise in this Empire or in any of the great things of our time.
>
> H. G. Wells, *Tono-Bungay*, Book IV, Chapter 3

The White Peacock has often been read as an apolitical, relatively innocent novel, its value lying mostly in its pastoral quality.[1] The novel, however, both implicitly and explicitly declares its preference for the values favoured by the middle classes, whose ideology influenced political discourses at that time. This preference becomes evident when the novel is compared with its earlier versions. The plot of the first draft, called *Laetitia*, was considerably different from that of the published version and arguably more ambitious and radical, or at least more provoking, for the middle-class readership. In *Laetitia*, the narrator's sister Lettie begets a child of Leslie Tempest, a wealthy young man, but she is abandoned by her fiancé. She marries George Saxton, a local farmer, but falls into hysteria and eventually emigrates to Canada. In *The White Peacock*, however, the marriage between social classes—the *Lady Chatterley* theme—is replaced with the more comfortable marriages within the same classes, such as those of Lettie and Leslie, George and Meg, and Emily and Tom. Furthermore, in the final manuscript, Lettie reads Ibsen's *Doll's House*, *Hedda Gabler* and Tolstoy's *Anna Karénina*—these writers and their works were severely attacked in Max Nordau's *Degeneration*, which was translated in English in 1895 and appealed widely to the bourgeois audience—but Lawrence deleted these specific names before publication.[2] The narrator Cyril Beardsall bears an obvious similarity to the author but is presented as a well-off middle-class character. Through the revisions, the novel became less upsetting, more

DOI: 10.4324/9781032675671-2

conventional and publishable, that is, more suitable for the middle-class readership.

The White Peacock centres on the relationship of the characters living in the world of Nethermere. The first-person narrator Cyril Beardsall spins the idyll of their lives. The story reaches its climax in the last scene wherein Cyril portrays the striking contrast between George in his drunken decline and the activity of Swineshed Farm:

> Like a tree that is falling, going soft and pale and rotten, clammy with small fungi, he [George] stood leaning against the gate, while the dim afternoon drifted with a sweet flow of thick sunshine past him, not touching him.
>
> In the stackyard, the summer's splendid monuments of wheat and grass were reared in gold and grey. The wheat was littered brightly round the rising stack. The loaded wagon clanked slowly up the incline, drew near, and rode like a ship at anchor against the scotches, brushing the stack with a crisp sharp sound. Tom climbed the ladder and stood a moment there against the sky, amid the brightness and fragrance of the gold corn, and waved his arm to his wife who was passing in the shadow of the buildings across the yard.
>
> (*WP* 324)

The misery of the wretched man is all the more emphasised by the celebration of rural life. This passage contains two essential elements in the text: the idyllic description of the traditional English rural life and the motif of degeneration.

The overtly idyllic tone is one of the central notes of the text. The landscape of Nethermere is saturated with tenderness and love for nature, and with nostalgia for the past. The aestheticised rural image was, however, not entirely original to Lawrence; this kind of idyllic narrative achieved its zenith at the turn of the nineteenth century when, with the growth of industry and urbanisation, the rural was supposed to represent the best part of English culture, the essence of England. Writers such as Richard Jefferies, W. H. Hudson and James Prior contributed to this movement.[3]

Although Cyril's narrative presents a romanticised vision of provincial life, it does not neglect urban and rural poverty, and starkly depicts the lives of people living at the bottom of society. George's decline in the quotation above represents the theme of degeneration that recurs throughout the text. At the beginning of the novel, a contrast is introduced between "the young days when the valley was lusty" and the inert and stagnant present (1). Cyril's father, who used to be "a tall, handsome, dark man" (33), appears as a miserable alcoholic. Likewise, the squire is described as the "head of an ancient, once even famous, but now decayed house" (57). The

Ram Inn used to be "an important farm", but it "declined" into a public house (139). This tone is not unique to *The White Peacock*, but appears in other works such as H. G. Wells' *Tono-Bungay* (1909), which Lawrence highly regarded when he was writing this novel. In *Tono-Bungay*, the first-person narrator George Ponderevo presents the country house Bladesover, where his mother is housekeeper, as a metaphor for "the broad slow decay of the great social organism of England" (*Tono-Bungay* 66).

This dominant motif represents the mood of British society at the turn of the century. From the last decades of the nineteenth century, fear of the decline of the Empire was a central issue to British citizens. People began to fear the downfall of the British Empire's political and economic hegemony. The meteoric rise of her chief competitors, Germany and America, was evident, and the threat of Germany grew before the Great War. Simultaneously, it was widely accepted that the people in Britain had been both physically and morally degenerated because of their lives of material prosperity and luxury. This idea, for example, shapes the Time Traveller's imagination on the characterisation of the "Eloi" in *The Time Machine* (1895) by H. G. Wells: "The too-perfect security of the Overworlders had led them to a slow movement of *degeneration*, to a general dwindling in size, strength, and intelligence" (109; my emphasis). As the quoted passage indicates, social theories such as racial degeneration and eugenics gained in popularity. The idea of degeneration was originally posed by the French psychiatrist B. A. Morel and the Italian criminal anthropologist Cesare Lombroso, and it was further developed by the English psychologist Henry Maudsley and others. The last decade of the nineteenth century witnessed the Oscar Wilde trial and the publication of the English version of *Degeneration* by Max Nordau, both of which contributed to the circulation of the idea of decadence and moral corruption. The science of eugenics was proposed by Charles Darwin's cousin Francis Galton. It sought to control desired heritable characteristics to improve the genetic make-up of the human population.[4] The influence of these theories peaked at the turn of the century, especially after a prolonged struggle in the Boer War was thought to be proof of the poor physical condition of British soldiers, and continued into the first decades of the twentieth century.[5]

In 1911, the year when *The White Peacock* was published, an article appeared in *The Times*. It was a "Manifesto on Public Morals" issued by the National Council of Public Morals and addressed "to the people of Great and Greater Britain". The article fully elucidates the atmosphere of British society in the early twentieth century. The manifesto begins with a warning against the tendency to disregard "racial instinct" because it "imperil[s] our very life as a nation" (5). In the next section, entitled "The Declining Birth-Rate", the neglect of parental obligations and the degradation of the marriage tie—which, according to the manifesto, results in the decline of the birth rate—are lamented. In "The Moral Education of the Young", it is insisted that young people "should be taught to entertain high conceptions of marriage, as involving duties to the future of the nation and the race" (5). The last section entitled "The Nation and the Feeble-Minded" argues that

> Certain laws of heredity and development ... must also receive due recognition, and govern our national policy. A high proportion of immorality and inebriety is due to neglect of the incurably defective-minded, whose progeny, lamentably numerous under present conditions, too frequently resemble their parents, and largely reinforce the ranks of degradation and shame. ...
>
> We believe that only along these lines—by raising the ideals of marriage, by education for parenthood, and by intervening to prevent degeneracy—can we cope with the demoralization which is sapping the foundations of national wellbeing.
>
> (5)

Thus, the manifesto calls for the urgent necessity of getting rid of the degenerate through correct breeding to rebuild the nation. In 1912, the first International Congress of Eugenics was held in London, and in the following year, 1913, the Mental Deficiency Act, which provided for the detention and segregation of the "feebleminded", was enacted.

This article in *The Times* also illustrates the ethos of British society from another angle. The signatories to the manifesto include Leonard Darwin, President of the Eugenics Education Society; William Booth, founder of the Salvation Army; Ramsay MacDonald, Leader of the Labour Party; Beatrice Webb, a prominent social reformer and key member of the Fabian Society; and Rider Haggard, an adventure story writer. The article mirrors the prevailing atmosphere of the time, when eugenics was not solely championed by right-wing extremists, but rather found considerable endorsement among British intellectuals.

Sally Ledger points out three significant causes for the penetration of the discourses on degeneration and eugenics into British society. These discourses arose from a constellation of middle-class fears and anxiety. Eugenicist thought was, Ledger argues, an ideological response to the fears of the decline of the British Empire, of the working-class revolt and of the uprising of the New Woman:

> Eugenic discourses reflected ... the political upheavals which dominated late-nineteenth century culture: the fears surrounding the perceived decline of the British Empire; the fear of working-class disorder and

> the rise in their numbers; and the resurgence of the bourgeois women's movement in the last years of the century, which meant that women's role as the mothers and nurturers of the "race" was felt to be under threat. Britain was perceived to be losing control of its colonial subjects just as it was losing control over its working-class subjects, and its women, at home.
>
> (Ledger 74)

Under these social and political circumstances, the condition of the poor was one of the prime concerns of the time since it could be used as the most powerful proof of the decline of the Empire. In London, for instance, Charles Booth's monumental survey of poverty culminated in the 17 volumes of *Life and Labour of the People of London* (1889–1902), and William Booth expounded his theory as to the eradication of poverty in *In Darkest England and the Way Out* (1890). As well as in the Metropolis, conditions in the countryside also became a matter of discussion. The publication of books and pamphlets on rural conditions burst forth from the beginning of the twentieth century, and even Rider Haggard, who is now remembered as a writer of romantic adventure stories set on foreign continents, lamented rural degeneration in England: "This is certain ... some parts of England are becoming almost as lonesome as the veld of Africa. ... Farming in this country is no longer what it was. In all parts of England the land is going more and more to grass ..." (Haggard 540). The fact that the outcasts in the world of Nethermere and the London slummers are described in *The White Peacock* shows the extent to which contemporary national concerns influenced the text. As well as the embellished visions of the countryside, *The White Peacock* depicts the social and political issues that contemporary British society confronted: rural and urban poverty, agrarian depression, emigration, socialism, the New Woman and degeneration of the lower classes. As the author's remark on this novel indicates—"a decorated idyll running to seed in realism" (*1L* 184)—Cyril's narrative is on the one hand furnished with (sometimes too excessive) pastoralism, but on the other hand it portrays the crude realities of life in the countryside and in town. *The White Peacock* consists of these apparently conflicting elements.

The function of these two elements will become evident by exploring the plot of the novel in relation to the contemporary evolutionary theories, the idyllic visions presented by the narrator and the textual ambivalence divulged by the fissures of the bourgeois embellishments. Lawrence imbibed Ernst Haeckel, T. H. Huxley and Herbert Spencer,[6] whose biological theory gave rise to such theories of cultural politics as social Darwinism, race degeneration and eugenics, which acquired wide currency in *fin-de-siècle* Britain. The first section examines how their influences infiltrate into the plot of *The White Peacock*. The next section will discuss the idyllic visions Cyril presents in his narrative and their affinity with landscape paintings. This analysis will disclose the affinity between Cyril's portrayal and the landscape paintings in which the artificially beautified country life was repeatedly taken up as a theme, as well as the ideology that both visions hold. The final section will explore several instances that reveal the fissures of these bourgeois embellishments. These analyses will eventually demonstrate the textual ambivalence *The White Peacock* entails within itself.

Degeneration and Ideology

In Britain, discourse on degeneration served to stereotype the poor as degenerate, thereby reinforcing the internal division within society. *The White Peacock* embodies this division between middle and lower classes, especially because the narrator adopts the privileged position favoured by the middle classes, and relates the vicissitudes of the life of a local farmer George Saxton. George falls in love with Lettie Beardsall, but he is abandoned. He becomes a minor voice of socialism, but makes some ruinous speculations, and is eventually drowned by drinking. His family gets into trouble with the squire and is forced to leave the country. On the other hand, Lettie and George's sister Emily withdraw from society to be devoted housewives. This plot assumes significance when put into the context of the contemporary social and political discourses on socialism, emigration and marriage.

The last decade of the nineteenth century witnessed the rapid growth of socialism. In *The White Peacock*, the Saxtons are attracted to the movement. The father reads "books on the land question" and becomes "an advanced radical, almost a socialist" (185). George, awakened by his encounter with the London slummers, also joins the socialist movement. On the other hand, the narrator is not convinced of the idea of socialism. While "George listened intently to the speaker, very much moved by him", Cyril is sceptical about the speaker, who he thinks exaggerates the misery of the poor: "… I [Cyril] felt a breathless pity for him, that his eyes should be always filled with mud, and never brightened" (282).

George and Cyril's opposite reactions towards the socialist's speech at Hyde Park Corner embody society's different class attitudes towards socialism. From the bourgeois point of view, the socialist movement was the cause of social unrest and disorder. One of the most prominent adherents of the degeneration theory, Henry Maudsley, was hostile to socialism and regarded it as working-class revolt with unavoidable danger. T. H. Huxley disregarded socialism thinking that it could not offer any solution to the problem of race degeneration. Herbert Spencer was also an anti-socialist on the grounds that socialism would preserve the unfit and deprive them of the ability of self-help, which was essential for social development. This *laissez-faire* individualist opposed public support to the poor, since it would allow them to survive.[7] Likewise, the influential sexologist Havelock Ellis argues against the social welfare in *The Problem of Race-Regeneration*, published in the same year as *The White Peacock*, as follows:

> But, whatever the exact action of natural selection may be, as soon as we begin to interfere with it and improve the conditions of life, by caring for the unfit, enabling them to survive and to propagate their like—as they will not fail to do in so far as they belong to unfit stocks—then we are certainly, without intending it, doing our best to lower the level of life. We increase, or at best retain, the unfit, while at the same time we burden the fit with the task of providing for the unfit. In this way we deteriorate the general quality of life in the next generation. (49)

The advertisement in this pamphlet lists eight titles that include the term "race-regeneration" among the 12 "New Tracts for the Times" series, which illuminates the degree to which British society was obsessed with the idea (see Figure 1.1). From this point of view, George in *The White Peacock* is to the bourgeois eye a fearful being who challenges the social-political status quo.

The Saxtons are virtually evicted by the squire and emigrate to Canada. In the text, Canada is represented as a place far from the Promised Land: "The talk is ... of Canada, where work is strenuous, but not life; where the plains are wide, and one is not lapped in a soft valley ..." (*WP* 59). Canada is regarded as a country where the so-called Indians live, as Will Bancroft's remark indicates: "'I came on snow-shoes,' said he. 'Real Indian,—came from Canada—they're just ripping'" (111). The Saxtons, who acquiesce in the colonial state of the repressed at home, are going to be the colonisers among Native Americans.

Emigration was an important issue of the period and one of the few choices for those without hope at home, as is shown in *Esther Waters* by George Moore. In the novel, the heroine's drunken stepfather loses his job and emigrates to Australia. Emigration assumed an ideological aspect because it meant to export economic victims to the colonies. During the last decades of the nineteenth century, many intellectuals, including Friedrich Nietzsche, whose works fascinated young Lawrence, believed that emigration would check the degenerative process.[8] Emigration was William Booth's favourite solution to the problems concerning the poor, and he called it the "final stage of the regenerative process" (*In Darkest England* 143). He promoted the large scale emigration of the poor, arguing

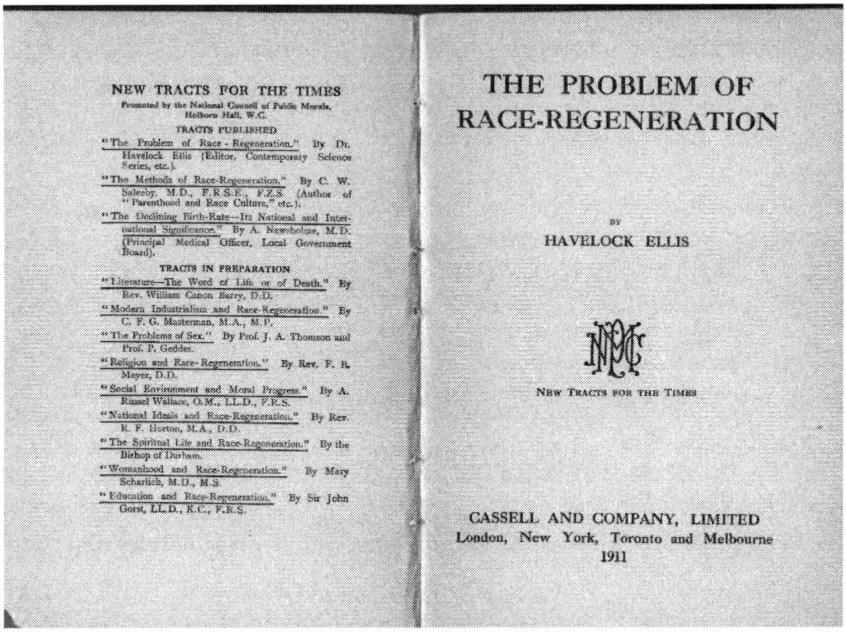

NEW TRACTS FOR THE TIMES

Promoted by the National Council of Public Morals, Holborn Hall, W.C.

TRACTS PUBLISHED

"The Problem of Race-Regeneration." By Dr. Havelock Ellis (Editor, Contemporary Science Series, etc.).

"The Methods of Race-Regeneration." By C. W. Saleeby, M.D., F.R.S.E., F.Z.S. (Author of "Parenthood and Race Culture," etc.).

"The Declining Birth-Rate—Its National and International Significance." By A. Newsholme, M.D. (Principal Medical Officer, Local Government Board).

TRACTS IN PREPARATION

"Literature—The Word of Life or of Death." By Rev. William Canon Barry, D.D.

"Modern Industrialism and Race-Regeneration." By C. F. G. Masterman, M.A., M.P.

"The Problems of Sex." By Prof. J. A. Thomson and Prof. P. Geddes.

"Religion and Race-Regeneration." By Rev. F. B. Meyer, D.D.

"Social Environment and Moral Progress." By A. Russel Wallace, O.M., LL.D., F.R.S.

"National Ideals and Race-Regeneration." By Rev. R. F. Horton, M.A., D.D.

"The Spiritual Life and Race-Regeneration." By the Bishop of Durham.

"Womanhood and Race-Regeneration." By Mary Scharlieb, M.D., M.S.

"Education and Race-Regeneration." By Sir John Gorst, LL.D., K.C., F.R.S.

THE PROBLEM OF RACE-REGENERATION

BY

HAVELOCK ELLIS

NEW TRACTS FOR THE TIMES

CASSELL AND COMPANY, LIMITED

London, New York, Toronto and Melbourne

1911

Figure 1.1 The title and the opposite page of *The Problem of Race-Regeneration* by Havelock Ellis.

that "emigration is the only remedy for this mighty evil" (145). Actually, such philanthropic organisations as the Salvation Army and Dr. Barnardo's paid for the journey of the orphans to the colonies and, furthermore, the Reformatory and Industrial Schools Act of 1891 gave the schools' governors the authority to send delinquent pupils to the colonies. As a result, in the 60 years after 1870, 100,000 emigrated to Canada.[9]

One of the causes of the decline of the Empire was ascribed to the poor working classes, which accelerated eugenics.[10] Eugenicists sought to control heritable characteristics through correct breeding, and hence, feared intermarriage between the "healthy" ruling class and the poor working class. They argued that crossbreeding between healthy and degenerate stock diffused the vice of degeneration and accelerated the deterioration of the whole British race. The ideology against inter-class marriage permeates *The White Peacock*. Annable's first marriage with Lady Christabel ends in what he calls "an unfortunate mésalliance" (151). His second wife is below him as she emphasises their unequal social position. The marriage between Mr. and Mrs. Beardsall is also unsuccessful, although we do not know if it is another "mésalliance" as the author imagined his parents' marriage was. Even in an anecdote which Cyril recounts to the bourgeois maidens, a tale of a secret love between "a fellow ... brown and strong" and a daughter of a squire, their romance ends with the sorrowful death of the girl by his mistaken shooting (232). Thus, the text follows the eugenicist argument against intermarriage and crossbreeding, and from this point of view, it is understandable that George's love for Lettie does not succeed.

The eugenicists, whose main concern was to reverse the degenerative process, emphasised the importance of the role of women as productive wives. Especially after the term "New Woman" entered the vocabulary in the last decade of the nineteenth century, womanhood or motherhood was highly regarded and defended by the middle classes as the key to the nation's future. Happy home and healthy, devoted mothers are the foundations for national prosperity. The "motto of the movement" of the National Council of Public Morals printed on the back cover of Ellis' *The Problem of Race-Regeneration* reads: "The foundations of National glory are set in the homes of the people. They will remain unshaken while the family life of our race and nation is strong, simple, and pure", which was actually the words by King George V. Ellis himself argues for the woman's role as a nurturing mother in *The Task of Social Hygiene*, published in the next year of *The White Peacock*:

> Woman's function in life can never be the same as man's, if only because women are the mothers of the race. ... The most vital problem before our civilization to-day is the problem of motherhood, the question of creating the human beings best fitted for modern life, the practical realization of a sound eugenics.
>
> (86)[11]

The female characters in *The White Peacock* follow their arguments and accept the role of self-negating housewives to nurture the "healthy race". Lettie is at first represented as a modern woman; she wages debates with Leslie on strike and business, reads all things that deal with modern women and joins The Woman's League. Lettie is, however, said to "have discovered the wonderful charm of her womanhood", and determines "to ignore her own self" (*WP* 255, 284). Likewise George's sister Emily, who has been a schoolmistress, willingly sacrifices her career for her expected role after her marriage:

> She was rich as always with her large beauty, and stately now with the stateliness of a strong woman six months gone with child. ... Emily had at last found her place, and had escaped from the torture of strange, complex modern life.
>
> (318–19)

Furthermore, watching Meg affectionately kiss her baby, the narrator remarks: "A woman who has her child in her arms is a tower of strength, a beautiful, unassailable tower of strength ..." (292). Thus, motherhood and women's reproductive function are praised in this text. The novel's female characters satisfy the bourgeois sense of value, as does Esther Waters: "She was only conscious that she had accomplished her woman's work—she had brought him [her son] up to man's estate; and that was her sufficient reward" (*Esther Waters* 394). The women in *The White Peacock* are neither Nora nor Hedda Gabler in Ibsen's dramas, but rather the ideal women of Victorian archetype that John Ruskin highly approved in his *Sesame and Lilies*, which Lawrence read while working on this novel.[12]

Thus, the contemporary discourses on degeneration and eugenics are inscribed in *The White Peacock*. In these discourses, heredity and economic failure were thought of as the two main factors in defining the degenerate, and both factors influence and determine George's destiny. George is born into a working class family, and although Cyril sometimes attempts to present him as a pastoral figure, George is in reality an economic victim: "As it is, we depend on the milk-round, and on the carting which I do for the Council. You can't call it farming. We're a miserable mixture of farmer, milkman, greengrocer, and carting contractor. It's a shabby business" (*WP* 61). After his marriage, he grows rich for a moment, but ruins himself by bad speculations. George is the loser of the competition that arises within capitalism, which signifies that he is stigmatised as the "unfit".[13]

George is eventually ruined by his heavy drinking. From the late nineteenth century, alcoholism was regarded both as a primary cause and as a result of degeneration, and was connected with other immoral behaviour such as idleness and sexual indulgence.[14] Lawrence was familiar with the idea of widespread alcoholism in rural districts. This theme was, for example, taken up by Richard Jefferies in *The Open Air* (1885), the book Lawrence was given by Louie Burrows as a gift for his twenty-fourth birthday:

> Harvest beer is probably the vilest drink in the world. ... It is beer rotting and decomposing in the stomach. Violent diarrhoea often follows, and then the exhaustion thus caused induces the men to drink more in order to regain the strength necessary to do their work. ... So vile a drink there is not elsewhere in the world.
>
> (Jefferies 84–85)[15]

In *The White Peacock*, alcoholism is represented as a vice that prevails throughout society: Cyril's father has kidney trouble, his doctor is a hopeless drunkard and Lettie tells Cyril of a drunken fellow who toppled into the canal and drowned. And George is also a victim of this vice. Born into a working-class family, suffering from financial difficulties and falling into alcoholic decrepitude, George embodies the typical image of the degenerate.

Aesthetic Ideology

George declines both mentally and physically towards the end. He is moved to Swineshed Farm where his sister Emily and her husband Tom Renshaw live. The life of the farming family is depicted as an idyllic landscape. Cyril from time to time portrays the country life as a landscape painting: farmers placed in the foreground, with the background of cultivated land and natural scenery. Throughout the novel, however, not only the narrator but also other middle-class characters see the world with a pictorial imagination. They admire landscape as they do paintings, as is indicated by Lettie's remark: "Doesn't Strelley Mill look pretty? Like a group of orange and scarlet fungi in a fairy picture" (127). Lettie views George mowing grain in the field as a part of a pastoral landscape painting: "'You are *picturesque*', she said, a trifle awkwardly, 'Quite fit for an Idyll'" (48; my emphasis).[16]

Lawrence devoted his whole life to painting as well as writing, and there are numerous references to various painters and paintings in *The White Peacock*, from the eighteenth-century landscape painters to the Pre-Raphaelites of the following century. In the quotation above, the word "picturesque" could suggest more than the ordinary meaning of "beautiful or striking, as in a picture"; in the context of landscape paintings, the "picturesque" indicates a particular mode of perceiving and visualising the world.

The nature of the picturesque was first theorised by the English painter William Gilpin, who gave the concept particular currency. In his three essays, he defines the essence of the picturesque landscape in terms of the rough and the rugged:

> A piece of Palladian architecture may be elegant in the last degree. … But if we introduce it in a picture, it immediately becomes a formal object, and ceases to please. Should we wish to give it picturesque beauty, … from a *smooth* building we must turn it into a *rough* ruin.
> (Gilpin 7; emphasis in original)

And Gilpin continues:

> But among all the objects of art, the picturesque eye is perhaps most inquisitive after the elegant relics of ancient architecture; the ruined

> tower, the Gothic arch, the remains of castles, and abbeys. These are the richest legacies of art.
>
> (46)

Gilpin argues that the beautiful is not an adequate component of a picturesque composition; only a mixture of the beautiful and the apparently opposite elements of shaggy trees, abandoned architecture and rough ruins generates pleasing pictures. Indispensable to the picturesque is not "the pampered horse" but "the worn-out cart-horse" (14), not gorgeous castles or rich and respectable people, but abandoned relics and humble farmers working in a field.

The historical context and meaning of the picturesque are fully examined by art and literary critic Wylie Sypher. The picturesque of the eighteenth and nineteenth centuries, Sypher argues, consists of two concepts: visual pleasure and nostalgia. A modest farm and its inhabitants, a central motif of the picturesque, are not only visually aesthetic, but they are also the source of sentiment and nostalgia:

> Even in the narrowest eighteenth-century sense of the word the picturesque is really more than a way of seeing. The picturesque scene is usually saturated with a mood … where shaggy oak trees, thatched roofs, domestic clutter, and the pastoral tasks of the submerged but honest poor are associated with a sentiment.
>
> (Sypher 86)

When rough nature or poor farmers are put into a composition, they make the landscape more pathetic and sentimental. Picturesque paintings aimed to evoke pathos and melancholy by depicting aestheticised rural images.

Lawrence was familiar with the eighteenth- and nineteenth-century landscape painters who took up the theme of the picturesque. Several critics have attempted to analyse *The White Peacock* in terms of the paintings mentioned in the text, but their arguments concentrate mostly on the mid and late nineteenth-century painters such as the Pre-Raphaelites, Impressionists and Aubrey Beardsley.[17] As well as these *fin-de-siècle* artists, Lawrence was also familiar with the eighteenth- and nineteenth-century British landscape painters, and they are the key figures in interpreting the text. He actually possessed and treasured six of the eight volumes of Charles Holme's *English Water-Colour* (1902), given by the Chambers for his twenty-first birthday. These volumes contain several painters referred to in *The White Peacock*, such as A. V. Copley Fielding and Thomas Girtin, who painted English rural scenery with picturesque sentimentalisations. Lawrence avidly copied some of these paintings, as he recalls later in his life:

> As I grew more ambitious, I copied Leader's landscapes, and Frank Brangwyn's cartoon-like pictures, then Peter de Wint and Girtin water-colours. I can never be sufficiently grateful for the series of English Water-Colour Painters, published by the Studio in eight parts, when I was a youth. I had only six of the eight parts, but they were invaluable to me. I copied them with the greatest joy.
>
> (*LEA* 230; see Figure 1.2)

The picturesque painters are key figures in interpreting *The White Peacock* as the narrator often views and visualises the world in terms of visual metaphors and the terminology of the picturesque.

Figure 1.2 Lawrence's copy (c. 1908) of "A Wind-swept Hill" by E. A. Waterlow, D. H. Lawrence Art Collection, 65.397.6, 1.2, Harry Ransom Center, The University of Texas at Austin. © Paper Lion Ltd and The Estate of Frieda Lawrence Ravagli.

The idyllic prose of *The White Peacock* conveys the picturesque sentimentality; Cyril Beardsall in his narrative portrays the landscape through the framework of the picturesque, depicting dishevelled nature, ruined architecture and the lower classes. Picturesque images abound in the text: "the sharp, wild, grassy hillside, … ruinous with the gaunt, ragged bones of old hedge-rows" around the mythical lake Nethermere (*WP* 57); the deserted "old farm" where Cyril and George explore (60); the "abandoned" church where Annable discloses his philosophy to Cyril (147); Mrs. Annable as a nursing mother surrounded by her children in their cottage; and the rustic life of the Saxtons and the Renshaws. These descriptions produce the lyricism pursued by the picturesque. Cyril portrays the pastoral landscape viewed by the picturesque eye—the sentimentalised, idyllic panorama of the Nethermere world.[18]

While several critics have admired the presentations of nature and the man-nature relation in the novel as true portraits of rural life, other critics perceive an ideological manipulation in these descriptions, which they regard as aesthetically modified. Graham Holderness argues that Eberwich is not a true representation of the mining village where Lawrence lived, but "a mythical social world" (Holderness 96). The colliery society in the novel is, he argues, metamorphosed into an aestheticised rural district:

> The image of society portrayed in *The White Peacock* should be seen … as a means of transforming the real historical society into a more compliant and satisfying myth, within which history can be controlled and ordered by the operation of an aesthetic ideology.
>
> (115)

John Worthen supports this view, arguing that the elements of industrialism are subtly dropped from the descriptions of the landscape. "As a result", Worthen argues,

> we tend to read *The White Peacock* rather in the same way as Cyril Beardsall looks at landscape; as a series of pictures, of beautifully observed details, of minor absurdities, drawn together not as a society is drawn together, but brought together in a common harmony by the tragic philosophy.
>
> ("Introduction" 26)

They point out that Cyril's pictures are distorted visions created by an aesthetic imagination.

As these critics suggest, the creation of a picturesque landscape necessarily entails an ideological manipulation through which a landscape is transformed into an aestheticised rural image. Gilpin describes in his essay

"On Picturesque Travel" the process in which a painter constructs his picturesque vision by selecting and arranging the materials he has actually seen:

> There is still another amusement arising from the correct knowledge of objects; and that is the power of creating, and representing *scenes of fancy*; which is still more a work of creation, than copying from nature. The imagination becomes a camera obscura, only with this difference, that the camera represents objects as they really are: while the imagination, impressed with the most beautiful scenes, and chastened by rules of art, forms its pictures, not only from the most admirable parts of nature; but in the best taste.
>
> (Gilpin 52; emphasis in original)

The picturesque is a way to articulate nature, and the paintings are the realisation and idealisation of a painter's vision. To construct a picturesque vision inevitably involves distorting and reconstructing the perception of nature.

The essence of this aestheticism lies in the fact that its distortion embodies the middle-class sense of values and perception. The romanticised vision of the rustic life of the peasants does not represent their actual situation but the image that is evocative and nostalgic to the bourgeois taste. Art historian Ann Bermingham, analysing the politics behind picturesque paintings, argues that these paintings conceal the misery and poverty of the farmers suffering from the enclosures:

> Although the picturesque celebrated the old order—by depicting a pastoral, preenclosed landscape—some of its features—the class snobbery, the distancing of the spectator from the picturesque object, and the aestheticization of rural poverty—suggest that at a deeper level the picturesque endorsed the results of agricultural industrialization. ... In this respect, the picturesque represented an attempt to wipe out the fact of enclosure and to minimize its consequences.
>
> (75)

Her argument was presumably inspired by Raymond Williams, who perceived that the celebration of rural England ironically "served to cover and to evade the actual and bitter contradictions of the time" (45) and as a result embraced capitalism. Thus, the picturesque embodies a romanticised vision of the country life appreciated by the middle classes, disguising the predicaments of the farmers.

The aestheticised pictures that middle-class narrator Cyril Beardsall portrays in his tableau are also an idealised vision from the middle-class point of view. The last few chapters of *The White Peacock* conceal the sufferings and misery of the Saxtons, who are virtually evicted by the squire, by highlighting another farming family, the Renshaws, as the central figures. The Renshaws represent the last in a series of romanticised rural images. The farmstead is secluded from the outside world and enjoys a good harvest. In this idyllic province lives Tom Renshaw, who marries George's sister Emily. His characterisation makes a striking contrast to that of George:

> He was twenty-nine years old, had been a *soldier* in China for five years. ... I liked Tom for his *handsome* bearing, and his *fresh*, winsome way. He was exceedingly *manly*: that is to say *he did not dream of questioning or analysing anything*. All that came his way was ready labelled nice or nasty, good or bad. He did not imagine that anything could be other than just what it appeared to be,—and with this appearance, he was quite content.
>
> (*WP* 308; my emphasis)

Tom Renshaw used to be a soldier, and his fresh and supple physique is opposed to George's awkward and clumsy manner. His simplistic mentality does not seem to challenge authority, unlike George, who joins the socialist movement. The Renshaws are healthy, and not liable to be the cause of social unease. Tom Renshaw's manly ideal, of which middle-class Cyril highly approves and the eugenicists must have also approved, dispels the fears of racial degeneration.[19] Tom Renshaw is a "healthy" farmer who deserves to propagate his breed. Thus, the celebration of bucolic life at Swineshed Farm serves to obscure actual social problems: exploitation by the landlord, agrarian capitalism and rural degeneracy. The prose of natural depiction and nostalgic evocation translates the misery and ruin into a romanticised vision. Cyril's portrayal represents the way in which the middle-class characters see the world of Nethermere; it is a romanticised vision, embellished and fabricated to fit into the picturesque composition.[20]

The White Peacock was composed in these social and political circumstances, and it has the aspect that allays the anxieties entertained by the middle-class readership. George and his family are eliminated as the "unfit", and marginalised in the text. The female characters submit themselves to patriarchal authority, and devote themselves to nurturing their children. At the end of the text, an idealised farmer and his household appear. The farm is free from the social unease that middle-class citizens were afraid of: the uproar by the labourers and the new women, and the poverty and degeneration of the lower classes. Cyril's idyllic narrative constructs ideologically romanticised visions.

Anti-Middle-Class Ideology

The White Peacock, however, does not merely serve to reinforce and strengthen middle-class ideology. What is significant in *The White Peacock* is that the text itself sometimes takes an ironic stance towards the bourgeois ideology and unmasks its deception. In the novel, idealised images of the land are always created and circulated by the middle and upper classes: Lady Christabel romanticised Annable and saw him as a Greek statue; the squire's wife writes a pot-pourri romance of the Mill; at the wedding picnic the middle-class picnickers see the life at Strelley Mill as a pastoral landscape. These incidents ironically imply that the middle-class narrator Cyril Beardsall's idyllic narrative also depicts the romanticised version of rustic life fabricated from the viewpoint of the richer people. His redundant and over-elaborate rhetorical prose also signifies that these descriptions are not the true representations of landscape but rather the reflections of Cyril's inner vision. For instance, personification which Cyril frequently adopts is the way to represent nature applied to human perspective—it is a distortion by the narrator, or what Ruskin called the pathetic fallacy. This final section will briefly examine the way in which the text adopts critical and ironic stances on the middle-class ideology, focusing on two scenes: the wedding picnic and the hare-hunt.

The chapter entitled "Pastorals and Peonies" indicates how the pastoral visions are fabricated through the middle-class sense of values and perceptions. In the chapter that concludes the second part, Lettie, Leslie and their wedding guests go on a picnic to the Saxtons' hayfields. To the picnickers, scything the crop or milking cows is not work but "a nice exercise" (47) and farmers working in the field are a part of romantic landscape: " 'Yes, let us go and fetch him [George],' said Miss D'Arcy 'I'm sure he doesn't know what a happy pastoral state he's in ...' " (228).

The text, however, indicates that the agricultural land is in actuality far from idyllic and that it can be "pastoral" only by a certain kind of detachment:

> "Oh, let us go—let us go—May we come and see the cows milked?" said Hilda. ...
>
> "No," drawled Freddy, "the stink o' live beef ain't salubrious. You be warned, and stop here."
>
> "I never could bear cows, except those lovely little highland cattle, all woolly, in pictures," said Louie Denys, smiling archly, with a little irony.
>
> "No," laughed Agnes D'Arcy "they—they're smelly,"—and she pursed up her mouth, and ended in a little trill of deprecatory laughter, as she often did.
>
> (230)

These responses by the bourgeois lad and maidens reveal that the romanticised vision is created by a certain kind of ignorance and hypocrisy. The middle classes ignore what they do not want to see and create romanticised images. The landscape must be seen as an object within a frame, and the duality of the spectator and the object must be strictly maintained. The picnic scene reveals the ideological deception inherent in the pastoral vision—the image is constructed to conform to the viewers' picturesque perspective. Thus, this episode is a critique of the pastoral mode of perception, and a self-parody since it discloses the deception and distortion in the novel's idyllic prose.

The Saxtons' rabbit-hunting is another intriguing scene as it deviates from the picturesque norm. Rabbit-hunting by farmers is a typical picturesque scene, as Gilpin explains: "A hare started before dogs is enough to set a whole country in an uproar. The plough, and the spade are deserted. Care is left behind; and every human faculty is dilated with joy" (Gilpin 48). This kind of idyllic scene is, Gilpin argues, the source of amusement "to the man of taste to pursue the beauties of nature" (48).

Nottinghamshire novelist James Prior, whose works Edward Garnett introduced to Lawrence, portrays in his *Forest Folk* hare-hunting with picturesque sentimentality:

> The young farmer had not long set out and was skirting the hedge and the dribbling brook ... when he heard a shout some distance in front of him, feminine but loud:
>
> "So ho! so ho!"
>
> "Theer goos Nell Rideout's grew [greyhound], mester!" said the lad. But Arthur had already seen a beautiful fallow hound start a hare in the next field. ...
>
> "She's got 'im, she's got 'im!" cried the lad with sportsmanlike enthusiasm.
>
> "I see that she has," said his master dryly, and called his setter to heel.
>
> "Theer's Nell hersen!"
>
> "So I perceive."
>
> She approached from the other side of the boundary which as the ground fell away rapidly was much lower. Just under them she stopped, and picked up the hare which the hound dropped at her feet.
>
> "Beautifully done, my beauty!" she said.
>
> (Prior 47)[21]

In contrast to the hare-hunting by Prior, the rabbit-hunting at Strelley Mill Farm is not the kind that satisfies the pastoral taste. In *The White Peacock*, the rabbits are a symbol of the squire's greed—the squire forbids his tenants to catch them since the rabbits are the source of his family's wealth. When the Saxtons find one, they chase it desperately with rakes, but the rabbits appear one after another, which infuriates the family. Eventually the father, afraid of the estate harmed by the rabbits, kills nearly 20 of them with his gun. Hare-hunting is here handled differently from the traditional norm, and the scene uncovers the actual situation of the world of Nethermere: agrarian depression, the local discord between the landowner and the tenants, and the destruction of the natural ecosystem that caused the abnormal multiplication of rabbits.

Thus, *The White Peacock* refuses to be simple propaganda of the middle classes. Unlike other works by Lawrence's contemporaries, this ambivalent text implicitly and explicitly discloses the deception inherent in bourgeois ideology and exposes the actual situation of the rural district hidden under the embellished visions. These anti-bourgeois qualities are, however, limited to certain parts of the text; its narrative is constructed by a pattern of attitude and reference at the turn of the century. Its plot shows the influence of the contemporary discourses on degeneration and eugenics which circulated among, and were supported by, the middle classes. Its aesthetic depictions represent the style of the picturesque, whose embellished visions work to disguise the dark side of the society that approves the elimination of the unfit. The alliance of degenerationism and aestheticism serves to alleviate fears and anxieties entertained by the middle classes, who cherished the idea that the essence of England consists fundamentally in the countryside and its people, uncontaminated by racial degeneration and expanding industrialism. Thus, this text is mostly a collage of bourgeois ideologies, informed by anxieties about the decline of the Empire and the degeneration of its race; although apparently innocent, *The White Peacock* is actually infiltrated by the bourgeois ideology that was prevalent at the turn of the century and in the early twentieth century, sometimes ambivalently indicating the crack of the embellished visions of the bourgeoisie.

Notes

1 Several critics have admired the depictions of nature and the man-nature relation in this novel, which they consider a true portrayal of rural life, where humans and nature coexist in perfect harmony. For example, Michael Squires, who reads the work as a modern version of pastoral novel, admires the idyllic passages in the novel, regarding them as the quintessence of Lawrence's artistic achievement: "Nature, and man amid nature, are the 'true' and the 'real' in the novel. They are what live in the novel with greatest independent life and with greatest impact on the imagination" (Squires 194–95). Similarly, Keith Alldritt argues that in this novel "the most striking visual category is landscape

description. ... It is directed by a keen determination to record fully and accurately a specific moment of perception" (Alldritt 11–13). From the viewpoint of ecocriticism, Anne Odenbring Ehlert celebrates the "ecological harmony of the Renshaw household", which is to her "the only comfort offered in *The White Peacock*" (Ehlert 59).

2 See the editor's note in *WP* 368.

3 See Howkins, especially 90–106. See also Chapter 8, section *Lady Chatterley's Lover*: Temptation to the Bourgeois Myth, of this book.

4 "The aim of Eugenics is", Galton argues in *Essays in Eugenics*, "to bring as many influences as can be reasonably employed, to cause the useful classes in the community to contribute *more* than their proportion to the next generation" (38). And he goes on: "Eugenics deal with what is more valuable than money or lands, namely the heritage of a high character, capable brains, fine physique, and vigour ..." (49).

5 The statistics of those rejected for military service in Britain at the turn of the century varies from 34 to 60 per cent. See Hynes, *Edwardian Turn of Mind* 22 and Richardson 21. For more detailed accounts on degeneration and eugenic matters, see Pick 176–221, Bowler 282–306, Kevles, Greenslade and Ledger. For the relationship between the popularity of eugenics and the declining birth rate in Britain before World War II, see Soloway. For the intellectuals and eugenics, see Greta Jones 43–65. For the cultural and political climate in early twentieth-century Britain, see Hynes' above-mentioned work and Searle. Most of the unattributed factual information in this book derives from these sources.

6 See Chambers 112–13, Ebbatson 28–60 and Rylance 15–21.

7 See Pick 203–16, Huxley 209–12 and 289–90, Spencer, "The Coming Slavery" in *The Man Versus the State* 18–43.

8 See Mosse xviii.

9 About four decades before the publication of Lawrence's novel, Galton argued in *Hereditary Genius* that

> as a rule, the very ablest men are strongly disinclined to emigrate. ... England has certainly got rid of a great deal of refuse, through means of emigration. She has found an outlet for men of adventurous and Bohemian natures, who are ... not wanted in old civilizations; and she has also been disembarrassed of a vast number of turbulent radicals and the like.
>
> (360–61)

In 1906, Hans Groß, with whose son Otto Lawrence's future wife Frieda had an affair, argued in his essay that in order not to hinder natural selection, degenerates and their descendants, who were considered a threat to the nation, must be deported to uncultivated lands for life. See Groß 285.

10 See "The Possible Improvement of the Human Breed, Under the Existing Conditions of Law and Science" in Galton, *Essays in Eugenics* 1–34, and "Eugenics and Love" in Ellis, *The Task of Social Hygiene* 193–216. In *Esther Waters*, the eugenicist discourse torments Esther, who is forced to attend to Mrs. Rivers' baby when her own baby is in danger:

> By what right, by what law, was she separated from her child? ... It was then a life for a life. It was more. For the children of two poor girls had been sacrificed so that this rich woman's child might be saved.
>
> (*Esther Waters* 146)

11 For more analysis of how womanhood and motherhood were defined in medicine and sociology in order to regulate fecundity in the interest of racial progress and how they were treated in fiction—mainly by Gissing—at the turn of the century, see Greenslade 134–50.

12 Ruskin argues in the second part of the book that a true wife "must be enduringly, incorruptibly good; instinctively, infallibly wise—wise, not for self-development, but for self-renunciation: wise ... with the passionate gentleness of an infinitely variable ... modesty of service ..." (Ruskin 123).

13 Roger Ebbatson briefly examines George's decline in terms of evolutionary theory. See Ebbatson 48–49.

14 For example, William Booth states:

> I will take the question of the drunkard, for the drink difficulty lies at the root of everything. Nine-tenths of our poverty, squalor, vice, and crime spring from this poisonous tap-root. Many of our social evils ... would dwindle away and die if they were not constantly watered with strong drink.
>
> (*In Darkest England* 47)

See also Valverde 258–62.

15 When Lawrence read this book, he wrote to Burrows: "I am very fond of Jefferies, and the pieces in the *Open Air* are so many of them down here" (*1L* 137). Ebbatson also examines Jeffries' influence on *The White Peacock*. See Ebbatson 249–51.

16 Nancy Kushigian analyses how Cyril, Lettie and their friends see the world through a visual filter. See Kushigian 22–25.

17 See Alldritt 8–10, Meyers 46–52, Sproles 299–300, Stewart, "Landscape Painting and Pre-Raphaelitism" 10–19, *The Vital Art* 9–24. Alldritt and Stewart briefly examines the influence of the landscape. My intention is not to refute these views, but to show another dimension of the text.

18 Among Lawrence's contemporaries, another example of the picturesque in prose can be found in W. H. Hudson. Hudson romanticised the South Downs with abundant nostalgia in his *Nature in Downland*, which Lawrence described as "very delightful" (*1L* 334). Its fourth chapter is subtitled "The shepherd as a picturesque figure", in which Hudson sentimentally depicts the solitary figure of a stolid shepherd, a good-looking peasant and a labourer's family (Hudson 103–25). Furthermore, Hudson often quoted Gilpin's travel writings. See Tomalin 178.

19 In this sense, the ending of *Esther Waters* also serves to alleviate bourgeois anxiety by depicting the heroine's son a healthy and manly soldier. Another example can be found in J. M. Barrie's *Peter and Wendy*, published in the same year as *The White Peacock*, in which the Lost Boys, strongly suggestive

of working-class orphans, bravely fight against the pirates, shouting "Rule Britannia!" (Barrie 177).

20 On the collusion of aesthetic ideology with the construction of the myth of rural England, including *The White Peacock*, see Brooker and Widdowson 158–65.

21 The characters themselves regard the scene as picturesque, as Arthur, the landlord, and his sister's conversation indicates:

> On the way she gave her brother in her young lady's manner a lively opinion of the exceeding dreariness of the country.
>
> "It isn't much to look at", said Arthur, "but the natives are *picturesque*—some of them".
>
> (Prior 52; my emphasis)

2 Bestwood and the Morels under Evolution

Parallelism through Procreation and Evolution in *Sons and Lovers*

> Now at some time this leisureliness was suddenly destroyed. ... The idyllic state collapsed under the pressure of a bitter competitive struggle. ... And, what is most important in this connection, it was not generally in such cases a stream of new money invested in the industry which brought about this revolution ... but the new spirit, the spirit of modern capitalism, had set to work.
>
> Max Weber, *The Protestant Ethic and the Spirit of Capitalism*

> On the basis of political economy itself, in its own words, we have shown that the worker sinks to the level of a commodity and becomes indeed the most wretched of commodities; ... and that the whole of society must fall apart into the two classes—the property-*owners* and the propertyless *workers*.
>
> Karl Marx, *Economic and Philosophic Manuscripts of 1844*

Like Lawrence's first novel, *Sons and Lovers* is set in a mining district in the Midlands, but the overt romanticism seen in his previous work becomes less evident and the novel becomes more realist. As the Introduction has previously noted, Paul's contradictory remarks and behaviours reveal his ambivalent feelings towards his parents and the social classes they represent. Because of the characterisation of the protagonist as the son of a miner and a middle-class woman, the text's ambivalent nature, which in the previous novel is embedded in the narrative, is more foregrounded and discernible. H. M. Daleski points to the inconsistency between hostile comments about the protagonist's father, Walter Morel, and the overt celebration of Mrs Morel on the one hand, and Morel's sympathetic presentation and Mrs Morel's harsh character on the other.[1] Michael Bell also analyses "a divided voice within its formally single narration" (Bell 39).[2] One of the most problematic scenes in the text is the closing episode where Paul turns from the mining village towards the town, attracted to "the city's gold phosphorescence" (*SL* 464). This is an ambiguous gesture which critics have interpreted as positive or negative according to

DOI: 10.4324/9781032675671-3

their analyses. Most literary criticism, from the humanist interpretation by Graham Hough to the psychoanalytical reading by Daniel J. Schneider, tends to conclude that Paul's final act represents his decision to choose life over death, rejecting his mother, to whom he is bound. Such interpretations, however, do not explain why the hero walks towards the town that is presented in the text as the centre of industry, which these critics regard as a negative force.[3] This question could be approached by focusing on two key concepts in *Sons and Lovers*, which would reveal how the narrative structure in this novel adheres to a dominant perspective widely accepted among the middle class at the turn of the century and in the early twentieth century.

The two key concepts to interpreting *Sons and Lovers* are procreation and evolution. These two ideas are respectively represented by Arthur Schopenhauer and Herbert Spencer, who had a considerable impact on philosophy, social theory and art from the late nineteenth to the early twentieth century. Schopenhauer postulated that the world is governed by the will to live and that sexual desire is the embodiment of the will. His influence ranged widely, from Friedrich Nietzsche's concept of tragedy and the "will to power" to Richard Wagner's music and Sigmund Freud's psychoanalysis. The English translation of a collection of his essays was published in 1897 and acquired wide readership in Britain, including Thomas Hardy, Joseph Conrad and James Joyce, not to mention Lawrence himself.[4] Schopenhauer argued in his essays, especially in "The Metaphysics of Love" (originally a chapter of the second volume of his monumental work *The World as Will and Representation* [1819]), that sexual attraction between certain persons is not an individual affair but is actually driven by the will of the species to produce their descendants. He believed that the "ultimate aim of all love-affairs ... is really more important than all other aims in human life. ... As a matter of fact, love determines nothing less than the *establishment of the next generation*" ("Metaphysics of Love" 172; emphasis in original).[5]

Schopenhauer's theory of love can be summarised in two points. First, he argues that sexual attraction occurs between people of different natures:

> Here we shall find that a woman universally is attracted by the qualities of a man's heart or character, both of which are inherited from the father. It is mainly firmness of will, determination and courage, and may be honesty and goodness of heart too, that win a woman over. ... And so we frequently find a woman preferring a stupid, ugly, and ill-mannered man to one who is well-educated, intellectual, and agreeable. Hence, people of extremely different temperament frequently marry for

> love—that is to say, *he* is coarse, strong, and narrow-minded, while *she* is very sensitive, refined, cultured, and æsthetic, and so on.
>
> (185–86; emphasis in original)

Second, the philosopher suggests that a person's passionate feelings towards his/her lover are kindled only for a short time and that they are quenched shortly thereafter, and hence, the couple necessarily has a miserable conjugal life:

> People who marry for love do so in the interest of the species and not of the individuals. It is true that the persons concerned imagine they are promoting their own happiness; but their real aim, which is one they are unconscious of, is to bring forth an individual which can be begotten by them alone. This purpose having brought them together, they ought henceforth to try and make the best of things. But it very frequently happens that two people who have been brought together by this instinctive illusion, which is the essence of passionate love, are in every other respect temperamentally different. This becomes apparent when the illusion wears off, as it necessarily must.
>
> Accordingly, people who marry for love are generally unhappy, for such people look after the welfare of the future generation at the expense of the present.
>
> (204)

Lawrence imbibed "The Metaphysics of Love" and its influence is plainly evident. In the third manuscript of *Sons and Lovers*, titled *Paul Morel*, the narrator refers to the philosopher in mentioning the Morels' procreation: "Walter Morel had given his wife children, according to the doctrine of Schopenhauer" (*PM* 192). Schopenhauer's name was deleted in the final manuscript, but the philosopher's marked influence on *Sons and Lovers* is easily discernible in its plot: an educated middle-class woman falls in love with a rather coarse and vigorous illiterate miner; their passionate love produces offspring, but their love is only temporary; after their marriage, "for three months she [Mrs Morel] was perfectly happy: for six months she was very happy" (*SL* 19), but their "instinctive illusion" soon wears off, and their conjugal life turns out to be a miserable and tormenting one. Paul's later remark again coincides with Schopenhauer's theory:

> "Yes, but my mother, I believe, got *real* joy and satisfaction out of my father at first. I believe she had a passion for him. ... That's what one *must have*, I think," he continued; "the real, real flame of feeling through another person, once, only once, if it only lasts three months".
>
> (*SL* 361–62; emphasis in original)

Based on such details, the characterisation of the Morels cannot simply be ascribed to Lawrence's autobiographical facts.[6]

Herbert Spencer's theory of evolution similarly had an impact on Lawrence's thinking. Spencer was a hugely influential sociologist and philosopher and his ideas gave rise to a school of thought called social Darwinism, which in turn led to the (pseudo-)science of eugenics and provided an ideological justification for colonial imperialism. Spencer's basic idea is that human society inevitably advances from one stage to the next, ruled by the principle of "survival of the fittest". He furthermore saw a parallel between the evolutionary processes in society and in organisms. In his essay "The Social Organism", Spencer propounds a theory of parallel development between social bodies and living organisms from the simplest forms to the most complex ones:

> Such, then, is a general outline of the evidence which justifies the comparison of societies to living organisms. That they gradually increase in mass; that they become little by little more complex; that at the same time their parts grow more mutually dependent; and that they continue to live and grow as wholes, while successive generations of their units appear and disappear. ... And on carrying out the comparison in detail, we find that these major analogies involve many minor analogies, far closer than might have been expected.
>
> ("Social Organism" 306)

This evolutionary process is ruled by the law of the survival of the fittest, by which he believed a society evolved in the best way. This theory justified the idea that in the course of the struggle for survival, the "unfit" could be eliminated. As a laissez-faire liberal, he also insisted that politicians and the states should not interfere with these natural processes. The idea of social Darwinism wielded significant influence, defining the middle-class frame of mind at the turn of the century and leaving a discernible impact on such authors as Thomas Hardy and H. G. Wells, among others.

Schopenhauer's beliefs about love and procreation and Spencer's theory of evolution define the basic structure of *Sons and Lovers*: the offspring brought into the world by a couple who are in many ways opposites, become entangled in a society that is evolving. Schopenhauer's marked influence is rather easy to detect; it is as if his "doctrine" dominates the plot. Spencer's influence has also been noted by several critics. Indeed in the novel, Spencer's ideas are a shared interest of Paul and Miriam and his terminology is interspersed throughout the narrative.[7] I would argue, however, that in addition to these apparent coincidences, Spencer's social theory deeply permeates and defines the plot of the novel. It is true, as we shall see, that Spencer's view and the parallel evolution portrayed in

Sons and Lovers are not altogether identical. However, they unmistakably shared the basic frame of thought—the parallel development between society and living creatures. In actuality, the notion that a society evolves correspondingly with its constituents was widely pervasive, as expressed, for example, by South African militant feminist Olive Schreiner in *Woman and Labour* (1911), a bible of the Women's Movement:

> It cannot be too often repeated, even at the risk of the most wearisome reiteration, that our societies are societies in a state of rapid evolution and change. The continually changing material conditions of life, with their reaction on the intellectual, emotional, and moral aspects of human affairs, render our societies the most complex and probably the most mobile and unsettled which the world has ever seen.
>
> (260)

Lawrence read this book when he was composing *Sons and Lovers* and recommended it to Louie Burrows: "I send you *Woman and Labour.* … Myself I skip the rhetoric. But read the book, will you. I think it's worth it" (*1L* 288).[8] Schopenhauer's fascination with procreation and Spencer's parallelism are entwined with the narrative structure of *Sons and Lovers.*

Transition

" 'The Bottoms' succeeded to 'Hell Row' "—thus begins *Sons and Lovers*, followed by a description of how the group of cottages where the coal miners lived, The Bottoms, was improved over the earlier ones of Hell Row (*SL* 9). No one would wish to retitle the novel *Houses and Gardens*, but no one could fail to recognise the numerous references to, and much detailed description of, houses and gardens in the text. Only a few literary critics have paid attention to this fact, but houses and gardens afford a clue to interpreting this work.[9] It is no accident that the novel begins with an improvement in accommodation; houses and gardens reveal the extent of transition and disclose the essence of human activity in the mining country. One of the central preoccupations in *Sons and Lovers* is improvement, or social evolution. Bestwood itself is changing, and the countryside is becoming more and more industrialised and mechanised, moving towards a capitalist society.

The houses symbolise the stages of a metamorphosis. While the Bottoms represents a new phase of the industrialisation of Bestwood, Hell Row represents the pre-industrial era when mining activity was on a much smaller scale and less mechanised. Mining in the age of Hell Row was limited in scope, donkey powered and more manually controlled. The language at the beginning of the novel establishes a mythic landscape: "[T]he few colliers and the donkeys [were] burrowing down like ants into the earth, making queer mounds and little black places among the corn-fields and the meadows" (9). As seen here, men and animals worked together on the fertile land and human beings occupied only a small domain in nature. The opening paragraph implies that mining itself was the colliers' *raison d'être* and that it was a part of the workings of nature.

In this period miners lived in a world where time moved in cycles. The methods of mining activity in this district had not changed for many years, and the process was repeated year after year for almost 200 years: "And all over the countryside were these same pits, some of which had been worked in the time of Charles II …" (9). The inhabitants of Bestwood lived in this mythic world of repeated cycles. People did not have any desire for development or for transcending the cyclical pattern of their lives and work.

Then this idyllic district underwent a transformation into a large industrialised area. The arrival of capitalism caused the sudden change of this pre-industrial Arcadia into an industrial village. The agents of capitalism who discovered the coal and iron fields—"the financiers" such as "Carston, Waite and Co." (9)—came from the outside capitalist world. They opened large mechanised mines, constructed railways, built the Bottoms and began to exploit the local miners. As a result, a massive industrialised area appeared there. Thus, a huge industry was born of the marriage between alien capitalism and the native labour force.

The cycle that had governed the idyllic countryside was thus forced to change due to the arrival of capitalism. The reason for this was simply because capitalist activity does not content itself with simple repetition; capitalism necessarily involves growth and multiplication. The cyclical movement of time was thus replaced by the linear movement of evolution. As a result, big mechanistic organisations "succeeded to" the pre-industrial labour system. Bestwood is now no longer a pastoral countryside—it is a place endlessly advancing towards becoming an industrialised capitalist region.

Corresponding to the improvement that occurs in Bestwood, the Morels similarly undergo a change and advance socially. The Morels switch their accommodation several times, and each new house shows their rise in social and economic status. Although they have a side garden, the Bottoms is simply a grouping of terraced houses intended exclusively for miners. Their next house is, however, not one designated solely for miners and their next-door neighbour is a shopkeeper (which shows the extent to which the monetary economy has permeated the village). In front of the house stands a gas lamp post, which symbolises a new phase in the development of the village. Their last house is semi-detached and has a big sunny garden. Thus, the supersession of the houses illustrates the gradual development of the country as a whole and the corresponding social and economic rise of the Morels.

Bestwood and Capitalism

It is significant that the first episode in which the Morels are introduced begins with the scene at the fair in Bestwood, where the children are eager to go. Throughout the text it is emphasised that the Morels like to spend money at fairs and markets. Both Walter Morel and his kids love fairs:

> Morel ... was sure to make a holiday of it. He went off early on the Monday morning, the day of the fair. The two children were highly excited. William, a boy of seven, fled off immediately after breakfast, to prowl round the wakes ground, leaving Annie, who was only five, to whine all morning to go also.
>
> (11)

Even after he has grown up, William is glad to come back home from London at the time of Goose Fair, the biggest annual fair in the district: "He wrote in wild excitement saying he could come for Saturday and Sunday at Goose Fair, the first week in October" (164). Although she does not like big fairs, "Mrs Morel loved her marketing" (98), spending her time and money at the market held periodically in Bestwood (see Figure 2.1).

Figure 2.1 "Young colliers and Eastwood Market cheapjacks. June 1913", taken by the Reverend F. W. Cobb, Rector of Eastwood. Courtesy of The National Archives of the UK (TNA): COAL 13/74.

The wakes were originally festivals of the saints, but in the text they are fun fairs where people spend their money on entertainment. The wakes symbolise the activity related to the monetary economy, with which the mining village has been involved since the arrival of capitalism. In Bestwood, not only the miners but also the women have been gradually associated with the monetary economy, and their everyday activity becomes more and more related to the exchange of money. The women wait for "Hose", a worker in the hosiery trade, and exchange their stitched stockings for money. "Barm-O" drives a cart from street to street, selling yeast to the wives. And the women go to market regularly to purchase necessities for their households. In the novel, fairs and markets provide the setting for many scenes, with recurring minute accounts of wages, prices and living expenses, which emphasises how the monetary system has been pervading the mining village. The people in Bestwood have become more and more involved with capitalist activities.

Accordingly, the development of Bestwood causes a change in the population of the community. Bestwood becomes a village not only for miners and their families but also for newly arrived middle-class bourgeoisie: "The townlet contained nothing higher than the clergyman. Then came the bank-manager, then the doctors, then the tradespeople, and after that, the hosts of colliers" (73). Bestwood is thus becoming a capitalist and industrialised society which consists of a bourgeois middle class and proletarian miners.

Lights, trains and machinery in the pits function as metaphors indicating the degree to which the village has changed. Fire, the most basic form of light, is superseded by the oil lamp, the gaslight and the electric light, each of which signifies a phase of industrialisation.[10] Trains, which at the beginning of the novel were part of a small railway system connecting the mining pits and conveying coal, have evolved into a bigger network which connects large cities and transports a large number of people. In Paul's boyhood, the mining industry is not yet hostile to nature. For example, while he is convalescing from an attack of bronchitis as a boy, he sees from his bedroom window the miners as a part of the monotonous, silent world, going back to their nest before dark. He also sees the tiny presence of a timid train overwhelmed by the vast whiteness of snow:

> In convalescence he would sit up in bed, see the fluffy horses feeding at the troughs in the field, scattering their hay on the trodden yellow snow; watch the miners troop home, small, black figures trailing slowly in gangs across the white field. Then the night came up in dark blue vapor from the snow.
>
> In convalescence everything was wonderful. The snowflakes, suddenly arriving on the window-pane, clung there a moment like swallows,

> then were gone, and a drop of water was crawling down the glass. The snowflakes whirled round the corner of the house, like pigeons dashing by. Away across the valley, the little black train crawled doubtfully over the great whiteness.
>
> (92)

In this phase of the countryside, nature and industry are not necessarily alienated from each other. The pits are fused into the natural surroundings and are part of a rural landscape: "The valley was full of a lustrous dark haze, through which the ripe corn shimmered, and in which the steam from Minton pit melted swiftly" (127). The coal mining activity is part of the rural landscape and contributes to the peaceful atmosphere of the region. The rumbling of the machines does not disturb but rather heightens the liveliness of the environment as if it were the buzz of honeybees:

> It was a beautiful day. At Bretty pit the white steam melted slowly in the sunshine of a soft blue sky, the wheels of the headstocks twinkled high up, the screen, shuffling its coal into the trucks, made a busy noise.
>
> (166)

The only thing that breaks the peaceful stillness is the trains to and from the Metropolis, but they are still merely a temporal disturbance, as Paul sees on returning from Nottingham:

> He had to walk two and more miles from Keston home, up two long hills, down two short hills. He was often tired, and he counted the lamps climbing the hill above him, how many more to pass. And from the hill-top, on pitch dark nights, he looked round on the villages five or six miles away, that shone like swarms of glittering living things, almost a heaven against his feet. Marlpool and Heanor scattered the far off darkness with brilliance. And occasionally, the black valley space between was traced, violated by a great train rushing south to London, or north to Scotland. The trains roared by like projectiles level on the darkness, fuming and burning, making the valley clang with their passage. They were gone, and the lights of the towns and villages glittered in silence.
>
> (140)

As industry advances, however, it begins to take on a sinister undertone. On their way to the Hemlock Stone, Paul and his friends see the railway tracks shining ominously, on which express trains roar away to the Metropolis, and can see a roaring fire at an iron foundry:

> They stood on the footbridge over Boathouse Station, and looked at the metals gleaming coldly.
>
> "You should see the Flying Scotchman come through at half past six," said Leonard, whose father was a signalman. "Lad, but she doesn't half buzz!". ...
>
> In Ilkeston the colliers were waiting in gangs for the public houses to open. It was a town of idleness and lounging. At Stanton Gate the iron foundry blazed.
>
> (200)

In Paul's adulthood, industrialisation has obviously moved into the next phase. From Nottingham Castle, Paul, with Clara, looks out over the town, which is now invading the countryside:

> Away beyond the boulevard, the thin stripes of the metals showed upon the railway track, whose margin was crowded with little stacks of timber, beside which smoking toy engines fussed. Then the silver string of the canal lay at random among the black heaps. Beyond, the dwellings, very dense on the river flats, looked like black, poisonous herbage, in thick rows and crowded beds, stretching right away, broken now and then by taller plants, right to where the river glistened in a hieroglyph across the country. The steep scarp cliffs across the river looked puny. Great stretches of country, darkened with trees and faintly brightened with corn-land, spread towards the haze, where the hills rose blue beyond grey.
>
> (313)

Although industry has not yet overwhelmed nature, its invasive power is depicted in the ominous darkness and metallic colour. A locomotive runs on the iron rails and the land is penetrated by the artificial waterway, both of which contribute to transporting loads of hewn logs to towns. The human habitat grows unpleasantly like toxic plants, and the countryside is totally dark except for the faint glimmer of the corn. Thus, the intrusion of capitalism has been transforming the land into a sinister, gloomy and desolate place.[11]

Mrs Morel

Paul's mother Mrs Morel is a character who both metaphorically and literally represents the monetary economy in the novel. She comes originally from the commercial class, and is the solid bourgeois stock "of a good old burgher family" (15), the Coppards, who are the descendants of the famous middle class in Nottingham that goes back to the era of the Civil War. She was born in Nottingham and then moved to the mining district when she got married. Thus, Mrs Morel is one of those middle-class people who comes from outside of the local community. Her deep attachment to money can be ascribed to her lineage. The episode of her mammonist ex-boyfriend illustrates the affinity of their class for money. John Field was "the son of a well-to-do tradesman" with a distinguished academic background, but nonetheless gave up being a minister and married "his landlady, a woman of forty, a widow with property" (16–17). Mrs Morel loves money, and anything that concerns money can be the cause of her joy or grief: she feels privileged thinking that her end house at the Bottoms is six shillings higher than the other houses; she haggles over the price of a little dish at the market; she is exhilarated when she learns how much her son's picture sells for. Paul makes a design for his mother but changes his mind and sells it because, as he says to Miriam, "I think she'd rather have the money" (241). And her mistrust and contempt for her husband arises when she finds out that he is not financially independent—the house is not theirs and Morel has paid rent to his mother, to whom he is also in debt for their household effects. Mrs Morel applies capitalist norms to other people, judging them from the point of view of their economic success or failure.

Being "a puritan, like her father, high-minded, and really stern" (18), Mrs Morel is not content with living a recurring life cycle without any development taking place. It is emphasised that she is an incarnation of the Protestant ethic:

> She still had her high moral sense, inherited from generations of Puritans. It was now a religious instinct, and she was almost a fanatic with him [Mr Morel]. ... If he sinned, she tortured him. If he drank, and lied, was often a poltroon, sometimes a knave, she wielded the lash unmercifully.
>
> (25)

Her puritanical virtue motivates her to pursue progress and social aspirations. She joins the Women's Co-operative Guild, which aims at improving the conditions of the miners' and their families' lives. She refuses to reproduce children who go down the pit; instead, she desires for her sons to be promoted and to attain a higher position in society. Her thinking and behaviour are always motivated by the desire for upward mobility and transcendence of the repeated activity.[12] Thus, Mrs Morel embodies the bourgeois Protestant ethic, which, as Max Weber observed, contributed to the development of capitalism.

Walter Morel

Walter Morel is in many ways the opposite of his wife. He is a native of Bestwood, and, as Michael Black suggests, essentially a premodern man of a previous era when work at smaller mining pits was done by hand: "Morel is tribal, archaic, almost mythical: it might have been wonderful to have been him in some earlier time" (Black 65). His nature is suggested in much of his behaviour and many of his characteristics. At the pits he still works with an "oss" (Midlands dialect for a "horse") called Taffy. He believes in irrational superstitions: "Morel never in his life played cards, considering them as having some occult, malevolent power: 'the devil's pictures,' he called them" (*SL* 29). At meals he drinks tea out of a saucer, uses a pocketknife and loathes a fork, which is to him "a modern introduction" (37). He cannot keep up with the trends of the times and does not accept new types of tools or utensils.

Although ignorant of the modern way of life, Morel is a sage about medicinal plants and a knowledgeable collector of dried herbs:

> And he made himself a jug of wormwood tea. He had hanging in the attic great bunches of dried herbs: wormwood, rue, horehound, elderflowers, parsley-purt, marsh-mallow, hyssop, dandelion and centaury. Usually there was a jug of one or other decoction standing on the hob, from which he drank largely.
>
> (61)

And although he is close to illiterate and able to write hardly more than his name, he is a remarkable storyteller: "Morel had a warm way of telling a story. He made one feel Taffy's cunning" (89). Thus, he is presented as the image of a successor—or a living relic—of age-old wisdom and the oral tradition.

This representation of him as a "tribal, archaic, almost mythical" man is supported by the fact that he lives a life regulated by one discipline: repetition. He does not accept change and lives a life that repeats itself in a consistent cycle. Morel follows what the older generations in Bestwood have done: like his father, he began to work in the pits when he was still ten, and he wants his sons to go down into the pits as well. His everyday life is also based on simple repetition: there is little need to revise the schedule of his working day. He does not challenge social norms and obeys the traditional roles assigned to men. Being afraid of the outside, unknown world, he does not leave his customary area. He is content to be a man who accepts the cyclical life of the mining country.[13] Thus, he is essentially an archaic miner of the previous era, living in a world where time moves in cycles.

Therefore, it is significant that fire, the most primitive means of obtaining light, is attributed to this miner. Just as Mrs Morel loves money, Morel loves fire: "Then Morel came again, and crouched before the bedroom fire. He loved a fire dearly" (92). He is offended if the fire is low at home. It must be kept burning in the house all through the day and night, and Morel himself tends and controls the fire:

> On Sunday morning he would get up and prepare breakfast. The fire was never let to go out. It was raked just at bed-time. That is, a great piece of coal, a raker, was placed so that it would be nearly burned through by morning. ... When she [Mrs Morel] came downstairs, a great fire glowed in the grate, the room was hot, the breakfast was roughly laid. And seated in his armchair, against the chimney piece, sat Morel.
>
> (23)

He makes a fire even when it is unnecessary: "He preferred to keep the blinds down and the candle lit, even when it was daylight" (38).

Not only does he actually love fire but he is also symbolically connected to it. A candle flame is his life force, which used to attract his wife:

> Therefore the dusky, golden softness of this man's *sensuous flame of life*, that flowed from off his flesh *like the flame from a candle*, not baffled and gripped into incandescence by thought and spirit as her life was, seemed to her something wonderful, beyond her.
>
> (18; my emphasis)

Morel's metaphorical and actual association with fire characterises him as a man of the pre-industrial era.

While in the world of wages and hiring he is only an alienated labourer and by degrees is kicked out of good pits, at home he can be a good worker. There he is skilled with his hands and can make anything necessary or useful: "He was a remarkably handy man, could make or mend anything" (20). He creates fuses for the pit himself as well as repairs his own boots and mends the kettle or his pit bottle. His love and enthusiasm for such manual work warms his chilly relationships with his children, if only for a while. It reveals that, although in the pit he is merely a cog in the wheel of the regulated labour system, he can be a craftsman at home who is not alienated from his labour. At such times he is a worker, idealised by Karl Marx as a labourer before the rise of predatory capitalism.

The decline of Morel is obstinately emphasised in the text. He has a strong physique, which his children lack, as his wife tells him: " 'You've had a constitution like iron,' she said. 'And never a man had a better start, if it was body that counted' " (236). Considering this remark, his downfall comes remarkably fast. Even before his son Paul is born, Morel's decay—both mental and physical—has begun:

> Yet there was a slight shrinking, a diminishing in his assurance. Physically even, he shrank, and his fine full presence waned. He never grew in the least stout, so that, as he sank from his erect, assertive

> bearing, his physique seemed to contract along with his pride and moral strength.
>
> (37)

When his last child, Arthur, is born, Morel's decline is again emphasised: "As he grew older, Morel fell into a slow ruin. His body, which had been beautiful in movement and in being, shrank, did not seem to ripen with the years, but to get mean and rather despicable" (141).

It is suggestive that his trip to Nottingham, a commercial centre, accentuates his decline. After the trip he contracts an illness which is incurable even with his favourite herbal teas:

> This time, however, neither pills nor vitriol nor all his herbs would shift the "nasty peens in his head." He was sickening for an attack of an inflammation of the brain. He had never been well since his sleeping on the ground when he went with Jerry to Nottingham.
>
> (61)

Later he has an accident twice in the pits and is brought to a hospital in Nottingham, but his wounds never fully heal. The hospital is a modern place which is run mechanically and methodically, as Paul notices when he goes to visit his mother's doctor at a Nottingham hospital. All the patients are assigned numbers and are treated systematically: "Paul told his name, and his mother's. The doctor did not remember. / 'Number 46M.' said the nurse, and the doctor looked up the case in his book" (417). Such an organised place is alien to Morel: "'And of course,' Mrs Morel continued, 'for a man like your father, the hospital *is* hard. He *can't* understand rules and regulations'" (112; emphasis in original). As a result he falls lame to the end of his life. He has come to look dispossessed and has none of his former blazing vitality: "He was a forlorn figure, looking rather as if nobody owned him" (421).

Some critics ascribe his decline to his labour in the mines or to his unsuccessful marriage,[14] but putting it in a wider context within the novel its metaphorical implications are evident. The mining country advances towards becoming an urbanised area. The oil or gas lamps, which produce more intense light than fire, are set at home, and the street lamps begin to brighten the night. The mining village is in transition to a more developed capitalist society. There remains little space for Walter Morel to live in this predatory society which is continually evolving into a more industrialised area. This man, representing the pre-industrial era, adhering to a pre-modern way of life, cannot adjust to the evolution of a society where only the fittest survive. He can be an ideal labourer only sometimes at home where a fire still burns in the hearth. In the pits the miners bring oil lamps with them, and on the streets stand gas lamp posts. A candle flame cannot keep burning forever; it must go out some day.[15]

Another metaphorical attribute associated with Morel is flowers: "Gertrude Coppard watched the young miner as he danced, a certain subtle exultation like glamour in his movement, and his face the *flower* of his body, ruddy, with tumbled black hair, and laughing alike whatever partner he bowed above" (17–18; my emphasis). Flowers have a significant metaphorical meaning in *Sons and Lovers*. In Bestwood, flowers are grown in gardens and these areas are not merely accessories to houses. The extra garden of the Bottoms makes Mrs Morel feel economically superior to other families. The garden of the third house is presented as a different world full of brightness in the sunshine, separated from the hideous, gloomy reality. In these gardens some of the novel's major events take place: Mrs Morel, kicked out of the house by her husband, experiences an epiphany in the garden of the Bottoms; Paul is at one time attracted to and, at another time, repelled by Miriam in the garden of her farm; and Paul, Clara and Miriam have a clumsy encounter in the garden of the Morels' third house.

The narrator describes in minute detail these gardens, in which are arranged many kinds of flowers and plants, from purely an aesthetic point of view, not an ecological or environmental one. Flowers in the gardens serve to provide human pleasure and happiness: "The garden was an endless joy to her [Mrs Morel]. … Every morning after breakfast she went out and was happy pottering about in it" (200). The garden is thus a space of the exploitation of nature by human beings—and it thereby symbolises the activity of the mining country: the digging of coal. Flowers are an emblem of exploited nature, much like Morel himself, who is an exploited labourer.

In Nottingham, people no longer tend the gardens but instead buy flowers at flower shops. Mrs Morel is fascinated by the flowers at a florist's when she goes to Nottingham with Paul, who is bewildered by her excessive excitement before the display. In a capitalist society, flowers are commodities bought at a shop. It suggests the destiny of Morel, whose life force is attributed to fire and flowers. He is doomed to decline as a commodity in a capitalist world, where a candle flame is no longer used and flowers have lost their natural strength and vitality.

The Morels

Thus, Morel and Mrs Morel are of different—in many senses contrary—natures. Morel represents archaic, pre-modern principles of life in accordance with nature, while Mrs Morel embodies the spirit of modern capitalism. Morel is an alienated labourer, whereas Mrs Morel is a *homo economicus* with a Protestant ethic. Fire is attributed to Morel, and, as Black suggests, the artificial light of the oil lamp to Mrs Morel.[16] Morel seeks continuity, following the norms and conventions of the community, while Mrs Morel, representing upward, linear movement, seeks change and improvement. Morel lives in a cyclical life pattern, while Mrs Morel intends to transcend the cyclical movement of time. In other words, Morel represents the native miners of the pre-industrialised era, and Mrs Morel the middle-class people from outside the coal mining community.

Therefore, the marriage between Walter Morel and Gertrude Coppard symbolises what happened in the mining country. Their marriage embodies an encounter between the native labour force and the capitalists from the outside world, which is depicted at the very beginning of *Sons and Lovers*. Since this contact has taken place, the mining countryside has undergone a metamorphosis. The idyllic world where men and animals once worked together in the small, manually oriented pits for nearly two centuries has changed into a commercial world where local labourers are exploited under the control of the colliery companies.

Capitalist society, as Marx observed, suffers from an essential division between workers and managers. In Bestwood the workers are the native miners, and the middle class, who come from the outside world—"the financiers" such as "Carston, Waite and Co."—manage and control the mines. The same frame can be applied to the Morels. Morel works for wages, and he is himself a worker as a commodity. In contrast, Mrs Morel does not allow herself to be exploited by taking on the outwork which the other women in Bestwood do: " 'Well!' said Mrs Morel, 'I'd starve before I'd sit down and seam twenty four stockings for twopence ha'penny' " (40). Instead she undertakes intellectual activity by joining the Women's Guild located at a grocery shop. Morel is a labourer whose work is measured by his wages, while Mrs Morel is a manager who nags her husband/worker for more wages, controls the money at home and manages the household.[17]

Attempting to adapt themselves to the development of society, the Morel offspring abandon the province, which is a realm where the same activity is repeated in an endless cycle, and launch themselves into the world of progress and evolution. They do not follow in their father's footsteps but go to Nottingham and London, centres of industry and capitalism. The differences between the children and their father are in many ways obvious. For example, they are no longer good storytellers as their father is: "Then he [Paul] told her [Mrs Morel] the budget of the day. His life-story, like an *Arabian Nights*, but much duller, was told night after night to his mother" (140). In a public house Paul propounds his own theory, which only bores the audience, contrary to his father, who is a popular figure in the pubs: "He [Paul] was not a favourite debater in the public house, being too quick and overbearing. He irritated the older men by his assertive manner, and his cock-sureness. They listened in silence, and were not sorry when he finished" (386–87). The children lack natural wisdom and never enjoy the herbal teas which their father has always favoured: " 'It's better than any of your tea or your cocoa stews,' he [Morel] vowed. But they [the children] were not to be tempted" (61). Morel is a *promeneur naturel* and loves to immerse himself in nature, exploring the fields for mushrooms: "He loved the early morning. ... Usually he went over the fields, and often, in summer, would look in the gin-close for mushrooms, straying through the thick wet grass in his pit-boots, looking for the lurking, white-fleshed things" (38). His children also love foraging mushrooms in the fields, but they have another reason for doing that—frugality:

> While they were so poor, the children were delighted if they could do anything to help, economically. Annie and Paul and Arthur went out early in the morning, in summer, looking for mushrooms, hunting through the wet grass, from which the larks were rising, for the white skinned, wonderful naked bodies crouched secretly in the green. And if they got half a pound, they felt exceedingly happy: there was the joy of finding something, the joy of accepting something straight from the hand of nature, and the joy of contributing to the family exchequer.
> (92)

While Morel loves the fire, his children are attracted to gas or electric light. They gather around the lamp post in front of their second house. Once they are grown up, they use electric lamps, as is shown in William's letter and in Paul's "penny-in-the-slot meter" (456) in his Nottingham lodgings, which supplies electric light when some penny coins are inserted, also suggesting the relation between urbanisation and the capitalist system. Arthur, who loves his father most among his brothers, comes back from Nottingham and works in the pits. He, however, does not go down the pit as a miner but, significantly, as an electrician.

Leaving the pastoral world, William and Paul devote themselves to capitalist activity in town. William is engaged in the sugar trade in London Port as a customs inspector. Paul enters the world of the merchandising trade at Jordan's, carrying out business with his uncertain French. His art also contributes to his earning power. He makes an attempt at creating conventional designs for the sake of money. He sends them to Liberty's and boasts to Clara's mother of earning more than 30 guineas a year. Liberty's, London's fashionable department store, started its business by selling imported goods from the Far East, but at the turn of the century, it sold wares and textiles all over Europe, in Canada, Australia, China, Japan, India and South Africa.[18] In the world of commerce, William and

Paul thus play a role in the transnational movement of capital, which establishes the international capitalist network.

William, however, eventually dies in London. In Chapter 6 titled "Death in the Family", first William and then Paul are confined to bed. This chapter is multilayered as it offers harsh criticism of mechanical industry and capitalism while simultaneously embracing contemporary reactionary discourse. Mrs Morel finds in his lodgings that William is laid in bed in an unhygienic, cold room in London, with no fire, with no one to attend to him. Her son suffers from hallucinations and moans as if he were at work: "Owing to a leakage in the hold of the vessel, the sugar had set, and become converted into rock. It needed hacking—" (166). He eventually expires miserably. Later in the same chapter, Paul is forced to be in bed for seven weeks suffering from bronchitis, which is caused by his work in an insanitary office at Jordan's in Nottingham. The description of the office implies the fact that the well-mechanised factory curiously resembles the modernised mines:

> Paul followed him [a clerk] round the rectangle of counters. The room was second storey. It had a great *hole* in the middle of the floor, fenced as with a wall of counters, and down this wide *shaft* the *lifts* went, and the light for the bottom storey. Also there was a corresponding big, oblong *hole* in the ceiling, and one could see above, over the fence of the top floor, some machinery. And right away overhead was the glass roof, and all light for the three storeys came downwards, getting dimmer, so that it was always night on the ground floor, and rather gloomy on the second floor. The factory was the top floor, the warehouse the second, the storehouse the ground floor. It was an insanitary ancient place.
>
> (128; my emphasis)

The similarity between the dark factory and the mines is explicitly presented with such words as "hole", "shaft" and "lifts". The resemblance of these places is actually affirmed by the narrator, who asserts that "the place was like a pit" (118). Paul goes to this dark, unhygienic office early in the morning, works in "the darkness, and lack of air, and the long hours" (135). Paul likes the feeling of comradeship and togetherness of the workers, which was also a popular image related to the coal miners: "The factory had a homely feel. No one was rushed or driven. Paul always enjoyed it when the work got faster, towards post-time, and all the men united in labour" (139–40).[19] The text indicates that through mechanisation and the expansion of industry, the essence of capitalism is succeeded from one place to another in the capitalist world. Workplaces remain dark, dirty and dangerous, with capitalism persistently exploiting labourers, producing substantial profits and making numerous victims, whether in mines in the country or factories in towns.

This critique of modern industry and capitalism is intermingled with contemporary conservative discourse in the narrative of *Sons and Lovers*. Urban degeneration, one of the often-debated issues among the intellectuals at the turn of the century, hastens William's death, along with an influence by a Spencerian concept of "the survival of the fittest" as Helen Baron notes.[20] As Chapter 1 of this study has previously noted, British people at that time thought that the nation had both physically and morally degenerated. In contrast to *The White Peacock*, which depicts rural degeneration, *Sons and Lovers* takes up urban degeneracy. At the turn of the century, the cause of urban degeneration was ascribed to their lives of material prosperity and luxury and to mechanised labour in the city. In his influential book *Degeneration*, Max Nordau attributed one major cause of degeneration to "residence in large towns" and argued that the

> inhabitant of a large town, even the richest, who is surrounded by the greatest luxury, is continually exposed to unfavourable influences which diminish his vital powers far more than what is inevitable. ... The effect of a large town on the human organism offers the closest analogy to that of the Maremma, and its population falls victim to the same fatality of degeneracy and destruction as the victims of malaria. (Nordau 35)

After he moves to London, William becomes "quite swanky" (*SL* 115) and frequents London's high society. He buys an engagement ring costing eight guineas for his fiancée, Louisa Lily Denys Western. This young woman is a paragon of wealth, who spends her fiancé's and her aunt's money quite lavishly, sends a photo of herself with a naked bust and shoulders to her boyfriend's parents and even at the Morels wears gorgeous dresses inappropriate to a working-class household. William has overextended himself too much to adapt to urban life and eventually dies of pneumonia, suffering from a high fever and a complicating disease. Thus, ambivalent implications are embedded in the narrative. Traces of influence by the reactionary discourse of social Darwinism and urban degeneration can be acknowledged in the text which simultaneously exposes the harshness and ruthlessness of modern capitalism.[21]

To conclude, in *Sons and Lovers*, the evolution of a mining district occurs in parallel with that of a local household. The encounter between the local labour force and capitalism has transformed Bestwood into an industrialised area which is continually advancing towards becoming a civilised and capitalist society. Bestwood is a macrocosm which corresponds to the microcosm of the Morels' home. Walter Morel represents the eternal repetitive cycle signifying a pre-industrial time sequence, while Mrs Morel represents upward, linear movement and the endless growth of capital. The marriage between the native labourer and the incarnation of the capitalist spirit results in offspring who, in attempting to adapt to a new environment, engage in industrial and capitalist activities. Thus, the basic framework of the novel is determined and developed through the parallel development of society and living creatures—as indicated by Paul's remark that the far-off villages are "like swarms of glittering living things" (140). The text is intensely focused on evolution and procreation, both of which are entwined with the narrative structure of *Sons and Lovers*. A community inevitably evolves into a town, and only those who can fit themselves into the town can survive. When his brother dies, Paul says to Miriam that he knows which way he should progress to survive:

> "And if we follow the course of our lives, we don't die?" she asked.
> "No we don't. ..."
> "But do we know when we're following the true course?" she asked.
> "Yes! *I* do. I know I'm following mine."
> "You do?" she asked.
> "Yes—I'm certain."
> He had stood under a lamp to think.
>
> (193)

Paul understands the path he must take to survive, and so it is a natural choice for him at the end of the novel to walk towards the centre of industry and capitalism glittering with electric lights.

Notes

1 See Daleski 43.

2 For more on the ambivalence in the narrative of *Sons and Lovers*, see Martz 343–69, Schorer 67–78 and Littlewood 323–61.

3 For example, Graham Holderness argues that "Paul walks back—towards the town; back towards relationship, interdependence, social connection; back towards the community in which alone human life can have meaning and reality ..." (158). But elsewhere he asserts that

> once the working-class community is left behind, there is precisely nothing "there". ... Individualised entry into the idle class can never constitute a solution to the problems of Bestwood, or of the Morel family. ... Outside the working-class community there is nothing—a vacuum.
>
> (147)

See also Hough 52, Weiss 66–67 and Schneider 139–40.

4 See Bishop 337–43 and Chambers 98 and 111–12.

5 All quotations from "The Metaphysics of Love" are from *Essays of Schopenhauer*, translated by Mrs Rudolf Dircks and published by Walter Scott in 1897, which is the version Lawrence read in his youth, although her translation is now considered to be somewhat distorted and arbitrary.

6 Carl Krockel analyses Schopenhauer's (as well as Freud's) influence on Lawrence's method of characterisation in *Sons and Lovers* and its earlier versions. He argues that "Lawrence's characters are only puppets enacting his reading of the philosopher" (*Lawrence and Germany* 79), but through revision Lawrence departs from Schopenhauer and *Sons and Lovers* anticipates Freud. See Krockel, *Lawrence and Germany* 75–80. Conversely, Eleanor H. Green discusses how Schopenhauer's dualist vision is realised in Lawrence's works, from *The White Peacock* to *Women in Love*, and concludes that "Lawrence becomes a true Schopenhauer disciple" (91). For her analysis of Schopenhauer's influence on *Sons and Lovers*, see Green 87–88. Mitzi M. Brunsdale analyses Schopenhauer's influence on the young author through his annotations in the margin of the German philosopher's book. See Brunsdale 120–29. See also Worthen, *EY* 434–35. For a discussion of Schopenhauer's influence on Lawrence in general, see Rylance 21 and Zoll 1–20.

7 Spencer's influence on *Sons and Lovers* has already been noted by several critics, but they often primarily focus on identifying common terms and similar expressions between Spencer and Lawrence. For example, Helen Baron argues that the words "gravitation", "protoplasm" and "force" found in Lawrence can be derived from Spencer's *First Principles* and *Principles of Biology*, and, referring to William's death, concludes that "Spencer stood for a central preoccupation in the novel: evolution and its implications for the relations between Man, Nature and God" (Baron 270). See Baron 268–71 and 276–77. Alternatively, from the posthumanist approach, Jeff Wallace analyses in detail how Lawrence, as an "alert" materialist, encountered and reacted to the construction of scientific discourse through writings by Darwin, Spencer, Haeckel, T. H. Huxley and William James. See Wallace, *Posthuman* 58–97.

8 *Woman and Labour* contains several passages that are reminiscent of later Lawrence: in the new conditions of life, women are now aiming for "a higher appreciation of the sacredness of all sex relations, and a clearer perception of the sex relation between man and woman …" (25); "sex and the sexual relation between man and woman have distinct æsthetic, intellectual, and spiritual functions and ends, apart entirely from physical reproduction" (26–27).

9 One of the few exceptions is Stefania Michelucci, who argues that

> Places play a primary role in *Sons and Lovers*, and are closely connected to the characters' experience. … [T]he place is the home, vital center and locus of struggle for its inhabitants. … In relation to the protagonist and his home, places correspond as well to modes of being, types of sensibility, different languages and viewpoints.
>
> (33)

See Michelucci 32–54. Seamus O'Malley, on the other hand, focuses on flowers as "complex and conflicting symbols of English culture's relationship to the natural world" and, positioning garden in opposition to wild nature, concludes: "Gertrude's garden emerges as the meager compensation for the technological ravaging of the English countryside" (26, 41).

10 Michael Black also discusses the correlation between the supersession of lights and industrialisation. See Black 66–69. For the introduction of electricity that superseded gas in Croydon, Nottingham and Eastwood, as well as its portrayal in some of Lawrence's novels, see Harrison, *D. H. Lawrence and Italian Futurism* 140–47.

11 Interpreting *Sons and Lovers* from the point of view of the historical transition of transport and of what transport—trains, bicycles and tramcars—stood for literally and metaphorically, Andrew F. Humphries explores the ambivalence in the novel: transport in *Sons and Lovers* represents the mechanised male culture and is a focal point of male privilege, but it also promotes awareness of gender inequality that challenges Paul's assertion of masculine need. See Humphries 35–77.

12 Her nature is implied by her fascination with lofty Lincoln Cathedral. Terry Eagleton argues that "she represents an impulse within the traditional settlement for extension and transcendence" (197).

13 Eagleton makes the same point: "Morel moves within the close, restricted limits of a routine working life, instinctively hostile to change and extension ..." (195).

14 For example, Daniel J. Schneider suggests that "If the pits do not kill him, they cripple him. ... But the deepest crippling occurs, of course, in his marriage" (136). From an Oedipal perspective, Daniel A. Weiss ascribes Morel's decline to the strong bond between Paul and his mother. See Weiss 23–25. Likewise, Eagleton ascribes the main cause of his decline to "the shaming consciousness of his failure to shoulder the burden of family life" (196).

15 Tony Pinkney also ascribes Morel's decline to the conflict between his nature and the change in the mining village. Pinkney argues that as "a miner, he is a creature of the underground, darkness, night; and he becomes increasingly ineffectual and ill at ease in the daylight world as the novel progresses" (47).

16 See Black 67.

17 Herbert Spencer also regarded the division of labour as an inevitable result in the process of social development: "You need but to ... observe social organization ... to see that these [the changes going on around] are ... consequent on general natural causes. The one case of the division of labour suffices to prove this" ("Social Organism" 266).

18 See Adburgham 83–101, Rieber 14 and 56.

19 Bernard Waites maintains that working-class solidarity has been a public image since the first decade of the twentieth century. See Waites 46.

20 See Baron 270. In addition, on his brother's death, Paul's idea that not the individual but the species matters directly corresponds to Schopenhauer's view.

21 Andrew Smith also recognises the connection between urban degeneracy and William's death. Smith maintains that in *Sons and Lovers*, Lawrence employs various Gothic images, specifically the vampire figure, which can be linked to theories of degeneration. One of the vampires in the novel is, Smith argues, Lily Western as the carrier of syphilis, haunting William and ultimately leading to his demise. See Smith 154–58.

3 The Brangwens and Construction of the Towns in *The Rainbow*

The Rainbow has often been regarded as a novel of Lawrence's new phase, whether *Sons and Lovers* is considered to be the last novel of Lawrence's apprenticeship or the first of his maturity. The styles of *Sons and Lovers* and *The Rainbow* outwardly show a marked difference; the former is composed by the traditional realism, while the latter adopts a more mythical style with full of Biblical allusions. The protagonist of the former is an immature young boy strongly resembling the author himself, while in the latter the attention moves to the female characters in a chronicle of successive generations.[1] Despite these differences, the basic framework found in *Sons and Lovers* is also employed in *The Rainbow*; the latter novel is also obsessed with procreation and evolution. In *Sons and Lovers*, the marriage of a local labourer and a bourgeois woman is overlapped with a historical moment of a mining country, after which they begin to evolve. In *The Rainbow*, the Brangwens, together with the Skrebenskies, contribute to the construction and development of the towns. Both texts portray in each family saga a transformation, where a repeated, prehistoric life in a rural district evolves into a linear, modern lifestyle of town, paralleling the development of a family and a town.

In the last scene of *The Rainbow*, Ursula sees a new hope in the upright form of a rainbow: a hope to transcend the corruption and ugliness of the newly bred towns which are rapidly spreading over the surface of the earth. To Ursula the swarm of the new houses seem to manifest the disorder and corruption of the place:

> She saw … the hard, cutting edges of the new houses, which seemed to spread over the hillside in their insentient triumph, … the amorphous, brittle, hard-edged new houses advancing from Beldover to meet the corrupt new houses from Lethley, the houses of Lethley advancing

DOI: 10.4324/9781032675671-4

> to mix with the houses of Hainor, a dry, brittle, terrible corruption spreading over the face of the land.
>
> (*R* 458)

This sordid disorder of new towns has already been presented at the middle of the novel: Wiggiston. This colliery town is a prototype of the throng of the houses Ursula is later to see. Wiggiston displays the same features of the later towns:

> He [Tom Brangwen Junior] lived in a large new house of red-brick standing outside a mass of homogeneous red-brick dwellings called Wiggiston. ... There was no meeting place, no centre, no artery, no organic formation. There it lay, like the new foundations of a red-brick confusion rapidly spreading, like a skin-disease.
>
> (320)

Thus, the development of the new towns reveals its characteristic nature: multiplication of the homogeneous shapes, rapid growth without discipline, and hence sombre, formless chaos.

The Marsh, where the Brangwens have for generations maintained their autonomous life with nature, is apparently opposite to this incarnation of industrialism and urbanisation. This conventional dualist view was formed and has been strengthened by F. R. Leavis onwards: the novel, written with Lawrence's shrewd eye as an "incomparable" "social historian" (Leavis 145), reflects England's actual social change from an agricultural society to an industrial country and, confronting the change, Ursula, or Lawrence, explores the human lives in both communal and individual dimensions.[2]

Graham Holderness, opposing this view of the novel as a record of social change, argues that Lawrence created an ahistorical pastoral world: "What *The Rainbow* does is to substitute a pleasant pastoral dream for the nightmare of bourgeois society" (Holderness 180). The "dream" is the Marsh, presented as a "myth of rural England" (180), and Holderness juxtaposes it with Wiggiston which he sees as "the primary image of that civilisation" (177). And then he interprets the conclusion of the novel as Ursula's return to the pastoral myth which she perceives in the form of the rainbow.

Leavis and Holderness nonetheless retain the same kind of schema: opposition of nature and civilisation or of the Marsh and Wiggiston. However, this simplistic dichotomy is, I would argue, not valid in this novel.[3] I propose to read the Marsh not as an ideal pastoral myth to which Ursula returns, but as a myth in which the Brangwen life pattern is presented as a kind of archetype, which Ursula eventually rejects. The Marsh world represents the archetypal myth into which the Brangwens are, even after their departure from the Marsh, incorporated. A close examination of the

Brangwens' descendants will, then, reveal the essence of the primary force and motive which urge the development of the new towns: procreation and evolution.

The Ur-Brangwens

The novel begins with the Brangwens living in a typical pre-industrial pastoral world. Here is depicted the rural life of the Brangwens who live and work in the Marsh, feeling the pulse of their cattle and beat of the earth, in harmony with the rhythm of natural process. In the Marsh their life goes on in the rhythm of the day and the year, their life pattern succeeds from one generation to another. Their life is productive; the Brangwens themselves are prolific as well as the crops they produce: "They had never become rich, because there were always children, and the patrimony was divided every time. But always, at the Marsh, there was ample" (*R* 9). In this secluded life, they are not individuals but a collective entity; their community is constituted only by "Brangwen men" and "Brangwen women". However, the seed of discord is introduced; the Brangwens yearn for something beyond the enclosed life pattern: "There was a look in the eyes of the Brangwens as if they were expecting something unknown, about which they were eager" (9); "And the Brangwen wife at the Marsh aspired beyond herself, towards the further life of the finer woman, towards the extended being she revealed …" (12–13). Yet, there is a circuit in which all individual aspirations are forgotten, and eventually, men and women are, as the "Brangwens", incorporated into the Brangwen cycle. This is the life of the Brangwens in the Marsh. The essential features of the Brangwen archetype are thus presented: repetition, unindividuality and fertility.

The second section begins with the date: 1840. A sense of history and change is introduced in the story. It is a time of industrial development during which the Marsh is trespassed by the railways and the canal, the collapse of which is to kill Tom Brangwen later. The Brangwens lose their paradise where they have for generations maintained their life pattern.

They are nonetheless not the innocent, poor victims of civilisation. As we have seen, the text reveals the Brangwens' unconscious urge towards "something unknown". And the new pulse of the civilisation is, for them, neither torment nor disturbance, but a supreme ecstasy they have never experienced before:

> As they worked in the fields, from beyond the now familiar embankment came the rhythmic run of the winding engines, startling at first, but afterwards a narcotic to the brain. Then the shrill whistle of the trains re-echoed through the heart, with fearsome pleasure. … As they pulled the turnips in November, the sharp clink-clink-clink-clink-clink

> of empty trucks shunting on the line, vibrated in their hearts with the fact of other activity going on beyond them.
>
> (14)

Civilisation brings a new feeling which appeals to them in spite of themselves and the Brangwens begin to launch into the material and commercial world. The Brangwens, abandoning the rhythm of nature for the "fearsome pleasure" of civilisation, engage in something uncanny, the price of which is the death of Tom.

The First and Second Generation

The new lifestyle, however, does not change the essence of the Brangwens. They persistently follow their life pattern from one generation to another. They are, even outside of the Marsh, incorporated into the Brangwen myth, inheriting the Brangwen features—repetition, unindividuality and fertility. One of the prominent features of the Brangwen archetype is repetition. The recurrent images and episodes pervade the whole text both literally and metaphorically. The couples in the novel are always confronted by the continual repetition of affection and repulsion, "the recurrence of love and conflict" (155). The symbolic scene of sheaf-stacking consists of Will and Anna's rhythmic movement of coming and going. Ursula is tormented by successive phases of disillusionment, which obstinately repeat themselves and mercilessly betray her hopes: "Would the next move turn out the same? Always the shining doorway ahead: and then, upon approach, always the shining doorway was a gate into another ugly yard, dirty and active and dead" (404). Ursula sways backwards and forwards on the swing boats taken to by her father and by Skrebensky, who imperiously pendulates on a rocking chair. Not only the chapter title "The Widening Circle" appears twice, but persistent recurrence of same words and phrases bored Lady Ottoline Morrell: "I was shocked in reading it [*The Rainbow*] by ... the habit when he [Lawrence] then first began of repeating the same word about ten times in a paragraph" (Morrell 283). Thus, repetitious images, scenes and expressions are so pervasive in this Brangwen chronicle that the whole text seems to embody the Brangwen rhythm.[4]

Amid these multitudinous repetitions, the Brangwens keep their own repetitious cycle which is suggested in the Brangwen myth: aspirations to the outside world and eventual incorporation. Tom, Anna and Ursula do not like the lifestyle of their previous generation; they yearn for an outside world; they see in their lovers some quality which might take them out to the outside world. Nonetheless, the first two generations, as we shall see, eventually forget or fulfil their aspiration, and are incorporated into the Brangwen cycle, and Ursula also nearly accepts it. The pattern of the

Brangwens' behaviour repeats, recurs and cycles. As a result, the behaviour of one generation seems to correspond to that of others:

> Hesitating, they [Ursula and Skrebensky] continued to walk on, quivering like shadows under the ash-trees of the hill, where her grandfather had walked with his daffodils to make his proposal, and where her mother had gone with her young husband, walking close upon him as Ursula was now walking upon Skrebensky.
>
> (278)

Unindividuality, another feature of the Brangwen archetype, is realised together with the other one, fertility. In the collective Brangwen cycle, being mature is equivalent to losing his/her individuality:

> So, after three days of incessant brandy-drinking, he [Tom] had burned out the youth from his blood, he had achieved this kindled state of oneness with all the world, which is the end of youth's most passionate desire. But he had achieved his satisfaction by obliterating his own individuality.
>
> (28)

By producing the next generation, Lydia is incorporated into the Brangwens: "In the birth of the child she seemed to lose connection with her former self. She became now really English, really Mrs Brangwen" (78). The lifestyle of the couple begins to gain the tincture of the Brangwens when they begin to be called by their family name. As a result, Tom and Lydia's life represents that of their ancestors. Their physical, wordless communion is the one that has been presented in the first section of the Brangwen myth:

> There was over the house a kind of dark silence and intensity, in which passion worked its inevitable conclusions. There was in the house a sort of richness, a deep, inarticulate interchange which made other places seem thin and unsatisfying. Brangwen could sit silent, smoking in his chair, the mother could move about in her quiet, insidious way, and the sense of the two presences was powerful, sustaining. The whole intercourse was wordless, intense and close.
>
> (98)

Anna and Will's life starts outside of the Marsh. They marry and move to Cossethay, and later to Beldover. This geographical change, however, does not take them out of the Brangwen cycle. Through their move, their life is dominated by a more exact, persistent repetition of a rhythm than by a natural process; the church bell next to their cottage in Cossethay keeps striking, continually reminding them of the time: "They counted the strokes of the bell. And when they counted midday, they understood that it was midday, in the world, and for themselves also" (135). In Beldover the dominant rhythm which governs the whole area is much more mighty: "There were the strange sounds of the town, and the repeated chiming of the big church bells, so much harsher and more insistent than the little bells of Cossethay" (395).

Under this persistent rhythm, Will and Anna stick to the Brangwen life pattern. The couple's fecund power is truly remarkable. Locating herself in the Brangwen cycle, Anna concentrates on producing the next generation: "There were already seven children, yet Mrs Brangwen was again with child, the ninth she had borne" (328). Through her childbearing, Anna, now Mrs Brangwen, no longer wishes anything but to reproduce the next generation with her husband: "All these years, nothing had happened save the coming of the children, nothing had mattered but the bodies of her babies. … Calm, placid, unshakeable as ever, Mrs Brangwen went about in her dominance of physical maternity" (328–29).

Her obsession with childbearing is not peculiar among the Brangwens. The idea of producing offspring always haunts the Brangwens. Tom is, for example, satisfied with the fact that he has got his progeny:

> When they told him it was a boy, he had a thrill of pleasure. He liked the confirmation of fatherhood. It gave him satisfaction to know he had a son. But he felt not very much outgoing to the baby itself. He was its father, that was enough.
>
> (78)

His son Tom, who marries Winifred Inger, is also preoccupied with the idea of procreation: "Brangwen had reached the age when he wanted children. He wanted children. Neither marriage nor the domestic establishment meant anything to him. He wanted to propagate himself" (326). Procreation makes possible the succession of the generations which is repeated by the anonymous Brangwens.

William, who has gone out of the Marsh, cannot take part in the Brangwen men's productive business—to work for a good harvest of crops, and to multiply their cattle. Instead, he multiplies many objects through his handiwork:

> Modelling in clay, in plaster, he produced beautiful reproductions, really beautiful. … He continued to copy, or to make designs by selecting motives from classic stuff. … His work had some of the freshness, the naïve alertness of the early Italians. But it was only reproduction. … He

> took up jewellery, read Benvenuto Cellini, pored over reproductions of ornament, and began to make pendants in silver and pearl and matrix. (330)

In the first days of their love Will gives Anna a butter stamper which reproduces and multiplies the self-same figures of a phoenix. He is all the time enchanted by reproductions of pictures, and collects many books of them. He does not create new things: he does not complete "The Creation of Eve"; he fails to carve his own expression ("utterances of himself" [330]), to make the head of Ursula in clay and to paint a picture of his church-tower. Instead he is busy reproducing the objects without the aura, unless otherwise being absorbed in repairing the stuff in the church—which is indeed the reproduction of former shapes. His reproduction is his own style of work which his ancestors have done in the field.[5]

As a result, Will and Anna's life also comes to embody the essential elements of the Brangwens—repetition, unindividuality and fertility in their rich physical intimacy:

> Brangwen continued in a kind of rich drowse of physical heat, in connection with his wife. They were neither of them quite personal, quite defined as individuals, so much were they pervaded by the physical heat of breeding and rearing their young. (329)

The first two generations of the Brangwens are thus incorporated into the Brangwen myth. These features—repetition, unindividuality and fecundity—are the three wheels by which the Brangwen cycle keeps going.

The Third Generation: Ursula and Skrebensky

Ursula's refusal of the Brangwen nature draws her to Anton Skrebensky, who is apparently an alien to the Brangwens. Skrebensky, however, betrays her because he eventually takes part in the Brangwen activity. The latter half of the novel renders not only Ursula's oscillation between the Brangwen–Skrebensky world and its outside, but also the way in which Ursula resists her incorporation.

Ursula rejects almost all her ties with the Brangwens: she is stifled by her mother's way of living of fecundity and breeding; the gulf with her father becomes unbridgeable when he throws a duster to her face because she has left open the door of the parish room; she hates to take care of her noisy and troublesome siblings as a representative of "the little Brangwen club" (244).

Her definite rejection of the Brangwen family pattern can be seen in Ursula's refusal to multiply its kind. Ursula insistently denies the idea of (re-)productivity. She finds Rubens' "Fecundity" abhorrent. The words in Genesis in which God commands Noah to be fruitful and multiply the earth are to Ursula merely a vulgar business. The reason for her opposition to her mother lies with her mother's devotion to childbearing. Ursula's negation of the idea of procreation and fecundity, which her parents embody, indicates her rejection of the Brangwen quality.

Skrebensky seems to her to be a door to a new outside world. It is understandable that she thinks so because this scion is in every sense different from the Brangwens: he is a descendant of an émigré aristocrat; he is familiar with London or Paris, metropolises of civilisation; he is engaged with constructing railways and bridges, exerting the power of mechanism and materialism. Thus, he comes from high social hierarchy and represents civilisation, both of which the Brangwens have never known. Despite such apparent contrast, Skrebensky on a different level shows similar characteristics to the Brangwens: repetition, unindividuality and fecundity. It is suggestive that Skrebensky, on Lydia's rocking chair, keeps swaying to and fro like a pendulum. His answer to Gudrun, who teases him, is full of implications:

> "Can't you stop?" asked Gudrun.
> "No—it's the *perpetuum mobile.*"
> (273)

At the heart of Skrebensky lies perpetual repetition and the swing boats episode follows this scene. Furthermore, like the Brangwens, Skrebensky does not lay much emphasis on individuality. His idea of "the nation" is after all achieved by the negation of the individual. The narrator describes his inner thoughts:

> What did a man matter, personally? He was just a brick in the whole great social fabric, the nation, the modern humanity. ... What did personal intimacy matter? One had to fill one's place in the whole, the great scheme of man's elaborate civilisation, that was all. The Whole mattered—but the unit, the person, had no importance, except as he represented the Whole.
> (304)

His anti-individualism is also implied by the narrator, who keeps calling him by his family name.

The most prominent attribute which he shares with the Brangwens is his procreative power. Skrebensky's innate fecundity, which leads his lover to physical intimacy and understanding, is so potent as to overwhelm Ursula if only temporarily:

> Gradually he transferred to her the hot, *fecund* darkness that possessed his own blood. ... A turgid, teeming night, heavy with *fecundity* in which every molecule of matter grew big with increase, secretly urgent with *fecund* desire, seemed to come to pass.
>
> (413; my emphasis)

As well as their similarities, the differences between Skrebensky and the Brangwens are also evident. Skrebensky's unindividuality forms a social entity like a nation, which is bigger than, and includes, a race or a family. His own innate procreativity is described as more intense, and his social one—"making railways or bridges, working like a nigger" (288)—is more massive and on a larger scale than Will's handiwork. Skrebensky's mighty fecundity is, however, almost fruitless. His creation is for destruction, for death. Ursula perceives the nature of his creation: "But you'd only make them [railways or bridges] to be pulled down again when the armies had done with them. It seems just as much a game" (288). His sterile creations always end in death, just as his child with Ursula fails to be born.

Parallel Development of a Family and a Town

Ursula widens even more the circle which has been enlarged by her ancestors since their move from the Marsh to Cossethay and to Beldover. She accentuates this movement; she goes to Ilkeston for teaching, to Nottingham for school, to London and to Paris with Skrebensky, or even intends to go to India. The circle is widened and widened, but this topological and horizontal movement does not free her from the Brangwen–Skrebensky world—Ursula comes to realise that she has been entrapped by the world of towns.

Ursula, with her family, moves to Beldover, where she becomes a member of the new town. There she finds out that the place she lives in is not Willey Green where she has wished to live, but among the same kind of sordid houses which she has seen in her uncle's town Wiggiston: "Ursula was rather sad. Instead of having arrived at distinction, they had come to new red-brick suburbia in a grimy, small town" (391). Ursula becomes involved with the newly bred towns.

The towns which become predominant in the latter part of the text begin to reveal similar attributes to those of the Brangwens and Skrebensky: repetition, unindividuality and fertility. The similar houses form a monotonous pattern:

> The streets were like visions of pure ugliness: a grey-black, macadamised road, asphalt causeways, held in between a flat succession of wall, window and door, a new-brick channel that began nowhere and ended nowhere. Everything was amorphous, yet everything repeated itself endlessly.
>
> (320)

Not only the exterior but people's inner rhythms are repetitious: in Beldover, "the repeated chiming of the big church bells" is "much harsher and more insistent than the little bells of Cossethay" (395).

The mass in the towns are all deprived of their individuality. The miners must adapt themselves to the pits. It does not matter if a wife changes her husband among miners, as Mrs Smith's two sisters have done. Tom says: "One man or another, it doesn't matter all the world" (323). In Ilkeston, not only must Ursula treat her pupils as a mass, but she herself must throw away her own individual name to be a Standard Five Teacher of the school, where the dominant bourgeois ideologies are reproduced—system, order and discipline.[6] The towns' disorder of chaos seems to embody the confusion in the house of the Brangwens, where their increasing children are running, crying and "bading" (253), and Ursula groans: "The miserable weeks went on, in the poky house crammed with children. What was her life—a sordid, formless, disintegrated nothing ..." (332). The towns' rapid spread, multiplying and reproducing themselves endlessly, manifests the Brangwens' enormous procreativity and Skrebensky's sterile fecundity. The Brangwen household is presented as a microcosm of outside towns.

The reason why the towns possess the same kind of attributes as those of the Brangwens and Skrebensky can be ascribed to the fact that the new world is both symbolically and actually dominated and governed by them. The towns are formed by two kinds of power which is embodied by Skrebensky and the Brangwens. Skrebensky constructs the infrastructure, building houses, railways and canals. The Brangwens dominate the superstructure,[7] together with Tom, who manages his colliery in Wiggiston. Will is socially promoted, and involved with education as a Handwork Instructor of the Grammar School in Beldover, where he presumably propagates his skill of "reproduction". Will's family is also held to "represent culture", decorating their house with reproductions:

> They would represent culture. And ... they would shine, with their Della Robbia, beautiful Madonna, their lovely reliefs from Donatello, their reproductions from Botticelli. Nay, the large photographs of the

> Primavera and the Aphrodite and the Nativity in the dining-room, the ordinary reception room, would make dumb the mouth of Beldover.
> (391)

Thus, the new towns are their collaboration: Skrebensky constructs buildings, while the Brangwens dominate economy, knowledge and culture.

This is the structure which forms the newly established towns. The new towns are an incarnation of the Brangwen quality together with that of Skrebensky. Even after leaving the Marsh, the Brangwens have maintained their own life pattern, adhering to their archetypal attributes: repetition, unindividuality and fertility. Since their departure from the Marsh "with fearsome pleasure", the Brangwen circle has been widened through their geographical move. Their quality finds its culmination in the construction of the new towns with their massive disorder, helped and urged on by Skrebensky. Thus, *The Rainbow* portrays the parallel development of a family and a town. The text reveals that the quality found in the country and its folks is continuously succeeded to the town and its inhabitants, invalidating reductive dualisms such as the country versus the city, nature versus civilisation and the Marsh versus Beldover.

Ursula eventually refuses not only the ugliness and corruption of civilisation but also the principles that dominate the text. Unlike the women of her former generations, Ursula leaves the anonymous Brangwens for the town, but unfortunately there she finds only the growing anonymous mass of a mining town and a far much wider anonymous entity called "the nation". Ursula therefore cherishes her last hope in a rising arched figure of the rainbow, in opposition to the horizontal movement of the rapid multiplication of the disorder. She thus wishes to disrupt the text's obsession with procreation and evolution, which has permeated the narrative structure since *Sons and Lovers*. To Ursula, the rainbow embodies "a new germination" (459), like a phoenix rising from the ashes of the towns, transcending all the simple reproduction and multiplication created and dispersed by the Brangwens.

Notes

1 Graham Holderness remarks: "It is a commonplace that the period between *Sons and Lovers* (1913) and *The Rainbow* (1915) represents the most radical and decisive period of change in Lawrence's art ..." (159). Only a few critics have observed a thematic sequence of *Sons and Lovers* and *The Rainbow*. As one of them, for example, Jeff Wallace argues that these two novels attempt to portray an anti-liberal-humanist posthuman condition of the "allotropic"

realm of the inhuman through the human sexual relationship. See Wallace, *Posthuman* 190–201. See also Eagleton 200.

2 See Leavis 96–145.

3 Howard J. Booth also attempts to transcend the reductive dichotomy. Criticising both Holderness and Terry Eagleton, Booth argues that the novel portrays the influence of high imperialism and industrialisation upon the provincial lives of the Brangwens. See Booth 34–58.

4 This is exactly that which annoyed an anonymous reviewer of Westminster Gazette:

> Mr Lawrence … has chosen to write a book consisting entirely of the same climax, to describe it again and again and again. But it is the same adventure, and the reader, dazed and stunned by the first episode, wanders on into repetition after repetition, dimly conscious that this unique upheaval is taking place in Lydia or Tom or Anna or Ursula, or in an anonymous girl from Nottingham, or anyone else.
>
> ("New Novel: 'The Rainbow'" 3)

5 Will's whole-hearted dedication to churches and cathedrals can be ascribed to fertility attributed to them. Tony Pinkney argues that the

> churches and cathedrals of the novel certainly seem fecund enough: in Cossethay church … the Lamb in the stained-glass window remains sufficiently in touch with the actual lambs born on Marsh Farm to bring the natural cycles and rhythms of generation into the very body of the church.
>
> (67)

See Pinkney 67–68. Will's devotion to reproductive work and Anna's to breeding are reminiscent of what Lawrence in "Study of Thomas Hardy" calls "self-preservation": "It is humiliating to think, that … we are considering our own self-preservation, or the greater scheme for the preservation of mankind. … Seed and fruit and produce, these are only a minor aim: children and good works are a minor aim" (*STH* 12). Lawrence insists that those who are pre-occupied with self-preservation and hence merely with reproduction, lack the ability to create new beings.

6 This episode exemplifies Louis Althusser's postulate of "Ideological State Apparatus". Althusser argues in "Ideology and Ideological State Apparatuses" that the school functions as the place that transmits the ideology of the state and interpellates individuals affected by it, thereby maintaining order in a society. In the essay, he maintains that "In fact, the Church has been replaced today *in its role as the dominant Ideological State Apparatus* by the School. It is coupled with the Family just as the Church was once coupled with the Family" (157; emphasis in original). This transition corresponds to the shift from the second to the third generation in *The Rainbow*, in which church organist Will is succeeded by school teacher Ursula. Ursula, however, eventually leaves school and desires to sever family ties with both the Brangwens and Skrebensky. She

thereby refuses to become entangled with, as well as to help promulgate, the dominant ideology of the state.

7 The "superstructure" here aligns more with the Marxist sense rather than with the one Will himself employs when referring to human artefacts in general:

> How had helpless savages, running with their spears on the river-side, after fish, how had they come to rear up this great London, the ponderous, massive, ugly superstructure of a world of man upon a world of nature? ... Sweep away the whole monstrous superstructure of the world of today, cities and industries and civilisation, leave only the bare earth with plants growing and waters running.
>
> (*R* 179)

4 Lawrence and War

Historical Contexts

Lawrence and the First World War

One evening in September 1915, about a month after the final revision of *The Rainbow*, Lawrence encountered, with his wife Frieda, the raid by the large German airship, the Zeppelin, on the city of London. Lawrence wrote to Ottoline Morrell the next day:

> Last night when we were coming home the guns broke out, and there was a noise of bombs. Then we saw the Zeppelin above us, just ahead, amid a gleaming of clouds. … And underneath it were splashes of fire as the shells fired from earth burst. Then there were flashes near the ground—and the shaking noise. It was like Milton—then there was war in heaven. … It seemed as if the cosmic order were gone, as if there had come a new order, a new heavens above us. …
>
> So it seems our cosmos is burst, burst at last, the stars and moon blown away, the envelope of the sky burst out, and a new cosmos appeared. … So it is the end—our world is gone, and we are like dust in the air.
>
> (2*L* 389–90)

The indiscriminate attack deeply shocked the British citizens as well as the Lawrences and thoroughly changed their views on humanity, life and the world.

The First World War, known as the "Great War", started when Britain declared war against Germany, which had invaded neutral country Belgium. When the war started, people believed that it would be over by Christmas, and few people expected this war to be a disastrous experience that would leave inerasable scars on all over Europe. At the outbreak of war, many British writers such as Thomas Hardy, Rudyard Kipling, Arnold Bennett and H. G. Wells willingly assembled at Wellington House,

DOI: 10.4324/9781032675671-5

the British War Propaganda Bureau, and contributed to the promulgation of the nation's cause. Such popular figures as David Lloyd George and Horatio Bottomley strove to kindle jingoistic feelings in the public. As a result, newspaper articles at home and numerous posters on the streets aroused patriotic fervour and provoked hostility against the enemy among British citizens. Within six months, by the end of 1914, more than one million British young men rushed to the colours.[1]

Lawrence's reaction towards the Great War was ambivalent. He detested war enthusiasm among the British and was sceptical about the national ideology that justified the nation's cause of the war; yet at the same time he recognised the necessity of war in order to satisfy the destructive desire and to eliminate the nation's corruption. From the early phase of the war, Lawrence repeatedly expressed his deep loathing of the warfare; one month after the onset of war, in September 1914, Lawrence wrote in one of his letters:

> The war makes me depressed, the talk about the war makes me sick, and I have never come so near to hating mankind as I am now. They are fools, and vulgar fools, and cowards who will always make a noise because they are afraid of the silence. But I don't even mind if they're killed. I do mind those who, being sensitive, will receive such a blow from the ghastliness and mechanical, obsolete, hideous stupidity of war.
>
> (*2L* 218)

In December 1915 he moved to Cornwall to withdraw from the patriotic frenzy of the war, but it did not free him from the tentacles of war. The war continued to disturb and torment the novelist's mind; in May 1916 he wrote: "I do wish there was peace, so we could have a happy time together. But the state of affairs gnaws one's heart, and one has no rest" (*2L* 605). In the same month, conscription, initially introduced in January, was extended to include married men, and he was summoned for medical inspection the following month. Now, his disgust and rage at the war were so deep and uncontrollable as to disrupt the flow of his pen:

> I will only say, in the particular, that for *me* the war is utterly wrong, stupid, monstrous and contemptible, and nothing, neither life nor death, makes it any different, for *me*. For me, it is better to die than to do something which is utterly a violation to my soul. ... [W]ar cannot be thought of, for me, without the utmost repulsion and desecration of one's being. For me, the war is wrong, and nothing, neither life nor death, can make it right.
>
> (*3L* 32; emphasis in original)

His anti-war sentiments were deepened by the harassment and persecution he suffered during the war:

> When are we going to have a shot at preparing this nation for peace? … We should say "enough of war" while yet we are alive. We should say enough of war. … I think Lloyd Georges are toads.—I must here assert again, that the war is, and continues, because of the lust for hate and war, chiefly hate of each other.
>
> (*3L* 38–39)

Simultaneously, however, Lawrence expresses contradictory sentiment and views on the war. Despite his repulsion towards the real war, he accepts the necessity of fighting, insisting that the destructive impulse that is inherent in human beings must be satisfied:

> … I am not a conscientious objector. … I too believe man must fight. …
>
> What we want is the fulfilment of our desires, down to the deepest and most spiritual desire. …
>
> I would never *forbid* any man to make war, or to go to war. …
>
> They will prove to themselves, by fighting, that their greater desire, on the whole, was *not* to fight for their nation, or sea-power, but to know a new value: to recognize a new, stronger desire in themselves, more spiritual and gladdening.
>
> (*2L* 633–35; emphasis in original)

Another reason that Lawrence affirms the war is because he cherished the idea that the war would cure the nation's disease. The idea that war could function as a purifying force of corrupt country was not Lawrence's original, but was widely shared in wartime Britain from volunteered servicemen to illustrious figures. A year before the outbreak of the First World War, A. J. Grant, Professor of History at the University of Leeds, critically argued that a "few voices are raised to declare that war is in itself a good thing, and that without its severe discipline the moral fibre of Europe would degenerate" (Grant 650–51). After the outbreak of war, however, this idea was not of "a few voices" but of dominant ones. For example, Paul Jones, a former public school student educated at Dulwich College, penned his final letter to his brother from the battlefield:

> The follies, selfishness, luxury and general pettiness of the vile commercial sort of existence led by nine-tenths of the people of the world in peace-time are replaced in war by a savagery that is at least more honest and outspoken. Look at it this way: in peace-time one just lives one's own little life, engaged in trivialities, worrying about one's own

> comfort, about money matters, and all that sort of thing—just living for one's own self. What a sordid life it is! In war, on the other hand, even if you do get killed … you have the satisfaction of knowing that you have "pegged out" in the attempt to help your country. You have, in fact, realised an ideal, which, as far as I can see, you very rarely do in ordinary life. The reason is that ordinary life runs on a commercial and selfish basis. …
>
> I think that the War has given to everyone a chance to "get out of himself," as I might say.
>
> (Jones, *War Letters* 253)

Similarly, in 1915, S. P. B. Mais, a prolific writer and journalist, celebrated the Great War, which illustrates the war enthusiasm of the period:

> [W]e were perhaps in danger of becoming a little vapid, a little inclined to ease and luxury; life was becoming in every way a little too easy for us, but in August, 1914, we were suddenly aroused from our slightly tipsy condition; on the instant, like Cassio, we became sober, so that we now thank God as never before for so ordering our lives that we live in an age which is likely to be talked of in all future generations as the most glorious of all in the history of England, and, God helping us, we of the public schools are going to do our part to make it glorious.
>
> (Mais 147)

He goes on to argue that "even the most wilfully blind of us recognises that one great effect of this war will be an immediate demand for a thorough cleansing of all *Augean stables*, whether in economics, politics, or education" (148; my emphasis). In a letter written in the same year, Lawrence, using the same metaphor, emphasises the necessity for social reform based not on materialism but an inner nucleus of being:

> We must revolutionise this system of life, that is based on *outside* things, money, property, and establish a system of life which is based on *inside* things. The war will come to an end, and then the Augean stables are to be cleansed.
>
> (*2L* 280; italics in original, my underline)

A medical analogy was also used in referring to the war. Arthur Machen was a popular novelist who publicised a famous legend in a propagandistic story "The Bowmen", in which the ghosts of the victorious army of the Battle of Agincourt in the fifteenth century assist the British soldiers retreating from Mons in the Great War. In one of his essays, Machen stressed the necessity to cure the nation's disease by war in figurative prose: "There are terrible operations in surgery, burnings and cuttings, which give life to the individual; it may well be that there is a surgery of nations as well as of individuals" (Machen 18–19). Lawrence employs the same metaphor to defend the war as a purifier of the British social system, which was, to him, base and degraded:

> But if I have toothache I don't depend on hope nor faith nor love, but on surgery. ... And it is surgery we want, Cambridge wants, England wants, I want. There is in us what the common people call "proud flesh"—i.e., mortified flesh: which must be cut out: it cannot be kissed out, nor hoped out, nor removed by faith. It must be removed by surgery. And it is in us now "proud flesh".
>
> I thought the war would surgeon us. Still it may. But this England at home is as yet entirely unaffected, entirely unaware of the mortification in its own body.
>
> (*2L* 318)

Thus, although Lawrence detested warmongers and distrusted the masses who blindly supported the war, he lived within the confines of a world at war and occasionally expressed views synchronous with the dominant discourses, which justified the war as a purifying force.[2]

The idea that the war would purify the corrupt nation was a by-product of the idea of degeneration. As Chapters 1 and 2 have previously noted, it was widely accepted that the people in Britain had been both physically and morally degenerated because of their lives of material prosperity and luxury. *The Decline and Fall of the Roman Empire* by Edward Gibbon was widely read as an analogy to their own Empire indulged in material wealth and comfort. King Edward was considered to represent luxury and ostentation which embodied the atmosphere of the first decade of the twentieth century. Actually, even before the outbreak of war, John Hargrave, who was later to form the Kindred of the Kibbo Kift, entertained the idea that pre-war civilisation had been evil and degenerative and that the "Great War" would purify the nation. In *The Great War Brings It Home: The Natural Reconstruction of an Unnatural Existence*, which was "compiled long before the outbreak of war" (Hargrave viii), Hargrave advocates his view that pre-war civilisation in Britain caused both mental and physical degeneracy:

> It becomes more and more evident that our pre-war system of life and our outlook on civilisation was unsatisfactory. ... [W]e shall find behind it a vast amount of unnecessary evil; diseases mental and physical,

> starvation, luxury and lust, and all their attendant evils—deceit, selfishness, money-grabbing, and the rest.
>
> (3)

The result was the degeneration of the entire British race:

> It is impossible to deny that *the race as a whole* under our system of civilisation was becoming weak, mentally and physically—and it was obvious that the more we "bolstered" it up by medical science and greater comfort *the weaker we were becoming.*
>
> (4; emphasis in original)

Here again, the "Great War" functions as a purifier; the War offers us a chance to realise our corruption and leads to social reform and racial regeneration:

> The wild hardy life is natural and permanent. The other artificial and temporary. To get "out of touch with Nature" is to get out of touch with life itself, and yet under our modern civilisation we did our best to ignore nature in every possible way. Such a civilisation tends to destroy life, and,—the Great War brings it home.
>
> (xvi)

With his return-to-nature doctrine and admiration for physical fitness, which are somewhat analogous to Lawrence's, Hargrave continues to reinforce his argument, persistently repeating the phrase "the Great War brings it home" like a chant. Thus, the feeling that the Great War was a good opportunity to purify the nation for regeneration had been fermented among British citizens.[3]

Lawrence and Anti-German Propaganda

> There are only two divisions in the world today: human beings and Germans.
>
> Rudyard Kipling, *Morning Post*, 22 June 1915

The First World War was different from previous wars in that propaganda was widely employed as one of the major weapons. Not only did massive propaganda campaigns boost patriotism, they also stirred up hatred against Britain's arch enemy: Germany. Hence, as a patriotic sentiment swelled among the British, antagonism towards Germany grew. Historically, however, Britain and Germany had in the past established a close alliance against France as their mutual potential enemy. Until the previous century, their relationship with each other had been forged through connections between the royal families, their religious ties as protestants, numerous cultural associations and their Germanic heritage, among others. The pro-German myth of Anglo-Saxonism had been favoured by critics and scholars such as Thomas Macaulay, Thomas Carlyle and J. R. Green. Green was one of the most influential historians of his generation, who argued in his authoritative *A Short History of the English People* (1874), which sold more than 100,000 copies, that Britain's cultural, religious and political heritage was Germanic:

> Engle, Saxon, and Jute all belonged to the same Low German branch of the Teutonic family … and it is from the union of all of them when its conquest was complete that the English people has sprung. … [W]hen conquest had brought them to the shores of Britain, their political and social organization must have been that of the German race to which they belonged.
>
> (Green 2)

Nevertheless, Britain's affection for the Germans began to deteriorate during the Franco-Prussian War of 1870–71, and by the beginning of the First World War, Britain's sentiment towards Germany had been negatively altered. The typical British view at that time was that Germany had metamorphosed from a highly cultivated liberal country into a belligerent militant nation, which is illustrated in a rather vulgar poem titled "The Two Germanies", published in *Punch* magazine at the outbreak of war, on 9 September 1914:

> Marvellous the utter transformation
> Of the spirit of the German nation!
>
> Once the land of poets, seers and sages,
> Who enchant us in their deathless pages,
>
> Holding high the torch of Truth, and earning
> Endless honour by their zeal for learning.
>
> Such the land that in an age uncouther
> Bred the soul-emancipating Luther.
>
> Such the land that made our debt the greater
> By the gift of *Faust* and *Struwwelpeter*.
>
> Now the creed of Nietzsche, base, unholy,
> Guides the nation's brain and guides it solely.
>
> Now Mozart's serene and joyous magic
> Yields to Richard Strauss, the hæmorrhagic.

Now the eagle changing to the vulture
Preaches rapine in the name of culture.

Now the Prussian *Junker*, blind with fury,
Claims to be God's counsel, judge and jury,

While the authentic German genius slumbers,
Cast into the limbo of back numbers.
("The Two Germanies" 213)

In this fashion official and unofficial propaganda against Germany widely circulated in Britain, which further damaged the British people's view of the Germans.[4] As a consequence, Germanophobia was widespread among the British. Just before the outbreak of war, the famous historian G. M. Trevelyan wrote to his brother Charles, who was engaged in pacifist activities: "My feeling for the defence of Europe against Germany is very strong. … I support the war not *merely* for our own survival but because I think a German victory will probably be the worst thing for Europe …" (qtd. in Moorman 127).

Lawrence met this historian two weeks after the above-mentioned letter and wrote to Edward Marsh: "I … rather hated him. He's so God almighty serious … as if he was the schoolmaster and all the world his scholars, poor dear" (*2L* 211). Lawrence's own feelings towards Germany were rather ambivalent. In his next letter to Marsh, three weeks later, Lawrence did not express approval of Germany's victory, but he did defend Britain's enemy: "When I hear of the Germans, it breaks my heart. They must not win, I know—because also they cannot. But they are a young, only adolescent nation, and they don't know what to do with themselves" (*2L* 214). In the following year, however, upon hearing the news of the sinking of the *Lusitania* by a German submarine, Lawrence revealed his rage in a letter he wrote to Ottoline Morrell:

> Soon we in England shall go fully mad, with hate. I too hate the Germans so much, I could kill every one of them. … I am mad with rage myself. I would like to kill a million Germans—two million.
>
> (*2L* 340)

The next day, 15 May 1915, an article was printed in a notoriously jingoistic journal, *John Bull*, written by the infamous chauvinist Horatio Bottomley. Although Lawrence's style was much less vulgar, he shared anti-German sentiments with Bottomley, whom he detested as a demagogue. "I call for a Vendetta", Bottomley bawls, "a vendetta against every German in Britain, whether 'naturalised' or not. As I have said elsewhere, you cannot naturalise an unnatural beast—a human abortion—a hellish freak. But you can exterminate it. And now the time has come" (Bottomley 6). Bottomley goes on to vociferate:

> Remember that the German is by instinct a spy, a sneak, a murderer, a ruffian, a barbarian. ... Too long have we tolerated that beast. He has no place in the human family—to say nothing of the Anglo-Saxon branch of it.
>
> (7)

It might also be argued that Lawrence's Germanophobia influenced his relationship with his wife, Frieda, the daughter of a Prussian officer, Baron Friedrich von Richthofen. Several weeks after the sinking of the *Lusitania*, Lawrence wrote to E. M. Forster:

> We [Lawrence and Frieda] should be in town probably in a fortnight. Mrs Lawrence is up there looking for her flat—unless a bomb has dropped on her—killed by her own countrymen—it is the kind of fate she is cut out for.
>
> (2*L* 351)

Nevertheless, Lawrence maintained some sympathy towards Germany. In November 1915, five months after writing the letter above, he wrote to Cynthia Asquith, arguing that it was England and the Allies that had driven Germany into madness and that they were therefore responsible for settling the problem:

> Besides, Germany, Prussia, is not evil through and through. Her mood is now *evil*. But we reap what we have sowed. It is as with a child: if with a sullen, evil soul one provokes an evil mood in the child, there is destruction. But no child is all evil. And Germany is the child of Europe: and senile Europe, with her conventions and arbitrary rules of conduct and life and very being, has provoked Germany into a purely destructive mood.
>
> (2*L* 425)

Amid the storm of Germanophobia among the British, Lawrence's feelings towards Germany were complex and ambivalent.

History Books in Context

The prolonged war eventually lasted for four years. As the war continued, hostility and weariness to the long-lasting war spread among the British. The introduction of conscription in 1916 made pacifism a political issue and inspired subsequent pacifist movements. In the following year food rations started. Many soldiers came back home physically disabled or shell shocked, if they had escaped futile deaths. As a natural consequence, anti-war sentiment began to arouse among the British. The intellectuals gathered at Garsington Manor of Philip and Ottoline Morrell as conscientious objectors. In due course, not only pacifists but also the conservative scholars and the MPs, and some ex-soldiers like Siegfried Sassoon began to raise the voice of protest.

Movements in European History was composed just before and after the armistice (the opening chapters in July 1918, the rest in the few months after the armistice). It is a history textbook for adolescents, composed with simple prose. Therefore, the work has often been considered a mere potboiler and it has been dedicated a relatively small place in the literature on Lawrence.[5] *Movements in European History* is, however, a significant text to decipher Lawrence's other wartime texts because it offers a good example of how contemporary discourses and the author's responses to them are inextricably entwined. For this reason, before his wartime novel and short stories, *Movements in European History* is analysed in this and the following chapter, which will elucidate the way to interpret Lawrence's other wartime texts.

Despite the fact that *Movements* was written during a period of political upheaval in Europe, and that the experience of war forced the author to accept a new reality, there is little description of the First World War in this book. Even when Lawrence was asked to bring the narrative up to date five years later, the description of historical events of World War I was not included in it. This makes a striking contrast to *The Outline of History*, written at almost the same period by H. G. Wells, who compiled a 60-page chapter titled "The International Catastrophe of 1914".

Instead, *Movements* presents the author's unique vision of history. Lawrence selected historical events and episodes from sources such as *The Decline and Fall of the Roman Empire* by Edward Gibbon, but they were reorganised in the textbook through the Lawrentian dichotomy. The main thesis of *Movements* is that history has been constructed through the eternal conflict between two opposites, an idea that he had explored elsewhere, for example, in his short story "The Prussian Officer" or in his essay "The Crown". In *Movements*, Lawrence portrays mankind as contradictory beings who hold in themselves opposing instincts: "There are two great passions that rule mankind—the passion of pride and power and conquest, and the passion of peace and production" (241–42). This text presents a unique view of European history that this Eros-Thanatos conflict has moved and formed the history of Europe from Ancient Rome to Modern Europe. The variations of this dualism of peace and war are presented as conflicts between love and violence, production and destruction, material prosperity and martial glory. Thus, this book gives us the impression of portraying the author's unique view of history, one that is not dimmed by patriotic frenzy or wartime propaganda.

This impression is all the more strengthened when the text is compared to other history books written by contemporary British authors, which are either excessively patriotic or noticeably pacifist. As the Great War approached, patriotism was boosted all the more, and the historians and the educationists thought of the cultivation of patriotism and civic virtue as their task. A year before the outbreak of war, H. B. Gray, Headmaster of Bradfield College, published *The Public Schools and the Empire*. In this book, Gray maintained that because of blind self-confidence in their superiority, the British people had declined both in physique and morals like the ancient Romans, and therefore Britain would be beaten by Germany and America unless she cultivated a "decreasing sense of national responsibility and self-sacrificing patriotism" (Gray 12) by the reform of the educational system. Likewise, W. H. Webb, a Fellow of the Royal Historical Society, argued the point:

> I am by no means a rabid "jingoist", but I am of opinion that ... unless the younger generation is more thoroughly taught the eternal principles of History and Patriotism, the Britain of the future must be a declining power. ... What I plead for is a more thorough and comprehensive dissemination of the teachings of History and Patriotism.
>
> (Webb 53–54)

Naturally, therefore, the history textbooks turned nationalistic and belligerent.

In 1911, *A School History of England*, co-authored by Rudyard Kipling and the historian C. R. L. Fletcher (who was later to reject Lawrence's "Epilogue" attached to *Movements*), was published by Oxford University Press, the same publisher that later issued *Movements*. Fletcher wrote the prose section, which is punctuated and embellished by 23 verses specially composed for and dedicated to this volume by Kipling. Their history book had an overtly propagandist purpose; the authors intended it to be a Tory history that stood against new liberalism and socialism, which in their eyes threatened to destroy the British Empire and obliterate its traditions. The book describes the formation of England and the development of its national character, glorifying "the English race as one people and ... England as a great power in Europe" (Kipling 45). It celebrates British imperialism as "the White Man's Burthen" and shows an abysmal lack of sympathy and respect for the colonised.[6] Identifying Germany as Britain's potential enemy, it also encourages readers to take up arms at any moment.[7]

In 1917, in the midst of war, G. K. Chesterton published *A Short History of England*. His *History* is not a compendium of historical dates and events; his unique view of the movements of English history is presented with his typical irony and cynicism. This text also served to strengthen the national propaganda during the Great War. For example, he entitled the chapter on modern Germany "The Return of the Barbarians" and urged the British people to fight against Germany, declaring that "we are back in the war with the barbarians" (Chesterton 240).[8]

H. G. Wells certainly contributed to boosting wartime fervour, joining other well-known authors at Wellington House at the outbreak of war and coining the highly publicised phrase "the war to end war". Disillusioned by the reality of war, however, he subsequently converted to pacifism. Later in his life, he admitted that his patriotic frenzy at the onset of war had misled him in his thinking and clouded his sanity:

> I was reluctant to admit how gravely I had compromised myself by my much too forward belligerence and my rash and eager confidence in the liberalism, intelligence and good faith of our Foreign Office and War Office in the first month or so of the war. My pro-war zeal was inconsistent with my pre-war utterances and against my profounder convictions.
>
> (*Experiment in Autobiography* 678)

Wells confessed his realisation that his "war to end war" was no better than a fantasy and that the war could not be justified—the British were fighting for the "King and Country" just as their adversary was fighting for the "Kaiser and Fatherland". Thus, in October 1918—a few months after Lawrence had begun his history—he endeavoured to compose his massive volume of *The Outline of History* from a pacifist viewpoint. In the introduction, Wells argued that the

> need for a common knowledge of the general facts of human history throughout the world has become very evident during the tragic happenings of the last few years. ... There can be no peace now, we realize, but a common peace in all the world. ... Without such ideas to hold them together in harmonious co-operation, with nothing but narrow, selfish, and conflicting nationalist traditions, races and peoples are bound to drift towards conflict and destruction.
>
> (*Outline* 2)

Wells' pacifist idea and war-weariness that urged the composition of his history of an unusually wide scope and length was shared among the public, and hence it became an unexpected bestselling history.

Another history written from the pacifist point of view is *A History of Europe* by A. J. Grant, published a year before the outbreak of war. This book was composed with the eye of a historian that was not clouded by downright hostility at the dawn of war, and hence, the author's observation of modern Germany was totally different from the stereotypical views during wartime. Grant argued that while Germany had developed into the most powerful state organisation in Europe, socialist movements had concurrently grown within her, which he thought posed the possibility of internal disruption. Grant, however, did not necessarily regard this internal division as a great problem, but rather saw it as an opportunity to advance international bonds among workers. He showed how organisation of labour and socialist movements had been widely recognised in Germany, presenting these international movements in opposition to narrow-minded nationalism.[9]

Internationalism became in vogue later after the war, but before and during the war, when Grant's book was published, people's mind was rather more insular in Britain. As for teaching history in schools before the Great War, it meant teaching national history as an imperial past. Grant had insisted on widening the scope and teaching European history, but his proposal did not gain much support in pre-war Britain. Its necessity was, however, recognised through the Great War experiences, and the Ministry of Education came to encourage schools to do more in teaching European history. It is at this time that Lawrence was commissioned to write a history of Europe by Oxford University Press.[10] Grant's *History* offered a major source for the last chapter of Lawrence's *Movements*, "The Unification of Germany".

After the war, internationalism and unity became key words. Thus, Grant became the president of the Historical Association (1920–23). "The Unity Series", edited by F. S. Marvin, began to be published by Oxford University Press during the war, and the series was printed and reprinted after the war in such titles as *The Unity of Western Civilization* and *The Evolution of World Peace* with such contributors as J. A. Hobson and H. G. Wells, who titled the last chapter of his *Outline* "The Possible Unification of the World into One Community of Knowledge and Will". The League of Nations Union, an influential liberal internationalist group in Britain, was formed in 1918 to raise support for the League of Nations.[11]

Compared to these politically infused histories published before and after the First World War, Lawrence's *Movements in European History* dramatically differs from them. He abhorred the militant nationalism that Kipling and Chesterton preached and his history is far from narrow patriotism; yet at the same time, he did not support the internationalism and world peace that Grant and Wells advocated. In spite of this fact, however, Lawrence's *Movements* is not entirely immune to discourses of patriotism and pacifism during the war. The next chapter investigates how and to what degree *Movements in European History* was influenced by wartime discourses, especially the Germanophobia that was widespread in Britain during the Great War, focusing on its chapters that discuss the early Germanic tribes, the Huns and modern Germany.

Notes

1 For the facts about the First World War and wartime Britain, see Winter, *Great War* and *World War I*, Storey and Housego, Hynes, *Edwardian Turn of Mind* and *A War Imagined*, Ceadel and Searle. Most of the unattributed factual information about the First World War in this book derives from these works.

2 Some critics have referred to Lawrence's ambivalence towards the war. For example, Ronald Granofsky mentions that "the war was [to Lawrence] an anathema most of the time, but occasionally it was welcomed as the force that would cleanse Europe of its disease" (Granofsky 18). Likewise, Andrew Harrison remarks on Lawrence's "embrace of war as a means to clearing away the old and ushering in the new" (*D. H. Lawrence and Italian Futurism* 111). Harrison argues that Lawrence's optimism about the war is influenced by the Futurist works, whose aesthetic informs the final draft of *The Rainbow* and influences the struggles of the protagonists in *Women in Love*. See Harrison, *D. H. Lawrence and Italian Futurism* 106–25, 133–40. Alternatively, Sarah Bouttier, analysing Lawrence's wartime poems and *The Lady Bird*, contends that within Lawrence's narratives, the war functions as a "catalyst" that actualises a latent potential existing before the war rather than a "cataclysm" for a total renewal. See Bouttier, "War and Continuity in D. H. Lawrence's Works".

3 For a detailed account on the national ideology of the Great War as a cleansing force, see Hynes, *War Imagined* 10–19, 57–67 and passim. Hynes suggests that Lawrence did not embrace the idea of purifying war (139–41), but, as I argue, Lawrence was not uncontaminated by the ideology.

4 On the British view of Germany before and during the war, see, for example, MacDougall 31–130, Kennedy 119 and 184–204 and Searle 248–49.

5 For example, L. D. Clark asserts that

> for all its imaginative reach, *Movements in European History* remains a lesser work, partly because it was not directed to an adult audience with whom Lawrence could be completely open, and partly because any such reconstruction of historical events must inevitably emphasize the political movements of the past, and Lawrence was never at his best when dealing with actual politics. (211)

One of the few exceptions is P. I. Crumpton's "D. H. Lawrence and the Sources of *Movements in European History*", in which Crumpton identified all the probable sourcebooks for *Movements*. This and the following chapter are indebted to his study.

6 In *The Outline of History*, Wells harshly criticises this imperialist attitude: "With a hypocritical pretence of reluctant benevolent effort the European mind prepared itself to take up what Mr. Rudyard Kipling called 'the White Man's Burthen'—that is to say, the loot and lordship of the earth" (*Outline* 681).

7 For more detailed analyses of this textbook, see Keating 170–84 and J. J. Ross 38.

8 The fact that both of these books sold fairly well indicates the belligerent atmosphere in British society during that period. Kipling and Fletcher's *School History* reached the top of the *Daily Graphic*'s monthly best-seller list, and was acclaimed as "the most popular book of the year" by the *Glasgow News*. See Sutcliffe 158–62. Chesterton's *Short History* reached its third impression in the month following its publication.

9 Grant's position becomes evident in the last few pages of his history. While challenging the logic of those who supported the war, he emphasised that despite increasing stress, European nations had managed to maintain and enjoy peace for over 40 years:

> A few voices are raised to declare that war is in itself a good thing, and that without its severe discipline the moral fibre of Europe would degenerate. But the almost universal feeling is that the burden of armaments and war preparations is a crushing load. ... There never has been a time when more thought has been devoted to discovering the "way of peace". ... Peace breeds peace, as war breeds war, and it may without optimism be anticipated that the practice of arbitration will grow, and that, if the European powers are restrained from actual conflict for some time, they will become more and more unwilling to plunge into war and more and more ready to adopt a more excellent way.
>
> (Grant 650–51)

To this historian, learning history meant to explore a way to peace:

> The study of history itself may lead to the encouragement of the same hopes. We may see the periods of war growing shorter and the periods of peace longer; we may see peace preserved over ever wider and wider areas. ... [I]t can hardly be doubted that the history of man shows us the evolution of peace.
>
> (652)

10 For more detailed discussions on teaching history at schools in England in the early twentieth century, see Robbins 1–26, Sutcliffe 158–200. On Oxford University Press and *Movements*, see Sutcliffe 195–96 and Nehls 471.

11 For the emergence of internationalism in Britain after the First World War, see, for example, Gorman 450–77.

5 Wartime Discourses on War and Peace in *Movements in European History*

The Germanic Race

In *Movements in European History*, Lawrence dedicated three chapters to the early Germanic tribes (Chapter 4: The Germans; Chapter 5: The Goths and Vandals; Chapter 8: The Franks and Charlemagne) and favourably portrayed them as a race that had contributed to the birth of European civilisation. For example, Lawrence writes: "Where the Germans stayed, they settled, and out of their rooting in the new lands rose in time the perfected civilisations of our history" (*MEH* 64). This approving portrayal is, however, in striking contrast to his sources or to other histories written in the early twentieth century. In these sources, the Germans are not necessarily presented as a race that laid the foundation of European civilisation. In writing the chapters on the Germans, Lawrence mainly relied on Edward Gibbon's *The Decline and Fall of the Roman Empire*, along with *The Gallic War* by Julius Caesar and *Germania* by Publius Cornelius Tacitus. It is true that Gibbon states that the "most civilised nations of modern Europe issued from the woods of Germany, and in the rude institutions of those barbarians we may still distinguish the original principles of our present laws and manners" (Gibbon 1: 208). In contrast to *Movements*, however, in which this assertion is expanded and allowed to flourish in the narrative, the statement in *Decline and Fall* is much less favourable. In Gibbon's text, the Germanic tribes, the Iranian Scythians and the Huns are classified as barbarians who threatened the Roman Empire and precipitated its decline: "In the disastrous period of the fall of the Roman empire ... the happiness and security of each individual were personally attacked, and the arts and labours of ages were rudely defaced by the barbarians of Scythia and Germany" (Gibbon 3: 2).

In contrast to the final version, Lawrence's portrayal of the Germans in the first draft of *Movements* largely relied on his sources. In the first draft, the Germans were not introduced as a race which had played any decisive

DOI: 10.4324/9781032675671-6

role in the founding of European civilisation; they were, on the contrary, frequently designated as "barbarians":

> The naked bodies of the barbarians could do little against the walled steel of the legions. Once they were repulsed, they were defeated, for they could not gather into order again. And yet these fearless barbarians were the limit, really, to Roman power.

The aim of Roman policy was furthermore "to set the Germans to destroy one another: for every barbarian destroyed was one enemy less to Rome".[1]

Through the revisions, however, Lawrence's Germans managed to achieve a certain status as a significant race. The published text of *Movements in European History* describes how a relationship developed between the Teutonic race and the Romans, how their bloods were mixed after the decline of the Empire and how, consequently, a higher civilisation was dialectically created. *Movements* argues that it was the fusion of the Germans and Romans that led to the establishment of European civilisation:

> The spirit of German independence and individual liberty had combined with the old Roman ideal of social unity, and the first signs of real European life appeared. …
>
> Churches also were built, and fine abbeys, in a new style, in which the Roman manner was modified by the German spirit. Everywhere the German spirit was pervading old forms, to give birth to a new world.
>
> (*MEH* 94–95)

In another chapter, the importance of the Germanic element in modern Europe is again emphasised:

> These barbarians [from Germany, Russia and Asia] settled down at last, and, mingling or not mingling with the natives of the lands they occupied, formed the base of the great modern nations: English, French, Spanish, Lombard, Swiss, Bulgarian, and so on. All these are formed from a wild mixture of races, in which … the Germanic element was dominant during the Dark Ages.
>
> (63)

Thus, in *Movements in European History*, the Germanic tribes are presented as a race indispensable for the birth of modern Europe.

The uniqueness of the Germanic race in *Movements* is all the more noteworthy when placed in the context of the early twentieth century, when the popularity of the Germanic tribes had diminished among the British.

A School History of England, for example, opens with Rudyard Kipling's poem "The River's Tale", in which the River Thames recounts its own history from ancient times:

> And Norseman and Negro and Gaul and Greek
> Drank with the Britons in Barking Creek,
> And life was gay, and the world was new,
> And I was a mile across at Kew!
> But the Roman came with a heavy hand,
> And bridged and roaded and ruled the land,
> And the Roman left and the Danes blew in—
> And that's where your history books begin!
> (Kipling and Fletcher 10)

All the races which immigrated to Britain before the Norman Conquest are enumerated here, with the exception of the Anglo-Saxons, who arrived in Britain between the fifth and sixth centuries, before the Danes. Does the narrator wish to shut his eyes to the unpalatable fact that Britain shares a common ancestor with its arch enemy? In the second chapter of this history, the Saxons, one of the Germanic tribes, are discussed, and a Saxon man is described as "a truth-teller, a brave, patient, and cool-headed fellow", but at the same time "remorseless and destructive" and "a savage, with the vices and cruelties of an overgrown boy; a drunkard and a gambler, and very stupid" (27, 28).

G. K. Chesterton is also not pleased that the English originated from the Germanic race. In his book, he repeatedly criticises J. R. Green for his idealisation of Teutonic society. Chesterton makes no attempt to conceal his contempt not only for the contemporary Germans but also for the Germanic tribes of the past, arguing that the "value of the Anglo-Saxon is exaggerated" (Chesterton 46). Since the seventeenth century, he argues, England has been overly influenced by this country, which distorted Britain's both internal and foreign policy and which resulted in harmful effects upon the English people's mind. To Chesterton, it is not the Germans, but the Romans, who are the spiritual heritage and foundation of the British people: "The important thing about France and England is not that they have Roman remains. They are Roman remains. In truth they are not so much remains as relics; for they are still working miracles" (9). Thus, both Kipling and Chesterton attempted to subvert the idea that Britain and Germany shared a common ancestor, an idea which had been dominant until late in the previous century.

As shown above, these jingoistic histories make a striking contrast to Lawrence's *Movements*. The difference between their views on the English race does not lie, however, merely in the degree to which the authors place importance on the Germans. Another difference is that while the conservatives assert the purity of their own race, Lawrence espouses the idea of hybridity. Kipling and Fletcher stick to the pure origins of the English race:

> The Saxons brought [to Britain] their wives and children with them, though it is difficult to believe that they were so stupid as to kill *all* the Britons instead of enslaving them and marrying their wives. Yet, if they had not done this, surely there would have been some traces left of Latin or Celtic speech, law and religion. But there were practically none. When, in the seventh and eighth centuries, we begin to see a little into the darkness, we find that England has become a purely English country, with a purely English ... system of law, and a purely English language.
>
> (Kipling and Fletcher 28)

It is, in the end, the spirit of the place that transformed the Saxons into decent English: "the spirit of the land entered into him, even more than into any of those who lived before or came after him" (29).

This theory differs fundamentally from that of Lawrence, who repeatedly propounds the idea that races of human beings, to say nothing of the English, have been produced through intermarriage: "the Saxons, Danes, and Normans were all of Germanic blood, and the fusion of these tribes with the native Briton has resulted in our modern English race" (*MEH* 64). In the late 1910s, Lawrence was not alone in advocating the idea of hybridity. In his *Outline of History*, H. G. Wells also insisted that people had essentially mixed and mingled with each other and that the nationalism that contrived to divide people into certain groups was merely a political fabrication:

> [O]ur story ... has demonstrated the mingling of races and peoples, the instability of human divisions, the swirling variety of human groups. ... The "nationality" ... is really no more than the romantic and emotional exaggeration of the stresses produced by the discord of the natural political map with unsuitable political arrangements.
>
> (Outline 666)

The early chapters of *Movements* align more with Wells' history than merely the idea of the intermingling of the races; they also subscribe to Wells' pacifist framework. In the early chapters of his history, Lawrence repeatedly portrays people as suffering from the devastation of war. He observes that in the fifth and the sixth centuries, "some men were weary to death of fighting, robbing, burning, thieving, snatching, they wanted peace and the stillness of the soul above all things" (87). Also, in the Roman Empire, "in a world weary of strife and excitement, and clogged with slavery, the thought of peace and innocent love, and of a life of still, gentle, everlasting happiness, was most beautiful" (30). The emphasis placed by Lawrence and by Wells on the fusion and mixing of the different races was a reaction against the period in which they composed their works, when European nations were devoting their energy to waging futile battles against each other:

> [T]he German races mingled and mixed with the dark-eyed races [the Romans], and it is from this intermingling of the two opposite spirits, two different and opposite streams of blood, that modern Europe has arisen. The *fusion* of the two opposites brought us the greatness of modern days: just as the *hostility* of the two brings disaster, now as in the old past.
>
> (*MEH* 52; my emphasis)[2]

Employing "fusion" and "hostility" as opposing concepts, this passage implies that the First World War is a devastating clash that brings forth nothing but disaster and misery, caused by mutual antagonism. In the early chapters of *Movements in European History*, reconciliation and harmonious relationships between different races are thus reiterated, as Wells' history. Consequently, these chapters, composed before the armistice, makes a marked contrast to the jingoistic histories that contributed to boosting patriotic fervour during the war; the early chapters of Lawrence's history are infused with war-weariness and anti-war feelings.

The Huns

As demonstrated in the previous section, the first several chapters of *Movements* present a marked contrast to the jingoistic histories. Nevertheless, Lawrence's history book does demonstrate susceptibility to permeation by belligerent atmosphere, especially the feeling of Germanophobia that was rife during the war. Lawrence's portrayal of the Huns is a significant clue to it. In contrast to contemporary historians such as A. J. Grant and G. W. Kitchin, who allocated only one page to the Huns in their *A History of Europe* and *A History of France* respectively (Grant 207–08, Kitchin 60–61; both were Lawrence's sources), Lawrence dedicated a whole chapter to the tribe, following Gibbon, who gave a comprehensive account of the Huns as a threat to the Western Roman Empire. A comparison between Lawrence's Huns and those of Gibbon in the context of the Great War illustrates the degree to which the anti-German discourse influenced its composition.

From the first reference to them in Chapter 5 of *Movements*, the Huns are presented as a continual threat to civilisation:

> The year 375 is marked as an epoch in the world's history, for it was the year in which the Huns, *coming out of the vast unknown Asia*, crossed the Volga on their way to Europe. ...
>
> Suddenly, as a volcano bursts and the lava pours down on a doomed people, the Huns burst *out of Asia* and came down in their black myriads upon the Goths. The Huns were hideous little people on horseback, savage, terribly fierce, and numerous like *clouds of locusts*.
>
> (*MEH* 56; my emphasis)

The sixth chapter "The Huns" accentuates the emphasis which is placed on the race as the destroyers of civilisation:

> Thus we see that from the distribution of German tribes among native nations ... the modern nations of Europe have arisen. There is one great barbarian race, however, ... and this is the race whose name rang terror through the whole ancient world. ... Yet the Hunnish force ... did nothing towards building up a new world. The Germanic races entered in and formed the basis of a new Europe. The Hunnish force rolled away like a thunder-cloud that has burst and struck the land.
>
> (64–65)

The Huns were born destroyers who not only devastated the land of Europe but also "brought ruin on the beautiful, civilised empire of China" (65). As the passages quoted above suggest, the destruction brought about by the Huns was not something that was necessary to achieve a higher level of dialectic creation, which Lawrence often advocated, but rather a sterile demolition which led to nothing. The Huns were aliens who came from outside of Europe (from "the vast unknown Asia"), and they were associated with beasts and small creatures: they are "more like baboons than men", living in black tents "like a bee-hive ... darting here and there over the plain like clouds of flies" (56, 65). Thus, *Movements* emphasises their otherness and their inhumane cruelty by overlaying them with images of apes and small creatures, which Gibbon did not employ.

The portrayal of Attila, who led a band of these untameable barbarians, is added to the gruesome portrait of the Huns. This ugly looking tyrant guided them with an exuberant vitality:

> Attila is the greatest of the Huns. He was a squat, broad-backed man with a large head and a flat face. But his little eyes sparkled with tremendous passions, his body had great nervous energy. A haughty little

> creature, he had a prancing way of walking, and he rolled his eyes fiercely, filling the onlookers with terror, and enjoying the terror he inspired.
>
> (69)

This passage is copied almost faithfully from the first half of Gibbon's portrait of Attila. Lawrence, however, omitted the latter part in which Gibbon stresses Attila's ability as a leader:

> [A]nd he had a custom of fiercely rolling his eyes, as if he wished to enjoy the terror which he inspired. Yet this savage hero was not inaccessible to pity; his suppliant enemies might confide in the assurance of peace or pardon; and Attila was considered by his subjects as a just and indulgent master. He delighted in war; but, after he had ascended the throne in a mature age, his head, rather than his hand, achieved the conquest of the North; and the fame of an adventurous soldier was usefully exchanged for that of a prudent and successful general. The effects of personal valour are so inconsiderable … that victory, even among barbarians, must depend on the degree of skill with which the passions of the multitude are combined and guided for the service of a single man.
>
> (Gibbon 3: 346)

In *Decline and Fall*, Attila is repeatedly praised as "a king, who had often fought and conquered at their head" (3: 389), as a hero who delivered a fatal blow to the declining Roman Empire. Conversely, in *Movements*, he is merely a despot who heads up a band of savage tribes with excessive vigour. In *Movements*, these barbarian hordes led by Attila unleash a storm of terror among the peoples of Europe and destroy civilisation:

> These untamable people were like animals. They were very swift and sudden in their movements, and the first hordes seem to have been almost without human feelings. When they came down on the Goths they slaughtered indiscriminately, opening their wide mouths and slashing and slaying anything that was alive and was not Hunnish. They spoke with shrill, high voices, calling shrilly, using strange, savage gestures. And when they had finished killing, they collected all the booty they wanted, for they were very greedy, and then they set fire to all that would burn, and that they did not want.
>
> No wonder the fleeing Goths were horrified. They felt that behind these fearful faces there was no human spirit. They felt that no human speech could reach these creatures. The Hunnish speech seemed like the

shrill, neighing communication of animals. And the Huns were avaricious as demons.

(*MEH* 67)

The text persistently portrays the Huns as beasts and devils, emphasising their inhumanity. A salient point here is that these representations of the Huns must have reminded the contemporary readers of the brutality of the Germans.

"The Hun" was an insulting epithet designating German soldiers, frequently used in anti-German propaganda during the First World War. For example, *The Times* printed an article titled "The March of the Huns" only three weeks after the outbreak of war. The article unashamedly sought to boost patriotic fervour by condemning "an atrocious act" by German soldiers, who were dubbed "ruthless barbarians" with an image of the Huns:

> Such is the character of the warfare of the modern Huns. They seek to strike terror into the hearts of their foes by methods which belong to the days of the old barbaric hosts, who were thought to have vanished from the world for ever.
>
> ("The March of the Huns" 9)

In the article, the German Kaiser is called "The modern ATTILA", and it is predicted that "the Monarch who unblushingly aspires to be regarded as ATTILA's successor" (9) will suffer the same fate as the former lord of the Huns. Thus, the idea that the Germans were as savage and cruel as the barbarous Huns was widely circulated from the beginning of the war.

On 13 September 1914, one month after the onset of war, Frieda wrote a letter to Edward Marsh arguing that these projected images of the Germans were merely an exaggerated, fabricated representation that always recurred during wartime:

> And this abstract hate of a fairytale German ogre (they used of Napoleon to say that he ate little children for breakfast,) it's mostly an artificial thing—Also in the Boer war they used to my horror tell ghastly stories of British cruelty in Germany—Of course in war all the madnesses come out in a man, that is the fault of *war* not of a *man* or a *nation*.
>
> (*2L* 214)

However, the widespread anti-German discourse was officially certified as "truth" when, in May 1915, the so-called *Bryce Report* was published, in which atrocious acts claimed to have been committed by German soldiers were documented. Published five days after the sinking of the *Lusitania*, the *Report* enumerated the brutality of the German army in Belgium. The land which the German troops had invaded was littered with the corpses of children and pregnant women who had been shot and bayonetted, and with charred bodies. Houses were looted and burnt down; a whole town was reduced to ashes:

> Though the cause of the massacre is in dispute, the results are known with certainty. … [M]any inhabitants were burnt alive in their houses, their efforts to escape being prevented by rifle fire. Twenty people were shot, while trying to escape. … The fire burnt on through the night and the murders continued on the following day, the 21st [August 1914]. Thirty-two civilians were killed on that day in the Place de l'Université alone, and a witness states that this was followed by the rape in open day of 15 or 20 women on tables in the square itself. …
>
> Hardly were we there [Belgian border] when we had a horrible sight. Houses were burnt down, the inhabitants chased away and some of them shot. Not one of the hundreds of houses were spared. Everything was plundered and burnt. … We then arrived at the town of Wandre. Here the houses were spared, but everything was examined. At last we were out of the town and everything went in ruins. In one house a whole collection of weapons was found. The inhabitants without exception were brought out and shot. This shooting was heart-breaking as they all knelt down and prayed, but that was no ground for mercy.
>
> (*BR* 12–13)

The report goes on:

> A shocking case of the murder of a baby by a drunken soldier at Malines is thus recorded by one eye-witness and confirmed by another:—
>
> One day when the Germans were not actualling [sic] bombarding the town I left my house to go to my mother's house in High Street. … As the German soldiers came along the street I saw a small child, whether boy or girl I could not see, come out of a house. The child was about two years of age. The child came into the middle of the street so as to be in the way of the soldiers. The soldiers were walking in twos. The first line of two passed the child; one of the second line, the man on the left, stepped aside and drove his bayonet with both hands into the child's stomach, lifting the child into the air on his bayonet and carrying it away on his bayonet, he and his comrades still singing. The child screamed when the soldier struck it with his bayonet, but not afterwards.
>
> (*BR* 52)

Furthermore, the following year, the book *German Atrocities: An Official Investigation* was published, which professed to be "a postscript to the Bryce Report" (Morgan 2). Somewhat different from the style of the *Bryce Report*, which evenly but persistently recounted the "truth", *German Atrocities* was, in its aggressive and sensational tone, the epitome of crude propaganda. This book, which sold over 1.5 million copies, contained typical representations of anti-German discourse. The author, J. H. Morgan, a professor at London University, argued that, unlike other Europeans, the Germans were in a state of "mental degeneration" (28), and suggested that they were descended from the savage Asians and that the British did not share common ancestors with them:

> It is not in their ignorance but in their turpitude that the clue to these barbarities is to be found. ... [A]nd there may be force in the contention of those who believe that the Prussian is not a member of the Teutonic family at all, but a "throw-back" to some Tartar stock.
>
> (29)

The author went on to insist that the Germans "retain the instincts of Asia or rather of some pre-Asiatic horde", and "the progress of German troops is like a plague of locusts over the land" (45, 84). Through various media such as pamphlets, posters and newspaper articles, the Germans' "atrocious acts"—including the invasion of Belgium, the use of poison gas in Ypres, the use of torpedoes by U-boats and the bombing of the Zeppelin—were exaggerated, strengthening the link between the Germans and the savage Huns. Thus, it was as a matter of course that in her diary Cynthia Asquith called Frieda "the exuberant Hun" (Asquith 37). It is significant that a series of images which Lawrence adopted to portray the Huns—savagery, atavism, Asia and small creatures—was actually used to describe the Germans in anti-German propaganda (see Figure 5.1).

In *The Decline and Fall of the Roman Empire*, Gibbon does depict the atrocious acts of the Huns, who invaded the land of the Gauls across the Rhine:

> But as the greatest part of the Gallic cities were alike destitute of saints and soldiers, they were besieged and stormed by the Huns, who practised, in the example of Metz, their customary maxims of war. They involved in a promiscuous massacre the priests who served at the altar and the infants who, in the hour of danger, had been providently baptised by the bishop; the flourishing city was delivered to the flames, and a solitary chapel of St. Stephen marked the place where it formerly stood.
>
> (3: 385)

Figure 5.1 Edmund J. Sullivan, "The Prussian Butcher" in *The Kaiser's Garland* 73.

When compared to the Huns in Gibbon's description, Lawrence's portrayal is cruder, emphasising their ferocity and ruthlessness. *Movements* enumerates their inhumane acts so vividly and roughly that Gibbon's depiction seems rather plain and simple. The above-quoted passage by Gibbon was expanded upon by Lawrence as follows:

> In a sudden unexpected rush the Huns would be on the town. Grinning with war-excitement, the little men swarmed and slashed, killing every inhabitant in their glee of slaughter. They found priests and bishops hastily baptising the infants, lest death should overtake the unchristened babies and their helpless souls be lost. This sight made the savage little

> Huns grin wider. Swiftly the priests and bishops were cut down, the babies tossed on spears. ... Then the town was thoroughly pillaged, food and wine consumed. After the revel, when all was stripped, the retreating Huns fired the towns, and far-off Gauls knew by the redness of the sky what was happening. Cities burned to a blackened ruin. ...
>
> Such was the fate of beautiful Roman cities like Metz and Trèves, and many others. The Huns advanced into Gaul, leaving the earth like a cinder behind them, strewn with the charred remains of men and women.
>
> (*MEH* 70)

People are mercilessly slaughtered, towns are utterly plundered and burnt down, heaps of charred corpses are scattered after their invasion—this portrayal of the Huns evokes the atrocious acts of the German soldiers meticulously documented in the *Bryce Report* and the exaggerated depictions in *German Atrocities* or of the popular cartoons (see Figure 5.2). In these descriptions of the Huns invading westwards can be heard an ominous echo of the Germans advancing towards the west.

It is the Battle in Châlons, in north-east France, that is depicted in *Movements* as Attila's biggest battle, in which the Romans defeated this lord of the savage tribe. In this battle, which Lawrence describes in terms of its "unspeakable hand to hand murder" and "the roaring bloody carnage" (71), Attila's army was beaten by the Romans under Aëtius and driven out of the land of the Western Roman Empire:

> At last suddenly Attila broke up his camp, and retreated east. Aëtius followed. Attila moved northwards and re-crossed the Rhine. Gaul breathed free, and Europe was saved. For if, in 451, Attila had won this great battle of Châlons, on the Catalaunian plain beside the Marne, Europe would have fallen under Tartar sway.
>
> (71)

Gibbon refers to the battlefield as "the plain of Châlons" (Gibbon 3: 390), whereas Lawrence describes it as "the plain of Châlons, on the Marne" and "the Catalaunian plain beside the Marne" (*MEH* 70, 71). The word "Marne" could have reverberated in the minds of Lawrence's readers at the time because two major battles were fought at the Marne during the Great War. In the First Battle of the Marne, which took place at the beginning of the war, the Germans were thwarted by British and French forces in their attempt to rapidly conquer Paris. During the First World War, when the battles of the Marne were mentioned, the battle against Attila was invariably referred to. From the beginning of the fighting, *The Times* alluded to the fifth-century battle when reporting on the contemporary one:

Figure 5.2 Edmund J. Sullivan, "The Gentle German" in *The Kaiser's Garland* 71.

> More than fourteen hundred years ago Attila and his Huns came to Châlons on the Marne, and were forced to retreat to the Rhine after tremendous slaughter. On the same ground the forces of the Monarch who has styled himself the modern ATTILA are meeting a like fate.
>
> ("The Retreat of the New Attila", 9; see Figure 5.3)

Nearly four years later, in July 1918, several months before the armistice, the Second Battle of the Marne broke out when the Allies fought against the Germans, who were approaching Paris and were only 80 miles away. In this battle, which erupted at exactly the time when Lawrence was composing the first draft of *Movements*, the Germans were again forced

Figure 5.3 Bernard Partridge, "Hun to Hun" in *Punch, or the London Charivari* 24 July 1918, 57.

to retreat across the Marne, an episode which signalled the beginning of the end of the prolonged war. Thus, in the Great War, the battles that the two sides fought at the Marne acquired a symbolic significance for the Allies: they were the battles that thwarted the invasion of the detestable Huns, shattering their insane ambitions. Lawrence concludes the episode with an ominous sentence: "if, in 451, Attila had won this great battle of Châlons, on the Catalaunian plain beside the Marne, *Europe would have fallen under Tartar sway* ..." (71; my emphasis). In *Movements*, it is Europe that is said to have won the battle of the Marne against the Huns, a somewhat different conclusion from that of Gibbon, who refers to it as "the last victory which was achieved in the name of the Western [Roman] empire" (3: 393). Lawrence's portentous statement has grim echoes of a deep-seated fear of the contemporary "Huns" during the Great War. Thus, although Lawrence in *Movements* adopts the historical events and episodes concerning the Huns from Gibbon's *Decline and Fall*, his depiction of them is infused with the anti-German discourse that was in wide circulation during the First World War.

The Unification of Germany

> My brother, are war and battle evil? Necessary, however, is the evil. ...
> I say unto you: it is the good war which halloweth every cause.
> War and courage have done more great things than charity.
>
> Friedrich Nietzsche, *Thus Spake Zarathustra*, Part I

> The girl does not know what they mean by "cap-i-tal-izm" (or the other word they sometimes use, "ma-teer-ee-al-izum"), but, judging from the scornful tone they use whenever they speak the words, cap-i-tal-izum and ma-teer-ee-al-izum must be very twisted things that are opposed to nature and *rightness*. The girl has been taught that, in order to keep her body and her thoughts clean, she must limit her contact with the outside world. Otherwise, her mind will become "po-loo-ted".
>
> Haruki Murakami, *1Q84*, Book II, Chapter 19

The last chapter of *Movements*, titled "The Unification of Germany", recounts the unification of Germany by Otto von Bismarck and later events in relation to the movements of modern European history. Comparison of this chapter to the contemporary British view on Germany and to *A History of Europe* by A. J. Grant, Lawrence's main source for this chapter, reveals that Lawrence's description is in conflict with the contemporary view or that of Grant's, while simultaneously displaying a curious affinity with the chauvinist history books.

After the armistice, as we have seen, internationalism was in vogue. In 1920 John Middleton Murry, in an essay in *Athenaeum*, insisted that a new kind of internationalism through which people in different nations would understand and sympathise with each other without prejudice should be established:

> As … it becomes more evident that a political internationalism will be for many years to come a vain mirage, the need to foster intellectual internationalism grows more urgent. … [W]hatever can be done to diminish the irrational race-hatred that is bred by ignorance is a positive gain to the world.
>
> (Murry 365)

Lawrence was sceptical about Europe's movement towards internationalism. He argued in his essay "Democracy", written when *Movements* was almost complete (except for its final chapter), that the "thing to do is not to raise the idea of a Nation, or even of Internationalism, higher. The need is to take away every scrap of ideal drapery from nationalism and from internationalism …" (*RDP* 66). This attitude is maintained in *Movements*. Adopting again such dualisms as destruction and creation or war and peace, the narrator ironically portrays post-Renaissance Europe, where the ideology of creation and peace has achieved dominance:

> Nations, in the modern sense, arise when mankind chooses peace and production rather than war and glory. … And so the idea works itself out: it is the producer who matters, only the producer. Pride is nothing, glory is nothing, only production is important.
>
> (*MEH* 242)

People have striven only for material prosperity instead of satisfying their destructive impulses, and this is, according to the narrator, the cause of the disease that has afflicted contemporary Europe:

> In the pride of its heart, every nation desires to triumph over its neighbours. But pride of heart and the desire for triumph exhaust themselves, it seems. And then in their hearts peoples and nations only wish for ease and prosperity, they have no use for wars. And when they have no use for wars, they have no use for absolute kings with their ministers. Nothing further matters but the dead level of material prosperity.
>
> (246)

The outlook of Europe, governed by the workers, is ominously portrayed with a rather reactionary view:

> Europe seems to move towards unification, towards the institution of one vast state ruled by the infinite numbers of the people—the producers, the proletariat, the workmen.

> The national spirit brings us to this, which is ultimately the international or universal spirit. Nations, however, must, in the first instance, be pivoted upon a central power, a king.
>
> (242)

Thus, although the events of history in "The Unification of Germany" in *Movements* are indebted to Grant's history, the narrator's view on modern Europe is quite contrary. Its passage is overtly belligerent and reactionary and deeply pessimistic about Europe's future.

Otto von Bismarck is celebrated in this chapter as a leader who built a nation that was not afflicted with materialism. He was appointed as Prime Minister when Emperor Wilhelm I had difficulty in dealing with liberals over military reform, and, as if swinging back the pendulum of European history, Bismarck ignored the parliament to expand military force and achieved German unification. *Movements* minutely describes how the national system this Iron Chancellor constructed stands in opposition to such merchant countries as Britain that were governed by the plutocratic middle classes:

> Now Bismarck founded the North German Federation, which was the beginning of the German Empire of our day. Bismarck did not follow the British model. He did not like the liberal middle classes of Germany. …
>
> It [the Reichstag] was not like the British House of Commons, a chamber of rich men. … The ministers governed. And the ministers were quite independent of the Reichstag. They represented the Crown. …
>
> The chief of the ministers was the Chancellor. He was a far more powerful person than the British Prime Minister. … The German Chancellor—and Bismarck was the first German Chancellor—answered only to the king. So his power was immense. It was his success in war which saved him, and made him a popular hero. Prussia was still a fighting state, not a commercial state.
>
> (248)

In *Movements* are recounted the Chancellor's glorious military achievements, but the annexation of Alsace-Lorraine or the colonial acquisitions, which aroused anti-German sentiment among the British, are not referred to. The overall tone of the concluding chapter of *Movements in European History* is expectant of a leader like Bismarck:

> But we must never forget that mankind lives by a twofold motive: the motive of peace and increase, and the motive of contest and martial triumph. As soon as the appetite for martial adventure and triumph in conflict is satisfied, the appetite for peace and increase manifests itself,

> and *vice versa*. It seems a law of life. Therefore a great united Europe of productive working people, all materially equal, will never be able to continue and remain firm unless it unites also round one great chosen figure, some hero who can lead a great war, as well as administer a wide peace.
>
> (252)

Half of the pages in this chapter are devoted to Bismarck and are favourable towards him, and hence the "one great chosen figure" mentioned at the conclusion explicitly refers to the Iron Chancellor, who dismantled democratic institutions and established a military regime as well as contributed to the industrialisation of Germany. Thus, the prevailing tone of this chapter differs dramatically from the contemporary British view of Germany as a rogue state. Likewise, it is quite opposite to the pacifist vision that is presented in Lawrence's source book by A. J. Grant.

Simultaneously, however, the concluding chapter of *Movements* reveals a link to contemporary dominant discourse. The last chapter reiterates that Britain had been corrupted by materialistic principles since the Renaissance and implies that the war was a historical necessity for dispelling the dead materialism that inflicted contemporary Western civilisation. The idea that Europe after the Renaissance was polluted by materialism is, however, by no means Lawrence's original theory; a similar notion is expressed in other history books as well. Despite his different political idea, religious faith and literary taste, Chesterton's *A Short History of England* adheres to a similar belief. In *Short History*, Chesterton idealises religious fervour and loyalty in medieval society and interprets post-Renaissance history as a process of degradation. He ascribes the cause of the corruption to the development of commercialism and propagation of materialism, or what this medievalist calls "plutocratic pillage" and "mercantile oligarchy" (Chesterton 164, 189). Similarly, in *A School History of England*, Kipling and Fletcher deplore the decline of Britain due to material prosperity, drawing an analogy that was too familiar to contemporary readers—the analogy with the Roman Empire: "The greatest empire that the world has ever seen was slowly dying at the heart, dying of too much power, too much prosperity, too much luxury. What a lesson for us all to-day!" (22).

In actuality, the idea that Britain had deteriorated by materialism was widely shared in the early twentieth century. In *The New Machiavelli* by H. G. Wells, published in the same year as *A School History* in 1911, the author-figure Richard Remington describes a sudden change of an idealised rural community of old England into a world of an urban disorder and proliferation dominated by mechanical industry and materialism, with a nostalgic evocation that is reminiscent of the beginning of *The Rainbow*:

> But after 1750 something got hold of the world, something that was destined to alter the scale of every human affair.
>
> That something was machinery and a vague energetic disposition to improve material things.
>
> (35)

In the same year, even in the music field, composer and critic Cecil Forsyth in his *Music and Nationalism* proposed to restore the British people's collective soul—the soul lost because of industrialism and imperial Germany—through the use of music.[3]

As demonstrated, Lawrence's history book does not merely portray his unique vision of history, nor does it simply chronicle events compiled from a variety of sources. *Movements in European History* is infused with contemporary discourses on war and peace. Lawrence's descriptions of Germany reveal the complex relationships between *Movements* and national ideologies. In the early chapters, it appears as if Lawrence was reacting against the anti-German propaganda of that time. His depiction of the Germanic race is uncommonly favourable compared to the chauvinist histories published before and during the war. The pacifist predilection exhibited in his portrayal aligns with Wells' history. Contrariwise, in his description of the Huns, Lawrence employs a series of atrocious images and metaphors that were a product of the wartime propaganda against German soldiers. Although based on Gibbon's *Decline and Fall*, Lawrence's portrayal of the Huns—his use of barbaric images, the exaggeration of their inhumane nature, the horror the savage tribe inspired among people—mirrors the widespread portrait of the contemporary "Hun".

Conversely, the last chapter of *Movements* is pro-German and makes a striking contrast to the Germanophobic attitude entertained by his British contemporaries. Bismarck's military regime is celebrated as a cleansing force of modern Europe that was ultimately tarnished because of extreme materialism. This perspective also sharply opposes Lawrence's sourcebook, A. J. Grant's *A History of Europe*, in which Grant foresaw the possibility of Germany moving towards internationalism after Bismarck's reign. Nevertheless, Lawrence's final chapter simultaneously evinces a curious affinity with chauvinist histories that blame plutocratic principles for causing the lamentable degeneration of the British race since the Renaissance. Thus, the ambivalent narrative of *Movements in European History* reveals entwined traces of controversial issues and anxieties swirling throughout a nation confronted with an unprecedented event of violence and destruction in human history.

Notes

1 Lawrence's autograph fragment "The Germans, Goths, and Vandals", La L 19/4R.

2 In his intriguing analysis, Michael Hollington explores these features in the context of contemporary frontier theory to show that the "conception of frontier cross-pollinating hybridity, of cultures and people open and receptive to one another and eventually assimilating one another and even fusing, is central to *Movements in European History* ..." (31). However, it is doubtful whether "many historians and geographers of the time would have accepted Lawrence's emphasis" (33) when compared to the history books of wartime examined in this and the previous chapters. Additionally, it should be noted that these passages in *Movements* resonate Lawrence's preoccupation with intermarriage, a recurring motif from *The White Peacock* to *Lady Chatterley's Lover.*

3 See Hughes and Stradling 115–25.

6 To Produce, or Not to Produce, That Is the Question

Materialism, Democracy and War in *Women in Love*

> You must drop all your democracy. You must not believe in "the people". …
> There must be an aristocracy of people who have wisdom, and there must be a Ruler: a Kaiser: no Presidents and democracies.
>
> D. H. Lawrence's letter to Bertrand Russell, 14 July 1915

The First World War started in the summer of 1914, and the following year, *The Rainbow* was banned on a charge of obscenity. Lawrence was forced to compose and revise *Women in Love* without any hope of publishing it. The war left inerasable scars on Lawrence's texts afterwards. It is true that the war is absent from *Women in Love* and no war erupts in it; despite this fact, contemporary discourses on war, materialism and democracy, which are found in the narrative of *Movements in European History*, are also interwoven within this text. *Women in Love* begins with a conversation between the Brangwen sisters, in which Ursula and Gudrun discuss the favourite topics of girls of a marriageable age. Gudrun gives a negative answer to her sister's question of whether she came back home to find an ideal partner and says, "Don't you find, that things fail to materialise? *Nothing materialises*!" (*WL* 8; emphasis in original). However, her lover, Gerald Crich, tells his best friend, Rupert Birkin, that "You've got to start with material things" (56) and as a mine owner he endeavours to increase coal production as much as possible: "He had a fight to fight with Matter, with the earth and the coal it enclosed" (227). In *Women in Love*, words related to substance such as "materialise", "material" and "matter" are employed from the beginning until the end of the novel. These are keywords as the development of this novel is bound up with the duality of production and barrenness.

These two attributes, production and barrenness, are embodied by Gerald and Birkin respectively. Gerald succeeds to the mining industry owned by his family and achieves massive growth in coal production through the introduction of modern technologies to his mines. This

DOI: 10.4324/9781032675671-7

Industrial Magnate represents the ethos of the time period when Lawrence produced this novel. L. T. Hobhouse, one of the major proponents of new liberalism, analysed British society in the early twentieth century in *Democracy and Reaction* (1904). He described the value system of the time, which placed more emphasis on economy than ethics, on private profits than mutual support:

> The principle of liberty may be converted into an unlovely gospel of commercial competition, in which mutual help is decried as a means of saving the feckless and inefficient from the consequences of their character, the impulses of pity and benevolence are repressed, and the promptings of self-interest invested with the sanctity of a stern duty. Merit is measured by success, and the standard of success is the money-making capacity.
>
> (227)

The setting of *Women in Love* is similar to the society which Hobhouse depicts, in which supreme value is placed on producing maximum profit through competition. Rejecting his father's philanthropic ways of managing the business, Gerald reorganises it and emphasises its profitability. In contrast, Birkin swims against the tide, following his own beliefs. He appears not interested in making a home or in creating family ties, nor is it clear how he earns his living after he quits his job as a school inspector. He stands aloof from society and produces nothing to contribute to it. Their opposite characters are illustrated in their conversation in the train to London:

> "You've got to start with material things," said Gerald.
> Which statement Birkin ignored. …
> "Tell me," said Birkin. "What do you live for?"
> Gerald's face went baffled.
> "What do I live for? … I suppose I live to work, to produce something. …"
>
> (*WL* 56)

Rather than adhering to the traditional dualistic reading that classifies Birkin and Ursula as representing the creative aspect and Gerald and Gudrun as the destructive one,[1] I propose analysing *Women in Love* focusing on the duality of production and barrenness, which ultimately melts into thin air and evaporates at the end of the novel. The key figure is Gerald, who epitomises the period of modern technology which affected various areas of activity from the trend of social theory to the strategy of war. Although the time period in which the novel is set is not identified, contemporary ideological discourses are engraved on *Women in Love*. The early twentieth century witnessed the development of modern technologies, the birth of a new trend of thought called new liberalism and the devastation wrought by the First World War. This chapter uncovers how these aspects influenced the text by placing it within the social and political context of the time when it was produced.

Technology, Labour-Management Strife and Democracy in the Early Twentieth Century

Chapter 17 of *Women in Love*, "The Industrial Magnate", depicts in great detail the drastic reform that Gerald introduces to the management of his company on confronting his labourers. Historically, coal mining was a source of national power in Britain from the last half of the nineteenth to the early twentieth century. The number of miners had increased, eventually exceeding one million in 1919, which was approximately 10 per cent of the working population of men. Coal production had also grown since the mid-nineteenth century and reached its peak in 1913—the year of the publication of *Sons and Lovers* and a year before the outbreak of World War I.[2] Thus, with the advance of modern technologies, the mining industry developed on a large scale at the turn of the century, and Gerald, like his contemporary mine owners, introduces extensive restructuring and mechanisation to the mines he inherited from his father.

Thomas Crich was one of the last middle-class philanthropists of the late Victorian era. This paternalistic man romanticised labourers and wished to create a (pseudo-)familial bond with them. Despite his benevolence, however, the miners began to feel dissatisfied with this patriarch, and the first labour strife erupted when Gerald was still a child. The miners embraced the concept of equality, which the narrator rather satirically describes:

> Seething masses of miners met daily, carried away by a new religious impulse. The idea flew through them: "All men are equal on earth," and they would carry the idea to its material fulfilment. ... Seething mobs of men marched about, their faces lighted up as for holy war, with a smoke of cupidity.
>
> (*WL* 225)

As this passage suggests, the early twentieth century witnessed the spread of the idea of democracy. Historically, the idea of democracy is not so old. In 1865, Lord Elcho, a Whig politician and grandfather of Lady Cynthia Asquith, made a speech in the parliamentary debate on the extension of the vote, in which he argued that

> by lowering the franchise as is proposed in this indiscriminate way, while you will get a certain number of good, prudent, and intelligent men, yet inasmuch as the mass of men are improvident and ignorant, ... and perhaps will be so till the end of time, the thoughtful and provident working people will be swamped. ... The measure is one which strikes at those of the working classes who are thoughtful and provident, and places the political power of the country in the hands of the thoughtless and improvident.
>
> (*Hansard's* 1402–03)

A half a century later, in the early twentieth century, many of the ruling classes still shared the anti-democratic idea. Liberal politician and journalist C. F. G. Masterman, in his *The Condition of England* (1909), stated that the "rich despise the Working People; the Middle Classes fear them" (71). Masterman went on to describe how the middle classes considered the multitude's demand for their political rights: the middle classes had "constructed in imagination the image of Democracy—a loud-voiced, independent, arrogant figure, with a thirst for drink, and imperfect standards of decency, and a determination to be supported at someone else's expense" (72). For the governing classes, democracy meant nothing more than mobocracy, or rule by the ignorant, greedy masses—"creeping democracy", as Mrs Crich calls it (*WL* 217).

At the turn of the century, however, a group of men began to propound democracy. They were called the new liberals. Liberalism had traditionally had a dualistic view of the individual versus the state, and it expressed disapproval of the state's intervention in the individuals. In contrast to this old, *laissez-faire* liberalism, which is represented by Herbert Spencer, new liberalism argued for using state power to help the individual. New liberalism promoted welfare policies, rather than self-help, to correct the economic inequality that affected the growing population of the urban working classes. And to the new liberals, democracy was a means of achieving a higher quality of life and true liberty. Hobhouse argued in "Government by the People" (1910) that the

> movement towards self-government ... is part of a more comprehensive effort to broaden the basis of civilization, to break down artificial barriers of birth, nationality and sex, to raise the masses of the people from a condition of subservience and tutelage, to give them their share in the common heritage and their part to play in the common life.
>
> (123)

And he continues, "Democracy may be nothing but an experiment. ... But it is an experiment worth the making in a world where no alternative mode of government holds out equal hopes of social progress" (135). In addition to Hobhouse and Masterman, those who advocated new liberalism at the turn of the century include the economist and anti-imperialist J. A. Hobson and the pacifistic economist John Maynard Keynes, among others. In *Women in Love*, Hermione's brother, Alexander Roddice, described as "democratic and lucid" (*WL* 90), is potentially characterised as a new liberal. Birkin, conversely, possesses a traditional liberal individualist temperament.[3]

Birkin bears obvious similarities to the author, who had a strong antagonism towards Bertrand Russell, a staunch defender of democracy and the model for Sir Joshua Malleson in the novel, and who was never involved in the pacifist movement, eventually turning into a misanthrope avoiding contact altogether with the human community. Lawrence had been critical of the idea of democracy, and his scepticism swelled when he witnessed the rise of jingoism among the British at the onset of war. During the war, he entertained a growing distrust for and disgust towards the masses of people who, boosted by agitators like Horatio Bottomley and David Lloyd George, were seized by a sudden enthusiasm for war. He moved to Zennor in Cornwall to withdraw from the patriotic frenzy, but it did not free him from the tentacles of war. In 1916, conscription was finally introduced, and he was summoned for medical inspection. At this point his misanthropy reached its peak:

> I must say I hate mankind. ... I think truly the only righteousness is the destruction of mankind, as in Sodom. Fire and brimstone should fall down. ... Oh, if one could but have a great box of insect powder, and shake it over them, in the heavens, and exterminate them. Only to clear and cleanse and purify the beautiful earth, and give room for some truth and pure living.
>
> (*2L* 650)

A man with serious scepticism towards mankind would never accept the idea of democracy. In his letters, Lawrence did not hide his deep distrust of this governmental system. For example, to Russell he wrote, "I don't want tyrants. But I don't believe in democratic control. ... Above all there must be no democratic control—that is the worst of all" (*2L* 370–71), and to Ottoline Morrell he howls, "I hate the 'public', the 'people', 'society', so much, that a madness possesses me when I think of them. I hate democracy so much. It almost kills me" (*2L* 593).[4]

In his fiction, Lawrence poses questions such as how to deal with the insatiable demands from the multitude and whether rights, individuality or self-government should be entrusted to them. For example, in *The Rainbow*, Ursula Brangwen, as a new schoolmistress, faces reality and finds that authoritative oppression is the only way of keeping the children of the mining district in order. The pupils are the automatised masses, lacking dignity, creativity and personality and regulated only by the authoritarian command. This novel portrays the working classes as incompatible with democratic self-government. After this harsh experience, Ursula says to her lover, Anton Skrebensky, "I hate democracy. ... Only degenerate races are democratic" (*R* 426–27).

Women in Love, Democracy and War

Most of the pupils Ursula teaches in *The Rainbow* will presumably become miners and their wives, and fight for democracy against their employers, as *Women in Love* depicts. In the latter novel, the working-class multitudes begin to press their audacious demands to their employer, which leads to serious labour strife. And yet, as the miners become engaged with new technologies through their work, their enthusiasm for equality transforms into an obsession with mechanised labour and the worship of Gerald. The Industrial Magnate succeeds in building his own authoritarian regime, and his miners curiously show the popular fervour, which resembles enthusiasm that drove the masses into a mad frenzy of war.

Gerald assumes his position as manager of the mining company when the conflict between labour and management is most critical. He breaks with the philanthropic management of his father and, abandoning "the whole democratic-equality problem as a problem of silliness" (*WL* 227), launches into a major reorganisation of the company by implementing the newest technologies. This endeavour fulfils his intense passion for efficiency:

> Gradually Gerald got hold of everything. And then began the great reform. Expert engineers were introduced in every department. An enormous electric plant was installed, both for lighting and for haulage underground, and for power. The electricity was carried to every mine. New machinery was brought from America, such as the miners had never seen before, great iron men, as the cutting machines were called, and unusual appliances. The working of the pits was thoroughly changed, all the control was taken out of the hands of the miners, the butty system was abolished. Everything was run on the most accurate and delicate scientific method, educated and expert men were in control everywhere, the miners were reduced to mere mechanical instruments. (230)

A comparison of the passage above with the one below from Hobhouse's *Democracy and Reaction* suggests that Gerald's new management style, which places great importance on efficiency with a Taylorist approach, is typical of that found in the early twentieth century:

> [A]s the "expert" comes to the front, and "efficiency" becomes the watchword of administration, all that was human in Socialism vanishes out of it. Its tenderness for the losers in the race, its protests against class tyranny, its revolt against commercial materialism, all the sources of the inspiration ... are gone like a dream, and instead of them we have the conception of society as a perfect piece of machinery pulled by wires radiating from a single centre, and all men and women are either "experts" or puppets. Humanity, Liberty, Justice are expunged from the banner, and the single word Efficiency replaces them.
>
> (228–29)[5]

This passage of social critique by Hobhouse could be seen as an appropriate commentary on *Women in Love*.

The novelist, however, had a deeper insight into psychological and physiological aspects than the socialist did, and revealed a strange effect to human mentality. That is, once a man accepts machines that are newly introduced into a company's work process and becomes inured to the inhumane principle of efficiency, he is, paradoxically, intoxicated by this process. This effect is already suggested at the beginning of *The Rainbow*. The Brangwens had lived in harmony with nature at the Marsh for generations, but as their surroundings are abruptly modernised, they begin to feel a morbid fascination with the rumbling or shrill noises of the machines:

> As they worked in the fields, from beyond the now familiar embankment came the rhythmic run of the winding engines, startling at first, but afterwards a narcotic to the brain. Then the shrill whistle of the trains re-echoed through the heart, with fearsome pleasure.
>
> (*R* 14)

In *Women in Love*, the miners, intoxicated by the rhythmic sound of the machines Gerald has introduced at the plant, begin to experience a gruesome sensation. The harder they are forced to work within the inhumane structure of a massive mechanism, the more they are obsessed with work, devoting themselves to producing coal with great efficiency. The miners' frenzy synchronises with that depicted in Mark Gertler's painting *Merry-Go-Round*, in which people on a carousel show a morbid fascination with the ride's mechanical repetition (see Figure 6.1). Lawrence saw a photograph of the painting in Zennor and sent his enthusiastic praise to the painter.[6] In effect, a weird obsession with endless repetition is one of the leitmotifs in *Women in Love*. For example, a rabbit called Bismarck

Figure 6.1 *Merry-Go-Round*, 1916. Mark Gertler. Tate, Purchased 1984. © Tate, Photo: Tate.

that the Criches own, suddenly erupts and "[r]ound and round the court it went, as if shot from a gun, round and round like a furry meteorite, in a tense hard circle that seemed to bind their brains" (243). The relief the German sculptor Loerke created represents "peasants and artizans in an orgy of enjoyment", "whirling ridiculously in roundabouts" in "a frenzy of chaotic motion" (423).[7] Furthermore, the industrial organisation Gerald constructs is the massive embodiment of repetitive movement:

> And for this fight with matter, one must have perfect instruments in perfect organisation, a mechanism [which] ... by its relentless repetition

> of given movement, will accomplish a purpose irresistibly, inhumanly. It was this inhuman principle in the mechanism he wanted to construct that inspired Gerald with an almost religious exaltation. … And between these [his will and the resistant Matter of the earth] he could establish the very expression of his will, the incarnation of his power, a great and perfect machine, a system, an activity of pure order, pure mechanical repetition, repetition ad infinitum, hence eternal and infinite. He found his eternal and his infinite in the pure machine-principle of perfect co-ordination into one pure, complex, infinitely repeated motion, like the spinning of a wheel; but a productive spinning … a productive repetition through eternity, to infinity. And this is the God-motion, this productive repetition ad infinitum.
>
> (227–28)

This passage itself embodies endless repetition in the persistent duplication of the same phrases. Consequently, the miners, who used to raise their voices to demand equality, are now fully satisfied with being cogs in a huge machine and wish to receive more and more stimuli, while simultaneously their essence as human beings is damaged by it:

> There was a new world, a new order, strict, terrible, inhuman, but satisfying in its very destructiveness. The men were satisfied to belong to the great and wonderful machine, even whilst it destroyed them. It was what they wanted, it was the highest that man had produced, the most wonderful and superhuman. They were exalted by belonging to this great and superhuman system which was beyond feeling or reason, something really godlike. Their hearts died within them, but their souls were satisfied.
>
> (231)

On the massive "merry-go-round" that Gerald has constructed, the miners are enraptured in a gruesome ecstasy, amplifying their wild excitement. The miners described in this passage are overlaid with the image of the masses who enthusiastically support the mass destruction caused by war. Gerald's empire, built through modern technology, is identical to a massive war machine in which people, driven by a patriotic frenzy, feel a morbid fascination with its mechanical destructive activity that harms the core of the humanity of those involved with them.[8]

The Network of Family, Nation and War

A series of passages on Gerald and his industrial empire reveal another crucial ideological aspect behind them—the connection of family, nation and war. *Women in Love* opens with the Brangwen sisters' conversation on marriage and a marriage ceremony in the Crich family. As the setting moves from one location to another, the focus broadens as we see a lavish party with a large number of guests at the Criches' mansion, Shortlands, and then their mining business, which dominates a large part of Beldover. The growing influence of the Criches eventually extends throughout the country, as is symbolised by the trains that run nationwide bearing the big white initials "C. B. & Co.". This sequence of events implies that the wealth of a family, which is a minimal unit of economic activity, is distributed throughout the country to contribute to the strengthening of the nation's power. The initial purpose of coal mining is "to obtain as much money from the earth" (*WL* 224) as possible, and the wealth it produces makes it possible to wage war, as indicated by the similarity between the modernised mining industry and the war machine. In contrast to *The Rainbow*, which approves the concept of family and naïvely narrates the Brangwen saga, *Women in Love* reveals the danger that family might become entangled with nation, and eventually with war, through apparatuses like Gerald's massive industrial institution.

Birkin on the other hand explores living a life of barrenness in order not to be implicated in this process. He does not wish to have a productive relationship with others—the relationship that people are supposed to have in a society. He lives alone, except for some housemaids, and there is no air of family or home about him. He vehemently rejects love and matrimony, which Ursula demands, associating the "old way of love" with the image of war and calling it "a sort of conscription" (199). He naturally rejects home, which traditional novels have always admired: "One should avoid this *home* instinct. It's not an instinct, it's a habit of cowardliness. One should never have a *home*" (352; emphasis in original). He impulsively buys an antique chair at a market, but abandons it when he realises that it could be an item for making a home with Ursula. By accepting his barrenness, Birkin perhaps instinctively strives to prevent his sexuality from becoming entangled in the web of family, nation and war.

Birkin's attempt to be singular is far more radical than traditional liberal humanism is supposed to be. I posit that his temperament is liberal individualist but I do not contend that he is an old-fashioned would-be revolutionist. Rather, he converts the old-school worldview into a radical and subversive alternative. The singularity of Birkin's being should not be interpreted in the modern, bourgeois sense of the "individual". Rather, his singular existence indicates what Raymond Williams labelled an "irreducible presence" that subverts "the modern nationalist and imperialist politics/rhetoric/aesthetics".[9] The bourgeois humanist conception of the subject romanticises the individual as a supreme autonomous being. However, Birkin is sceptical about this idea, which is inextricably implicated in the development of the capitalist world. He seeks to be singular so his being cannot be defined by other humans, let alone by bourgeois ideologies. Accepting his barrenness to be singular and irreducible denotes his unique attempt to eject the yoke of modern industrial society.[10]

Gerald and Germany

In contrast to his best friend, Gerald consolidates the network of family, nation and war by dominating the mining industry. His representation as the Industrial Magnate is all the more strengthened by his both apparent and metaphorical association with Germany because that nation was widely considered to be the source of the mechanised, large-scale industry that was in vogue in early twentieth-century Europe. For example, the magazine *New Age,* which the young Lawrence devoured and which turned conservative following the outbreak of war, published a series of essays titled "Provincialism the Enemy" by Ezra Pound in 1917. In these writings, which reflected the wartime Germanophobia, Pound examined education and industry in Germany. He argued that "the 'university system' of Germany is evil" (191), and that flourishing large-scale industry was the result of the influence of corrupt German academia:

> The bulk of scholarship has gone under completely; the fascinations of technical and mechanical education have been extremely seductive (I mean definitely the study of machines, the association with engines of all sorts, the inebriety of mechanical efficiency, in all the excitement of its very rapid evolution).
>
> The social theorist, springing, alas, a good deal from Germany, has not been careful enough to emphasise that no man is merely a unit. (195)

The empire of Gerald, who refused to go to Oxford and was educated in Germany on the science of mining, is built on the base of German science and industry.[11]

Gerald's representation as Cain is another feature that connects him with the Germans. Early in his childhood, he accidentally killed his younger brother when they were playing with a gun. Since then, he has been stigmatised as Cain: "He suffered badly. He had killed his brother when a boy, and was set apart, like Cain" (*WL* 172). It is significant that Gerald is associated with the fratricide because during World War I, "Cain" could remind the British of the Germans. In spite of the two countries' long-term close alliance and their religious and cultural ties, the Germans began raining down bombs on Britain from Zeppelins. Hence, during the war, the Germans were embodied as "Cain" in the minds of the British. In 1918, *Punch* magazine published a cartoon titled "Cain", in which a savage German was represented as the eponymous character (see Figure 6.2).

Figure 6.2 Bernard Partridge, "Cain" in *Punch, or the London Charivari* 13 February 1918, 105. © Punch Limited.

When deciphering German qualities embedded in Gerald's characterisation, *Movements in European History* also offers several crucial clues. First, Gerald's physical features show a striking resemblance to those which Lawrence described as unique to the ancient Germanic race in *Movements*. In the chapter titled "The Germans" in *Movements*, the narrator describes the Germanic tribes as having the "fair limbs of the men from the northern forests", "blue eyes" and "the yellow hair", "born from the northern sea, ... the perfect beautiful blue of ice" (*MEH* 43–44). In *Women in Love*, Gerald's most prominent physical quality is his "northernness". Birkin finds in him "a northern kind of beauty" and sees "a keen, yet cold light" in "his blue eyes" (*WL* 273, 60). Gudrun is magnetised by "something northern" in him and recognises in "his clear northern flesh and his fair hair ... a glisten like cold sunshine refracted through crystals of ice" (*WL* 14). In the author's imagination, Gerald is obviously connected to the Germanic race, which the author and his contemporaries called the "Germans".[12]

Furthermore, the image of Otto von Bismarck is superimposed on Gerald. In *Women in Love*, Gerald is compared to the Iron Chancellor by his lover Gudrun, who "had read Bismarck's letters, and had been deeply moved" (*WL* 418), along with the fact that he has a rabbit called "Bismarck". His connection to the founder of the new Reich is, however, more essential. As we have seen in the previous chapters, *Movements in European History* posits a view of European history as the perpetual conflict between the destructive and the creative impulse—"There are two great passions that rule mankind—the passion of pride and power and conquest, and the passion of peace and production" (*MEH* 241–42)—and argues that after the Renaissance, the creative impulse came to dominate over the destructive one, and kings no longer ruled the world but capitalists took their place, and hence, "mankind chooses peace and production rather than war and glory" (*MEH* 242). As the Industrial Magnate, Gerald indeed "causes the greatest production of necessary substance—[like] the greatest merchant, the greatest owner of industry" (*MEH* 242). He is, however, an ambivalent character with the opposite nature: destructivity—as is suggested by his fratricide. Birkin sees in him "the perfect good-humoured callousness, even strange, glistening malice, in Gerald, glistening through the plausible ethics of productivity" (*WL* 56), and, in a later chapter, while throwing stones at the moon on a face of a pond, Birkin thinks of him as "one of these strange white wonderful demons from the north, fulfilled in the destructive frost-mystery" (254). Thus, Gerald has these two opposing natures in himself; as a result, he succeeds in building up his huge industrial empire, which, while engaging in producing a large amount of coals, stimulates mechanical destructive activity and stirs up an excessive frenzy among the workers.

The significance of Gerald's characterisation would properly be appreciated when we recall that in its final chapter on modern Germany, *Movements in European History* argues that the ideal leader should possess both elements:

> Therefore a great united Europe of productive working people, all materially equal, will never be able to continue and remain firm unless it unites also round one great chosen figure, some hero who can lead a great war, as well as administer a wide peace.
>
> (*MEH* 252)

In the history book, the "one great chosen figure" clearly evokes Bismarck, who dismantled democratic institutions and established a military regime but also contributed to the industrialisation of Germany, as Keynes later states that the "German Empire has been built more truly on coal and iron than on blood and iron" (Keynes 74–75). The Iron Chancellor of the German Empire echoes in the characterisation of Gerald, who, refusing the miners' demand for democracy, builds a colossal industrial empire that is comparable to a war machine. Thus, German qualities are embedded in Gerald's representation. It is no mere coincidence that the spelling of his name suggests his connection with "German" and "Germany".

The End of the Matter

Gerald's fetish for production ends in his ironic demise. When he dies miserably on a snowy mountain, his empire collapses and the curtain is finally closed on a pageant of excitement and enthusiasm, haunted by the madness of production and destruction. At the same time, however, his friend Birkin cannot be a hero. He breaks up conventional human relationships to be free from the yoke of modern society, but in the end his bold endeavour is unsuccessful; he cannot establish his ideal relationship with either Ursula or Gerald, nor does he present a new vision to replace that of a world enslaved to materialism. At the end of the novel, Ursula sees Birkin sitting beside the corpse of his close friend, and her weeping lover reminds her of the contemporary German emperor, Kaiser Wilhelm II, who dismissed Bismarck and, eighteen years later, fled from the German Revolution and went into exile in Holland, where he met his end:

> But when he [Birkin] went in again, at evening, to look at Gerald … the tears broke out. He sat down in a chair, shaken by a sudden access. Ursula, who had followed him, recoiled aghast from him, as he sat with sunken head and body convulsively shaken, making a strange, horrible sound of tears.

> "I didn't want it to be like this—I didn't want it to be like this," he cried to himself.
>
> Ursula could but think of the Kaiser's: "Ich habe es nicht gewollt." She looked almost with horror on Birkin.
>
> (479)

The Kaiser's words that Ursula quotes are part of the statement he made on 31 July 1915 as a manifesto issued on the first anniversary of the outbreak of World War I. This remark was widely distributed through various forms of media such as newspapers and picture postcards (see Figure 6.3). Thus, in contrast to Gerald, on whom Bismarck is superimposed, on Birkin, ironically, is superimposed an ineffectual Kaiser, who discharged the Iron Chancellor and began the futile war to be forced into exile.[13]

There is a bitter irony on Gerald's side as well at the end. He dies and transforms into "Matter". Turning his back to Ursula, who would never accept his idea of an indispensable same-sex relationship, Birkin looks at his friend's body lying on his deathbed:

> He forgot her, and turned to look at Gerald. … [H]e watched the cold, mute, material face. It had a bluish cast. … Cold, mute, material! …
>
> But now he was dead, like clay, like bluish, corruptible ice. Birkin looked at the pale fingers, the inert mass. …
>
> And Gerald! The denier! He left the heart cold, frozen, hardly able to beat. Gerald's father had looked wistful, to break the heart: but not this last terrible look of cold, mute Matter.
>
> (480)

Gerald's corpse, which has turned into "cold, mute, material", makes a striking contrast to that of his father. The elderly man's corpse looks like him "in his teens, with his first beard on his face" and as if he is about to revive: "The dead man lay in repose, as if gently asleep, so gently, so peacefully, like a young man sleeping in purity. He was still warm" (334). The dead body is paradoxically rejuvenated and vital. This is a typical Lawrentian corpse, such as those portrayed in "Odour of Chrysanthemums" and "The Prussian Officer"—inanimate but full of energy, exactly like coal. Gerald's corpse is deliberately portrayed in such a way as to present a stark contrast: his dead body is cold, frozen "Matter" which allows no possibility of reawakening. Gerald, who has been absorbed in producing as much coal as possible by way of modern technology, turns into a material, but not a vital mineral like coal—merely worthless "cold, mute Matter". His body is buried in the soil of England as his bereaved family insists. The "cold, mute, material" body is, however,

Figure 6.3 Picture postcard depicting Kaiser Wilhelm II quoting "Ich habe es nicht gewollt".

buried only as decaying, unusable matter, unlike the vital substance to which he devoted his whole life, and, sadly and ironically, he will never be resurrected from the ashes. The industrial lord goes into the dark, and the rest is silence.

Notes

1 H. M. Daleski, for example, argues that the

> recurrence of the phrase "disintegration and dissolution" ... is the key motive of the book, indicative of a general process against which Birkin and Ursula pit themselves. ... That Gerald responds by laughing "dangerously, from the blood" is ... illustrative of his own suppressed desire for a similar sort of dissolution.
>
> (132)

See Daleski 126–87.

2 See Mitchell 104, 248 and 253.

3 In the 1906 General Election, the Liberals won a landslide victory, winning 400 seats. The first decade of this century was also the period of the rise of the Labour Party. The inaugural Labour Representation Committee Conference took place in 1900, and in the 1906 election, the Labour Party won 29 seats and elected Keir Hardie as its chairman. For more information on new liberalism, see Freeden, Collini, Cain 1–14 and *passim* and Fawcett 138–97.

4 As previous chapters have noted, material prosperity was considered to be one of the primary factors of the corruption that afflicted the country, and in Lawrence's mind, materialism and mechanical civilisation caused the rise of democracy as they brought forth the idea of material equality. In "Democracy", written shortly after the armistice, Lawrence argues that democracy in the materialist world transforms essentially unique human beings into mechanical automatons:

> Where each thing is unique in itself, there can be no comparison made. One man is neither equal nor unequal to another man. ... Comparison enters only when one of us departs from his own integral being, and enters the material-mechanical world. ...
>
> Men have reached the point where, in further fulfilling their ideals, they break down the living integrity of their being and fall into sheer mechanical materialism. They become automatic units, determined entirely by mechanical law.
>
> This is horribly true of modern democracy—socialism, conservatism, bolshevism, liberalism, republicanism, communism: all alike.
>
> (*RDP* 80–81)

Actually, anti-democratic sentiment was widely shared among contemporary intellectuals, who thought that the growing demand for democracy and the features related to it—popular elections, the emancipation of women, mass culture—would have harmful effects on the values the British had cherished, such as a sophisticated culture and the dignity of man. For the modernists' views on democracy, see, for example, Rachel Potter.

5 Taylorism is a "scientific management" system which was devised by an American mechanical engineer, F. W. Taylor, and which gained worldwide attention starting in the years before the outbreak of the Great War and lasted for a decade. For a comparative analysis of Taylorism and Gerald's management approach, see Zapf 129–39, Knapp 59–73 and Bradshaw, "Introduction" xxix.

6 Lawrence wrote to Gertler from Zennor on 9 October 1916 that

> it is the best *modern* picture I have seen: I think it is great, and true. But it is horrible and terrifying. ... I *do* think that in this combination of blaze, and violent mechanical rotation and complex involution, and ghastly, utterly mindless human intensity of sensational extremity, you have made a real and ultimate revelation.
>
> (*2L* 660)

7 J. B. Bullen maintains that Lawrence transformed Gertler's image of a merry-go-round into Loerke's relief. See Bullen 842. Anne Fernihough, on the other hand, recognises a similarity between Lawrence's critique of method through circular images and the essence of Heidegger's philosophy. See Fernihough 142–43.

8 Analysing the connection between Gerald's management of the mines and warfare, Graham Holderness compares the novel to "England, My England" (Holderness 207–08), but a more appropriate comparison would be to the 1915 version of "England, My England". The satisfaction Evelyn Daughtry, the protagonist, finds through engaging in destructive activities on the battlefield curiously resembles the one that the miners feel in *Women in Love*:

> He hated it, and yet he was fulfilling himself. He hated it violently, and yet it gave him the only real satisfaction he could have in life now. Deeply and satisfactorily it fulfilled him, this warring on men. This work of destruction alone satisfied his deepest desire.
>
> (*EME* 226)

Andrew Harrison also indicates the same point in "Men No More Than the Subjective Material of the Machine" 78–80. From a different perspective, Michael Hardt and Antonio Negri argue in *Multitude* that the mass workers who were assembled in factories and subjected to Taylorist strategies can be likened to the anonymous masses of soldiers in modern warfare:

> The "total mobilization" of modern warfare was really the turning of the entire society into a kind of war factory in which the project of amassing bodies in the battlefields was parallel to that of amassing bodies in the factories, the anonymous body of the mass worker corresponding to that of the mass soldier, the unknown soldier. Taylorist strategies of organizational efficiency, scientific planning, and technological innovations invested the battlefields just as they did the factories.
>
> (*Multitude* 43–44)

9 See Endo 93–107. The quoted extract occurs on p. 102. Endo perceives in Lawrence and Williams the possibility of subverting the "aesthetic organicism" constructed by bourgeois ideology.

10 Birkin's idea of the "singular being" can also be elucidated through the Deleuzian concept of the "singular". Hidenaga Arai draws upon Gilles Deleuze and Kojin Karatani's discussion on the concept of "singularity" posited in opposition to "particularity" to argue that "[f]ree from the nation-state, this community or world [which Birkin seeks for] postulates the relationship among singular persons" (24). See Arai 18–26.

11 Carl Krockel argues that "Gerald's management of his father's business mirrors the development of coal mining in Germany between Unification and the First World War" (*Lawrence and Germany* 164) and examines Gerald's association with Germany in terms of Bismarck's rule, Max Weber's sociology and the culture of Johann Wolfgang von Goethe and Friedrich Nietzsche. See Krockel, *Lawrence and Germany* 159–96. James F. Scott also analyses the similarities between Gerald and Bismarck. See Scott 119–24. Fernihough on the other hand argues that Gerald is partly characterised by Nietzsche's nihilism, becoming what Heidegger calls "technological man" and one of Marx's alienated workers. See Fernihough 145–50.

12 Nick Bennett examines the similarities between Gerald and the Norse Odin, one of the principal gods in Norse mythology. See Bennett 8–15.

13 For the historical context of the Kaiser's statement and a different interpretation of this scene, see Stevens 93–95.

7 Wartime Short Stories from "The Thimble" to "The Blind Man" and "Tickets Please"

The characters in Lawrence's wartime short stories are somewhat involved in the war, unlike those in his wartime novel *Women in Love*. The protagonist of "England, My England" experiences the battlefield, and volunteer soldiers return disfigured from the frontline in "The Thimble" and "The Blind Man". Some stories such as "Tickets Please", "The Thimble" and "The Fox" are set on the war's homefront. Some critics have, therefore, noted the functions of war in Lawrence's short stories. For example, Linda Ruth Williams has indicated the positive role enacted by war in Lawrence's tales: "it ['The Blind Man'] makes war injury and handicap positive. ... The negative of war acts upon the negative sense of sight to enable a positive, sexualised and essentially dark relationship with the natural world" (26). Likewise, Judith Punchner Breen has iterated that the protagonists in "Tickets Please" and "The Blind Man" embody the author's "ironic vision of World War I as an opportunity for the destruction of an exhausted culture and the rebirth of long-repressed erotic energies" (63). Other critics like Janice Hubbard Harris have argued that returned soldiers appear as intruders in some of Lawrence's short stories: "Hadrian too is a soldier back from the war, visiting his old home. In both tales ['Hadrian' and 'The Fox'], the intruder is presented as crude, young, dangerous, calculating, vibrant; he is very much the returning stranger" (151). Thus, critics have analysed the functions of war or of veterans in Lawrence's wartime short stories. However, the discussion of such issues has tended to focus on the author's personal experiences and views of war or the development of the author's philosophical ideas. Instead, I propose to expand the lens to spotlight a wider social and historical perspective.[1] The prolonged war lasted four years and varied wartime discourses were born and circulated during each phase of the war. Analyses of Lawrence's short stories must take into account the phase of the war in which they were composed.

DOI: 10.4324/9781032675671-8

Such an examination would reveal how and to what degree the positive function of war or the portrayal of ex-soldiers as intruders synchronise or conflict with the dominant discourses on war. In so doing, I hope to uncover the textual ambivalence inherent in Lawrence's wartime short stories. This chapter examines Lawrence's short fiction from two stages of the war: "The Thimble" and "England, My England", along with Lawrence's poems "New Heaven and Earth" and "Eloi, Eloi, Lama Sabachthani", composed in the early phase of the war in 1915; "The Blind Man" and "Tickets Please", composed in 1918, at the time of the armistice.

Popular Wartime Romance and Lawrence's Anti-Romance: Berta Ruck's "The Infant-in Arms" and Lawrence's "The Thimble"

> Half an hour later Prince Andrew was again called to Kutúzov. He found him reclining in an armchair, still in the same unbuttoned overcoat. He had in his hand a French book which he closed as Prince Andrew entered, marking the place with a knife. Prince Andrew saw by the cover that it was *Les Chevaliers du Cygne* by Madame de Genlis.
>
> Leo Tolstoy, *War and Peace*, Book X, Chapter XVI

During the First World War, Lawrence did not get along with publishers, and his works attracted only a small circle of readers. He published *The Rainbow* in 1915, but it was soon banned. He kept revising *Women in Love* without any hope of publishing it. He wrote several important essays, but *The Signature*, a journal that he launched with John Middleton Murry as a medium to publish his essays, released no more than three issues due to a shortage of subscribers. In this situation, understandably, Lawrence could not appreciate novelists or readers of popular books, which he considered shallow, sloppy and futile. In a letter to Cynthia Asquith in March 1916, Lawrence did not conceal his hostility towards and dislike of sentimental, popular stories and their readers: "… I can't write stories to make money, because I don't want to. Curse the idiotic editors and the more idiotic people who read: shall I pander to their maudlin taste. They bore me" (*2L* 587). In a letter to his literary agent, J. B. Pinker, Lawrence cynically approves of the war because, according to him, it would eradicate shallow, trendy books:

> I am glad of this war. It kicks the pasteboard bottom in the usual "good" popular novel. People have felt much more deeply and strongly these last few months, and they are not going to let themselves be taken in by "serious" works whose feeling is shallower than that of the official army reports. … Folk will either read sheer rubbish, or something that

> has in it as much or more emotional force as the newspaper has in *it* today. I am glad of the war. It sets a slump in trifling.
>
> (*2L* 240)

Thus, Lawrence watched the massive surge of patriotic frenzy with disgust, but neither did he participate in any political campaigns against the war. In another letter to Asquith, he wished the war would eliminate not only demagogues who unashamedly boosted patriotism but also intellectuals who advocated pacifist social reform:

> Here's a pretty state of affairs—Messrs Lloyd George and Lord Derby—funny—pretty! This is the last stage of all, that ends our sad eventful history. So be it. It is what the countryful of swine wanted, now let them have it. All we have to do is wait for the débâcle.
>
> ... I must say, I too expect a national disaster before very long. ... Perhaps when we've all had a ducking in the sea of fearful disaster, we shall be more wholesome and truthful. At any rate, then I feel we shall be able to do something, something new.—It is no use adhering to that old "advanced" crowd—Cambridge, Lowes Dickinson, Bertie Russell, young reformers, socialists, Fabians—they are our disease, not our hope. We want a clean sweep, and a new start.
>
> (*3L* 49)

He turned into a bitter misanthrope and remained in Cornwall separated from the hysteria of war and composed works that hardly any publishers would want to print.

In spite of his mental and geographical distance from reality, however, Lawrence lived within the confines of a world at war and was not totally free from the wartime ideology swirling around him. Chapter 4 has previously noted that he occasionally described the war from his contemporary point of view, using the same terminology as that of popular writers who were responsible for disseminating the dominant notions of the war. It was not unique to Lawrence, in fact, to disdain social reformers or best-selling writers as shallow and mediocre during the war. In *The First Hundred Thousand* by Ian Hay, published in 1915, the year when Lawrence composed "The Thimble", the K1 soldiers—volunteered soldiers of Kitchener's Army—have a conversation on the battlefield:

> "War is hell, and all that, but it has a good deal to recommend it. It wipes out all the small nuisances of peace-time."
>
> "Such as—?"
>
> "Well, Suffragettes, and Futurism, and—and—"
>
> "Bernard Shaw," suggested another voice. "Hall Caine—"
>
> (Hay 120)

These volunteered servicemen believe that the war would purify social evils, that is, social reformers, radical artists, pacifist writers and best-selling novelists such as the one who was dubbed "a Victorian Romancer".

In 1915, Lawrence composed a short piece titled "The Thimble", which was later developed into the novella *The Ladybird*. In this story, Lawrence explores the possibility of resurrection after the devastation of war. In a letter sent with the story's manuscript to Asquith, who served as the model for the story's heroine, he explains:

> This is the story: I don't know what you'll think of it. The fact of resurrection, in this life, is all in all to me now. ... The fact of resurrection is everything, now: whether we dead can rise from the dead, and love, and live, in a new life, here.
>
> (*2L* 420)

Lawrence composed "The Thimble" to test his concept of resurrection, implying the possibility of a reborn ex-soldier leading the population into regeneration.

The theme of this story is obviously different from that of popular romances, which Lawrence detested, calling them "stories to make money" with "maudlin taste". Nevertheless, a comparison of "The Thimble" with contemporary romances is not irrelevant because Lawrence's story is a satire of the popular romances that flourished during the First World War.[2] He employed the conventional settings of melodrama and created his own version as an anti-romance. This is demonstrated by a comparison of "The Thimble" with a story called "The Infant-in Arms" by Berta Ruck. Both stories were written in 1915 and exhibit a similar pattern: each heroine finds a new relationship with her sweetheart who returns disabled from the battlefield. A comparison illustrates an ambivalent dimension in Lawrence's text: "The Thimble" is composed as an anti-romance in its satirical use of romantic diction and norms; simultaneously, however, it embraces the wartime ideology that popular romance espoused.

Berta Ruck was a prolific writer who published more than 150 works of fiction. Her works during the First World War were topical, and she built a career on the success of her wartime writing. "The Infant-in Arms" is the opening story of her short story collection *Khaki and Kisses*. The first part of the story is set in June 1914, several weeks before the outbreak of war, and opens at a glittering costume party attended by members of London's fashionable society. At this party, an anonymous heroine dressed as Nijinsky's *Spectre of the Rose* dances with an anonymous young man dressed as a "Black Panther". The man woos her, but she dismisses him, calling him an infant in arms, and flatly refuses his proposal, saying, "*Not in the mood!*" (*KK* 11).

Nearly a year has passed when the second part of the story begins, wherein the heroine goes to a stately home that has hastily been refurbished as a hospital ward for invalid ex-soldiers. There, she sees the young man with whom she danced at the party and discovers that he has lost one of his legs in the Battle of Ypres. In spite of his injury, or rather because of it, she is attracted to this man who fought for the nation and accepts his proposal, saying, "I am in the mood, *now!*" (16).

This frothy piece represents typical aspects of wartime melodrama, such as undisguised patriotism and patriarchalism. Once he is wearing khaki, the inexperienced youth becomes manly and attractive. The heroine's impression of him changes when she sees the young man in uniform: "In his face, drawn and drained of blood, his eyes are bright and handsome as ever. ... He was a dilettante sculptor once, but he looks a thorough soldier now" (12). How the ladies are attracted to the men in uniform is repeatedly portrayed in the stories in *Khaki and Kisses*, as the title potently suggests. The heroine of a story of a rather unsuitable title for a romance, "The War Film", ponders:

> It was a pot-pourri of pictures taken at manœovres, at one time and another, of different regiments of horse and foot, marching, watering their mounts, closing up round a hill, taking cover behind brushwood. Horses, guns, uniforms! Woman is accused of "loving the uniform." Why be ashamed of that fact?
>
> (*KK* 188)

Of course the heroines of the romances would not be ashamed of their being a uniform fetish. She continues:

> Does not uniform seem to hide the shortcomings, the irritating "little ways" and uglinesses of the individual? Doesn't it merge him into a type with every fighter who was ever brave and chivalrous and enduring and handsome and all that a man should be?
>
> (188)

A stained uniform that bears the marks of battlefields all the more enhances his charisma; Molly, another heroine in a *Khaki and Kisses* story "The War-Bride", is thoroughly charmed by her childhood friend who came back from the battlefield:

> He was taller and browner than ever, the young sailor, with those broad, sloping shoulders and narrow, springy hips, with his clean-cut jaw and the eyes that looked so straight into hers. ... He'd changed. He was

> certainly better-looking. ... And the movement of his lithe, supple body in the worn uniform! That suit was old. Yet how well it looked!
>
> (*KK* 219–20)

This is not merely the case with Ruck. Another example from late-blooming romance writer Florence Barclay:

> Jim stood upon the hearth-rug in the bright little kitchen. ...
>
> His broad shoulders hid the portrait on the mantel-shelf, wreathed in Virginian creeper and Michaelmas daisies. But what matters a photograph, when the original is before you—large as life? And what smart uniform can compare with the stained worn suit of khaki, which has come through forced marches, hard fighting, days and nights in the trenches?
>
> (Barclay 41–42)

As with these heroines, the lady in "The Infant-in Arms" falls in love with the young man in uniform, who sheds his blood for king and country. His injury is a morally agreeable emblem and makes the ex-soldier more honourable and attractive. It is the beginning of a new romance:

> Nor has he expected what she does next. For she slips on her knees on the floor beside his couch, and falters. ...
>
> The radiant, kneeling girl beside him laughs and sobs together. "Oh, *can't* you understand that this has made everything different? You're just twice as much of a man, now that you'll have to get along with one leg, as you were when you were dancing and fooling about on two! As for me, I'm not even a woman unless you'll help to make me one."
>
> (*KK* 14–15)

The gender roles that the text depicts are stereotypical; it celebrates manly, chivalrous acts by men and virtuous, submissive behaviour of women. As an example of the popular romances published during the war, "The Infant-in Arms" is overtly propagandist, crammed with celebrations of honour and glory and hence, contributed to the promulgation of wartime ideology. Such escapist entertainment, which readers sought during that period, raised soldiers' spirits in the trenches and consoled women on the home front.[3]

By employing the conventional code of romantic stories, Lawrence's "The Thimble" denounces brief love affairs and relationships found in wartime melodrama. Its heroine, Daphne Hepburn, is a fashionable woman yearning for love and romance. Like the heroine of Ruck's story, she is initially presented as a woman with Edwardian ostentation: "She was a beautiful woman, … one for whom the modern fashions were perfect. … She knew she was a beauty, she knew it was expected of her that she should create an impression of modern beauty" (*EME* 192). She carefully maintains her attractive appearance, "wearing her jewels, her string of opals, her big, ruby brooch" (193), and gives meticulous directions to the maid who does her hair. She has perfectly learned the appropriate code of behaviour in high society: "She knew how to walk, how to hold her body according to the mode. She did it almost instinctively, so deep was her consciousness of the impression her own appearance must create" (193). This stylish lady had been swept away by the public's enthusiasm for the war and fell in love with Mr Hepburn when he wore a khaki uniform, although she had no interest in him prior to his enlistment:

> "If you want to love your husband," she had said to her friends, with splendid recklessness, "you should see him in khaki." And she had really loved him, he was so handsome in uniform, well-built, yet with a sort of reserve and remoteness that suited the neutral khaki perfectly.
>
> Before, as a barrister with nothing to do, he had been slack and unconvincing, a sort of hanger-on, and she had never come to the point of marrying him. …
>
> Then came the great shock of the war, his coming to her in a new light, as lieutenant in the artillery. And she had been carried away by his perfect calm manliness and significance, now he was a soldier. He seemed to have gained a fascinating importance, that made her seem quite unimportant. It was she who was insignificant and subservient, he who was dignified, with a sort of indifferent lordliness.
>
> (190)

The plot is appropriate for a light romance: an ostentatious and flamboyant lady falls in love with a manly soldier in uniform and becomes submissive. Machoism, stereotypical gender roles and uniform fetishism—the beginning of "The Thimble" ironically copies the conventions of wartime melodrama in vogue.

The irony in "The Thimble" lies in the fact that Daphne is not eligible to be a romantic heroine. Although she wishes to play the role of a heroine, imagining herself as a virgin girl, she is not young enough to play that role. In fact, she is obliged to accept that she is far from a heroine:

> She was getting dressed now to see her *bridegroom*. The phrase, with its association in all the *romances* of the world, made her snigger involuntarily to herself. She was still *like a schoolgirl*, always seeing herself in *her part*. She got curious satisfaction from it too. But also she was always humorously ironical when she found herself in these romantic

> situations. If brigands and robbers had carried her off, she would have played up to the event perfectly. In life, however, there was always a certain painful, laborious heaviness, a weight of self-responsibility. The event never carried her along, a helpless protagonist. She was always responsible, in whatever situation. ...
>
> Entering the small drawing-room she lifted her eyes slowly and looked at herself. ... She was aware also of the traces of weariness and illness and age, in her face. She was twenty-seven years old.
>
> (192–93; my emphasis)

Unlike her namesake in Greek mythology, Daphne is a middle-aged woman—at least in the context of the early twentieth century—worried about the burdens of real life.

The thimble retrieved from the sofa on which Daphne sits heightens the readers' expectations of pure romance, but its excavation is ironically related to the discoverer's unfulfilled sexual desire. While waiting for her husband's homecoming, Daphne puts her fingers into a crevice in the sofa. The passage in which she gropes into the depths of the crevice with a rhythmic movement in a trance is replete with sexual innuendo, implying her unsatisfied eroticism:

> She was unaware of what she was doing. ... But now she sat still in suspense in the silent drawing room, ... sliding hands of the woman, and her hands slid backwards and forwards, backwards and forwards like a pleading, a hope, a tension of madness. ...
>
> Her long white fingers pressed into the fissure, pressed and entered rhythmically, pressed and pressed further and further into the tight depth of the fissure, ... whilst her mind was in a trance of suspense. ...
>
> The working, slow, intent fingers pressed deeper and deeper in the fissure of the sofa, pressed and worked their way intently, to the bottom. It was the bottom. ... Making sure, they worked all along, very gradually, along the tight depth of the fissure.
>
> (194)

The excavated souvenir, the decorated thimble, looks gorgeous, but its authenticity is actually uncertain: "It was a thimble set with brilliants; it was an old, rather heavy thimble of tarnished gold, set round the base with little diamonds or rubies. Perhaps it was not gold, perhaps they were only paste" (195). This thimble, with a monogram indicating that it dates back to 1801, reflects an aspect of courtship that existed a century earlier. It is a relic of an old romance, when men were virile and women submissive, or, as the narrator expresses, "the days when women did stitching as a usual thing" (195). The thimble embodies values celebrated in romances—chivalry, loyalty, devotion and obedience. The faded antique with doubtful authenticity implies that these virtues are outmoded and illusory.

The text's satire on romance is also illustrated by its reversal of the pattern of a conventional fairy tale in which an ugly toad is revealed to be a handsome prince. In "The Thimble", an attractive husband turns into a repellent ex-serviceman. The heroine is horrified to see her husband's destroyed face:

> It [his mouth] was broken in, the bottom teeth all gone, the side of the chin battered small, whilst a deep seam, a deep horrible groove ran right into the middle of the cheek. But the mouth was the worst, sunk in at the bottom, with half the lip cut away.
>
> (196)[4]

In "The Thimble", this injury assumes a different function from that in "The Infant-in Arms". While the injury in the latter is meant to enhance the romantic effect, the disfigured face in "The Thimble" signifies the end of the romance.[5] The fact that Mr Hepburn's disfigurement is caused not by an honourable wound from battle, as is the young man's mutilation in "The Infant-in Arms", but rather by friendly fire amplifies the irony of the story. This scene reveals that the glittering image of love for disabled soldiers, celebrated in Ruck's story, is simply a romantic illusion. At the end of the story, Mr Hepburn throws the thimble away. This is a decisive moment in the text as it represents the negation of romance. Thus, the contrast between the two stories is obvious. In Ruck's story, the heroine, kindled by patriotic fervour, finds love for the disabled ex-serviceman. In Lawrence's anti-romance, the text's parodic descriptions subvert the embellished glitter of wartime love and romance.

Despite the fact that Lawrence's story satirises popular romances by parodying romantic diction and conventions, "The Thimble" and "The Infant-in Arms" exhibit a similar pattern: they demonstrate the war's power to transform British society and its people. Both stories presuppose that before the war, British society and its people were degraded and frivolous, and that the war would recondition them. "The Infant-in Arms" opens with a glittering costume party, and the text emphasises that corruption is widespread within the decadent society. The entire nation is enamoured with bacchanalian revelries:

> For we are at that brief, grotesque phase in English History when dancing and masquerading seem affairs of national importance, when columns of responsible newspapers are given up to accounts of some "brilliant carnival" or other, when tickets for artists' balls are gambled

> with as with stocks and shares, when prizes for costume ... run into hundreds of pounds, and when Society, the Arts, Commerce, and the "respectable" Middle Class join hands to dance the maddest Ring-o'-Roses round some mulberry-bush rooted in Heaven knows how deep a soil of slackness.
>
> (*KK* 8)

The second part of the story is set in the spring of 1915. The city is full of vitality because the war has dispelled the rottenness formerly prevalent in the capital:

> Spring, Nineteen fifteen.
>
> London's gayest finery of lilac and laburnum seems put on in special honour of the khaki boys that throng her streets. ... For the soil of slackness that produced those gay and bizarre blossoms of decadence has proved not so deep after all; there was British bedrock beneath it!
>
> (11)

The main characters in the story are also purified. The flippant and cynical young woman is transformed into a "sensible", patriotic lady who supports Britain's cause. The text modestly but explicitly asserts that it is the war that changed her: "Can it be that this War, which has cut all life in half for our nation, has worked another miracle in her?" (14). In the first part, the heroine teases the young man, calling him "an infant-in-arms". Through his sacrifice for the nation, however, the "dilettante sculptor" is also transformed into "a thorough soldier" and earns her love. Ruck's text embraces the Great War as a purifier.

Likewise, in "The Thimble", the war enables the characters' metamorphosis. Mr Hepburn, formerly an ineffectual fellow, is transformed through his ordeals on the battlefield into a man with a mystic, dark and taciturn aura. He becomes a typical Lawrentian hero who might be able to lead people to a resurrection. Daphne, a frivolous and fashionable lady who always dreams of romance, is also transformed into a woman who, at the instigation of the ex-soldier, discovers her new being and feels her soul newly born. As a result, the two main characters are resurrected into innocent beings and seek a new relationship: "The darkness of his eyes was now watching her, her soul was exposed and new-born. The triviality was gone, the dream-psychology, the self-dependence. They were naked and new-born in soul, and dependent on each other" (*EME* 198). Thus, the text is constructed within the framework of the period: it implies that the war functions as a purifier and a source of social regeneration. "The Thimble", similar to the melodrama which it aims to caricature, embraces the wartime ideology.

As demonstrated, "The Thimble" embodies the ambivalence that Lawrence's texts embrace. Lawrence detested unashamed patriotic agitation and abhorred people who enthusiastically followed propagandists, and in his fiction, he explored how mankind could resurrect itself from the ashes of a catastrophic disaster and construct new relationships in a new society. What this author sought was too unique, and he achieved little recognition among contemporary readers. Despite this alienation, however, his short story reflects the ethos of a society gone mad with war, and the dominant thinking of the era defines the text. While "The Thimble" criticises contemporary romances, which functioned as ideological vehicles and contributed to the circulation of wartime ideology, the text resonates with the widespread ideological conviction that the Great War would purify the corrupt British society. Thus, "The Thimble" is a revealing example of ambivalence in Lawrence's texts: it is a scathing critique of the period wherein it was composed, but it also bears discernible traces of the contemporary logic and frame of reference that it intends to subvert.

The Path to Resurrection or Becoming a War Machine in "New Heaven and Earth", "Eloi, Eloi, Lama Sabachthani" and "England, My England"

Despite their similar settings of London in spring, the optimism of Ruck's story composed during the first phase of war contrasts strikingly against the pessimism exhibited in T. S. Eliot's "The Waste Land", published four years after the armistice:

> April is the cruellest month, breeding
> Lilacs out of the dead land, mixing
> Memory and desire, stirring
> Dull roots with spring rain.
>
> (Eliot 61)

The indiscriminate bombing of British citizens was one reason why the nation's atmosphere changed from positivity to negativity. Chapter 4 has previously noted that Lawrence and Frieda were shocked and terrorised by the Zeppelin raids on London. Lawrence suggested in his letter to Ottoline Morrell that a new reality is to be born after the demolition of the present world:

> So it seems our cosmos is burst, burst at last, the stars and moon blown away, the envelope of the sky burst out, and a new cosmos

> appeared. … So it is the end—our world is gone, and we are like dust in the air.
>
> But there must be a new heaven and a new earth.
>
> (2*L* 390)

That same year, Lawrence composed a poem on the theme of resurrection and chose as its title the biblical phrase he cited in this letter. The poem, "New Heaven and Earth", portrays a man's "resurrection" after his symbolic death and describes his founding of a new relationship with his wife. Both this poem and "The Thimble" are themed on war and subsequent resurrection, but the latter does not specifically depict the characters' psychological mechanism of resurrection and consummation, which is the main focus of the poem. Therefore, it is advantageous to read these texts in tandem.

The speaker in "New Heaven and Earth" is "so weary of the world" and "so sick of it" because "everything was tainted with myself" (*Poems* 210). The speaker finds that he is one among the human beings who are captivated by their ego-selves and who imagined themselves as "the God" who controls the world. Thus, he was disgusted with the fact that he loves a woman solely for his own pleasure and not hers, which ultimately signifies self-love and the negation of the other:

> I shall never forget the maniacal horror of it all in the end
> when everything was me. …
> I was the God and the creation at once;
> …
> I was a lover, I kissed the woman I loved,
> and God of horror, I was kissing also myself.
>
> (211)

However, a war erupts and everyone including the speaker becomes a murderer and mercilessly slaughters each other, causing a brutal massacre: "War came, and every hand raised to murder; /… thousands and thousands of gaping, hideous foul dead" (211). Consequently, he dies a miserable death: "I am dead, and trodden to nought in the smoke-sodden tomb; / dead and trodden to nought in the sour black earth / of the tomb; dead and trodden to nought, trodden to nought" (211). The carnage is disastrous but here again, the war is presented as an opportunity to cleanse a corrupt world. The mass destruction generates a symbolic consequence: the death of his old ego-self, which eventually directs his resurrection as a totally new being:

> God, but it is good to have died and been trodden out
> . . .
> When I am trodden quite out, quite, quite out

> every vestige gone, then I am here
> risen, and setting my foot on another world
> risen, accomplishing a resurrection
> (212)

After his rebirth, the speaker senses the existence of another being nearby: "So I put my hand out further, a little further / and I felt that which was not I, / it verily was not I / it was the unknown" (212). This unknown entity is his wife, who has also been resurrected:

> It was the flank of my wife
> I touched with my hand, I clutched with my hand
> rising, new-awakened from the tomb!
> It was the flank of my wife
> whom I married years ago
> at whose side I have lain for over a thousand nights
> (213)

Before his rebirth, the speaker perceives all phenomena from his own perspective and behaves solely to attain personal satisfaction. However, he can achieve a new relationship with his wife who appears as a totally new being to him as he is released from his old self. This awakening is comparable to the realisation sensed by Elizabeth Bates in "Odour of Chrysanthemums", who comprehends the existence of a physical being as an other by touching her husband's dead body resurrected from the womb of the earth. The narrator of "New Heaven and Earth" constructs a completely new relationship with his wife in a new world with new consciousness: "I touched her flank and knew I was carried by the current in death / over to the new world … / to a new earth, a new I, a new knowledge, a new world of time" (213). The speaker attains to a consummation with his wife through this experience:

> Sightless and strong oblivion in utter life takes possession of me!
> The unknown, strong current of life supreme
> drowns me and sweeps me away and holds me down
> to the sources of mystery, in the depths,
> extinguishes there my risen resurrected life
> and kindles it further at the core of utter mystery.
> (214)

This poem articulates the psychological mechanism during the process of resurrection and consummation that is not depicted in the short story composed in the same year. This notion could provide the backdrop for the post-war relationship between the protagonists in "The

Thimble". "New Heaven and Earth" and "The Thimble" thus complement each other.

Yet, the consummation Lawrence envisages is not always accomplished via heterosexual relationships. "Eloi, Eloi, Lama Sabachthani" is presumably Lawrence's first attempt at war poetry. The first version of this poem was composed in November 1914 and the piece was finally published in May 1915. The poem portrays a battlefield scene through the eyes of a moribund soldier who achieves consummation by killing an enemy soldier. Andrew Harrison's succinct analysis of this poem indicates the ambivalent positioning of a soldier as both saviour and aggressor.[6] This poem is replete with ambivalence even besides the speaker's position. For example, the poem opens with the soldier's rather pathological aversion to his own body: "How I hate myself, this body which is me; / How it dogs me, what a galling shadow!" (*Poems* 1517). Then, the raconteur expresses contradictory feelings towards his body: "For I dote on them [my legs, my breast, my belly] with tenderness, and I hate them, / I hate them bitterly" (1517). We cannot oversimplify the poem's complex imagery to include every word and phrase utilised in this poem. Nevertheless, reading these lines alongside "New Heaven and Earth", the body in "Eloi" invokes the metaphor of the ego-self relinquished by the speaker of "New Heaven and Earth" to resurrect himself as a new being. In "Eloi", the speaker's ambivalence towards his body/self causes another dilemma: his ambivalence towards war. He is terrified of the incessant bombing but prefers it because it will bring death to his body/self. He desires the shelling earnestly but with horror: "God, how glad I am to hear the shells / Droning over, threatening me! / It is their threat, their loud, jeering threat, / Like screaming birds of Fate / ... That gives me peace" (1517). He then runs to the trenches, where he finds his enemy and bayonets him. This killing scene is overtly charged with homosexual eroticism. The murder is depicted as a homosexual marriage ritual in which the male combatants engage:

> So when I run at length thither across
> To the trenches, I see again a face with blue eyes,
> A blenched face, fixed and agonised,
> Waiting.—And I knew he wanted it.
> Like a bride he took my bayonet, wanting it,
> Like a virgin the blade of my bayonet, wanting it,
> And it sank to rest from me in him,
> And I, the lover, am consummate,
> And he is the bride, I have sown him with the seed
> And planted and fertilised him.
>
> (1518)

Women are presented in this poem as beings who infringe on the nuptial bed. Women are portrayed as "peering through the vents / In the purple veil" like "thieves" and "pilferers" (1518). They do not understand the clandestine bonds forged between soldiers on the battlefield. Rather, women merely glorify the battlefield injuries sustained by the men and worship the wounded soldiers, just like the heroines of romantic fiction: "And why do the women follow us satisfied, / Feed on our wounds like bread, receive our blood / Like glittering seed upon them for fulfilment?" (1519).

This poem thus dismisses women and depicts a male couple in a homosocial space. However, the process of consummation is paradoxically portrayed as a heterosexual marriage. The soldiers do not bayonet each other; instead, the speaker is the bridegroom and the enemy is his bride. More ambivalently, the protagonist's partner is not always presented as an enemy. The enemy character is imaged in multiple ways in the poem and his personality is constantly substituted. The enemy is also envisioned as a doppelganger or alter ego, a part of the speaker himself: the "shadow's shadow of me" (1517). Therefore, the enemy's death equals the protagonist's death: "But I kill my shadow's shadow of me! / ... And God is good, for I wanted him to die. / ... This death, his death, my death— / It is the same, this death" (1517). The enemy is further presented as the speaker's sibling: "that other, / The enemy, my brother" (1519). Notably, however, the speaker does not identify himself or his enemies with their nationalities.

The speaker eventually realises that he must sacrifice his body in order to atone for his sins: "Lord, what we have done we hereby expiate, / We expiate in our bodies' rents and rags / In our sheaf of self-gathered wounds ..." (1519). This sacrifice is accomplished through the murder/ marriage, which is, as previously noted, suicidal, fratricidal and homosexual that encompasses heterosexual role play. The protagonist is eventually resurrected through the ritual: "I walk the earth intact hereafterwards; / The crime full-expiate, ... we walk the earth / Unchallenged, intact, unabridged ..." (1519).

This denouement offers a contrast to the ending of the 1915 version of "England, My England", which also concludes with some battlefield clashes between soldiers. The killings perpetrated on each other by the male soldiers of this story evoke the murders in "Eloi, Eloi, Lama Sabachthani", but the soldiers of "England, My England" do not achieve consummation. The protagonist, Evelyn Daughtry, belongs to an old south-of-England family and loves the "peace and sunshine and loveliness" (*EME* 220) of the countryside. He cannot abide by the rules and systems of capitalist society and makes no money to maintain his family, merely tending to the garden full-time to make the place beautiful. He exhibits no trace of chauvinism and does not judge people on the grounds of nationality. He contemplates that "well, a German was as much mankind as an Englishman" (226). He nevertheless decides to join the army once the war breaks out, not because he is stirred by patriotic frenzy but because he is involuntarily thrilled about the idea of participating in "the positive activity of destruction" (224). Eventually, he is sent to France, where a shell damages his left brow and mutilates a part of his thigh. His ambivalent emotions are reminiscent of the feelings experienced by the soldier in "Eloi": "He felt very sick, and very peaceful at the same time" (*EME* 229). However, Evelyn does not attain to a consummation through combat. Unlike the anonymous soldiers of "Eloi, Eloi, Lama Sabachthani", the soldiers committing the murders in "England, My England" are labelled by their nationalities:

> A fine, transcendent spirituality was on the face of the Englishman, a white gleam. The other German, with a curious, almost ludicrous bustling movement had got out his revolver and was running forwards, when he saw the wounded, subtle Englishman luminous with an abstract smile on his face. At the same instant two bullets entered his body. ... The Englishman, still luminous and clear, fired at the dropped head. ...
>
> At the same moment the Englishman felt a sharp blow, and knew he was hit. ... He saw the red face of a German with blue, staring eyes coming upon him, and he knew a knife was striking him. For one moment he felt the searing of steel, another final agony of suffocating darkness.
>
> (231–32)

These soldiers die a futile death as victims of chauvinist patriotism. Evelyn is free from patriotic sentiment but the State intervenes effectively to define his frame of thought. He is no longer Evelyn Daughtry but an English soldier. These combatants are no longer bride and bridegroom; the Englishman's enemy is neither his "shadow's shadow" nor his "brother". Rather, they individually represent their nations as agents of war. This story illustrates how national ideologies can readily infiltrate even those who appear immune to wartime propaganda or patriotic enthusiasm, just as they penetrate into Lawrence's texts. The exploration for male bonding shifts away from the battlefield and an ex-soldier approaches a non-combatant in "The Blind Man".

Short Fiction in 1918: "The Fox", "The Blind Man" and "Tickets Please"

The prolonged war eventually lasted for four years. Many soldiers came back home physically disabled or shell shocked, if they had escaped futile deaths. By the end of the war in 1918, 6 million British men enlisted, nearly 750,000 soldiers died in the war, more than 240,000 suffered total or partial leg or arm amputations, 80,000 were diagnosed as shell shock.[7] Moreover, following the armistice, the gulf between the classes widened. A sense of fear spread extensively among the middle class, who viewed the working-class ex-soldiers as a potential threat to social stability. Sarah Cole explains ex-soldiers' uncertain status after the war:

> In the language of the old soldiers' journals, as well as in the visual imagery of mass demonstrations, a picture emerges of the returned soldier as, paradoxically, at both the center and the margins of the post-war world, an object of reverence and pathos as well as an instigator of potential trouble.
>
> (Cole 222)

Thus, the returned soldiers of the lower class found themselves in a paradoxical position—they were publicly admired as "heroes" of the war, but in reality isolated in post-war British society.

This section analyses Lawrence's short fiction composed at around the time of armistice to demonstrate how deeply the condition and atmosphere of late-war Britain is inscribed in his ambivalent texts. For example, the passage of March and Banford's vigilant days in the first version of "The Fox", written at the end of 1918, is full of allusions to the trench warfare images that were widely circulated during the war. As the soldiers were confined to the trenches, so was the couple confined to the domestic area. At night, March, in uniform, uncomfortable and disgusted with the filthy dirt, wades through the mud while Banford is frightened by furtive enemies:

> The months passed, the dark evenings came, heavy, dark November, when March went about in high boots, ankle deep in mud, when the night began to fall at four oclock, and the day never properly dawned. Both girls dreaded these times. They dreaded the almost continuous darkness that enveloped them on their desolate little farm near the wood. Banford was physically afraid. She was afraid of tramps, afraid lest someone should come prowling round. March was not so much afraid, as uncomfortable and disturbed. She felt discomfort and gloom in all her physique.
>
> ("Fox" 34)

Mud, discomfort, vigilance, fear: the life of the two ladies is portrayed within the framework of the publicised image of combat in entrenchments.[8]

Moreover, the chronicle of March and Banford's communal life at the beginning of the story can be interpreted as a metaphor of British society that had enthusiastically joined in the Great War, but which gradually lost hope and faith during the war's prolonged continuance. At first, the two women "set out quite gallantly with their enterprise" (28), but, as time passes, early glamour gradually dissipates, everything goes wrong, and the women are stuck in a total morass. Hostility is aroused between March and Banford, as if it represents the great chasm between the military personnel and non-combatants on the home front. At the end, they seem "to be losing ground, somehow, losing hope as the months went by. ... There was nothing to keep them up—and no hope" (31). The deteriorating life of the couple illustrates the declining morale and the shortage of daily commodities that British society experienced towards the end of the war.

On 23 November 1918, about a fortnight after the armistice, Lawrence wrote to Pinker: "I have written three short stories which ought to sell ..." (*3L* 299). The "three short stories" referred to in this letter are, along with "The Fox" examined above, "The Blind Man" and "Tickets Please". These stories exhibit a similar pattern. In each, an intruder trespasses on a homogeneous or homosocial community: in "The Fox", a returned soldier pays a surprise visit to a same-sex couple; in "The Blind Man", a Scottish barrister's visit to a couple gives the story its impetus; and in "Tickets Please", a male inspector rather thoughtlessly intrudes into the Furies' nest. As the following sections will demonstrate, "The Blind Man" and "Tickets Please" are, in some respects, at one with contemporary national ideology; simultaneously, however, these texts undermine the widely shared wartime discourses by exposing the unpalatable realities which haunted British society during the Great War.

"The Blind Man": Can a Returned Hero Purify Pre-War Corruption?

> What is our task? To make Britain a fit country for heroes to live in.
>
> David Lloyd George, Wolverhampton, November 1918

"The Blind Man" shows a similar setting as "The Thimble". In both stories, the husbands were each disfigured as a result of their wartime experiences at the war's front. Now, grave and taciturn, each seems to have some mysterious power. This fact indicates that the story of "The Blind Man" explores the same theme as the previously written story—the possibility of resurrection after the devastation of war. Lawrence composed these fictional stories to test his concept of resurrection, implying the possibility of reborn ex-soldiers leading the rest of the population into regeneration.

In the end, however, the returned war heroes do not fully succeed; the conclusions of these stories are not straightforward and optimistic, but rather ambiguous and uncertain, as the author refers to in his letter to Pinker in December 1918, concerning the ending of the first version of "The Blind Man", as "queer and ironical" (*3L* 303).

There are two versions of "The Blind Man". The first version was written in November 1918; this version was later revised for the publication in the July 1920 issue of *The English Review*. The plots of both the 1918 version and the published version are not appreciatively different. "The Blind Man" centres on the relationships among the three characters: the blind man, Maurice Pervin; his wife, Isabel; and her cousin and old friend, Bertie Reid, a barrister. Maurice has been dispatched twice to the Western Front and received a severe blow to his brow, resulting in a nasty scar on his forehead and total blindness. Maurice and Isabel's marital life is relatively satisfying but not entirely happy; sometimes it is tense and suffocating. Because of this, Isabel accepts Bertie's offer of a visit. The story culminates with Maurice's abortive attempt to establish a firm bond and mutual understanding with Bertie. Although the storyline of each version does not show noticeable differences, numerous minor revisions are added to the later text, especially to its ending.

In the published version, for example, Isabel shows a certain respect for motherhood, by which she somewhat responds to her husband's masculine potency. Both in the first and published versions, Isabel is expecting a baby in a few weeks' time, but in contrast to Isabel in the first version, who is afraid that "the child would be an obstacle to their [her and her husband's] close and important relationship" (*VicG* 178), in the later version, Isabel "looked with joy and relief to the coming of the second. ... She did so want to luxuriate in a rich, physical satisfaction of maternity"; "With hair knotted loosely behind, she had something of a warm, maternal look" (*EME* 47, 50). Additionally, in the published version, the blind man is presented as a more heroic and mysterious figure than that of the previous version. Isabel favourably describes her husband's hidden, hypnotic power:

> "There is something else, something *there*, which you never knew was there, and which you can't express."
>
> "What is there?" asked Bertie.
>
> "I don't know—it's awfully hard to define it—but something strong and immediate. There's something strange in Maurice's presence—indefinable—but I couldn't do without it. I agree that it seems to put one's mind to sleep. But when we're alone I miss nothing; it seems awfully rich, almost splendid, you know."
>
> (*EME* 59)

Thus, in the published version, Maurice is a more enigmatic character and Isabel, who has the maternal warmth, is more strongly attracted to his mysterious power, in contrast to the earlier 1918 version, in which, as we shall see, the blind man is characterised as an isolated figure from the middle-class allies of his wife and her childhood friend.

These differences inevitably lead to the significantly different endings. In the published text, alone in a dark barn, Maurice tells Bertie to touch his scar and insists on establishing a bond of friendship. In the end, the blind man's overflowing passion and energy completely destroys the barrister:

> "Touch my eyes, will you?—touch my scar."
>
> Now Bertie quivered with revulsion. Yet he was under the power of the blind man, as if hypnotised. He lifted his hand, and laid the fingers on the scar, on the scarred eyes. Maurice suddenly covered them with his own hand, pressed the fingers of the other man upon his disfigured eye-sockets, trembling in every fibre, and rocking slightly, slowly, from side to side. …
>
> "Oh, my God," he said, "we shall know each other now, shan't we? We shall know each other now."
>
> Bertie could not answer. He gazed mute and terror-struck, overcome by his own weakness. He knew he could not answer. He had an unreasonable fear, lest the other man should suddenly destroy him. Whereas Maurice was actually filled with hot, poignant love, the passion of friendship.
>
> . . .
>
> He was indeed so glad. Isabel took his hand with both hers, and held it fast.
>
> "You'll be happier now, dear," she said.
>
> But she was watching Bertie. She knew that he had one desire—to escape from this intimacy, this friendship, which had been thrust upon him. He could not bear it that he had been touched by the blind man, his insane reserve broken in. He was like a mollusc whose shell is broken.
>
> (*EME* 62–63)

With his dark, mysterious power, the blind man totally overwhelms the barrister and completely nullifies him. This denouement alludes to the supremacy of instinct and the sense of touch over the mind and intellect, each of which the two characters represent respectively.

In the longer ending of the earlier 1918 version, the blind man is again ecstatic about his success but he is less of a heroic but more of a bewildering figure. The blind man rather more craves to establish a firm friendship with the barrister, who reluctantly accepts the proposal:

Bertie lifted his hand and laid the fingers on the scarred eyes, moved them slowly along the brow. Maurice suddenly put his hand over Bertie's hand, pressing it on his brow, over his disfigurement, in a strange passion.

"You don't mind, do you?" he said at length, in a voice of unbearable emotion.

"No—I—I also love you," said Bertie, scarcely conscious of what he said.

A tremor ran over the blind man's frame.

. . .

"Shall we be friends for ever?" he repeated, with a strange smile on his disfigured face.

Now Bertie quivered through all his soul. He could not answer. But his hands clung to the other man's hand.

"Friends for ever!" repeated the blind man, with accent of strange joy.

"Shall it be so?" said Bertie.

"For me, yes. But for you?"

"Yes also."

Bertie felt faint, he almost fainted, as he committed himself.

"Friends for ever—for ever," Maurice repeated, in inexpressible exaltation.

. . .

"Bell!" said Maurice.

"Yes dear." She wondered at the strange, exultant smile on her husband's lips. She was terribly startled.

"Tell her," he said to Bertie.

"We have become friends," said Bertie. His eyes were dilated, his look was strange.

"For ever!" added Maurice.

"*Really*!" cried Isabel, a little dazed. …

"Are you glad, dear?" she asked.

"Yes," he said, drawing her to him and taking her in his arms. "Don't call me blind, Bell."

He pressed her close to him. She suddenly started to cry, sobbing violently on his shoulder. His arms winced and tightened. He turned to Bertie with the same strange smile on his blind face.

"She's glad," he said.

(*VicG* 190–91)

This ending of the first version is indeed "queer and ironical" as Lawrence himself referred to in his letter. Is his wife really glad, as the blind man insists with his "strange smile" at the end of the story? Or is she merely upset and bewildered? His plea to his wife not to call him blind ironically illustrates how much he is stigmatised by the war wound. This ex-soldier is an extremely embarrassing figure to the civilians with his excessively persistent demand for mutual, everlasting friendship, which ironically reveals a deep gulf between the protagonist and the two cousins. This ending highlights the hero's total alienation from the civilians rather than showing the triumph of instinct and blood over mind and intellect.[9] The following analysis focuses on this first version of "The Blind Man" since the impact of the Great War is more vividly engraved on it; the text reveals crude realities of the returned soldiers' awkward position in the British society at around the time of the armistice.

In the first version, despite his blindness, Maurice Pervin is presented as a skilled farmer; he discusses all matters with his tenant farmers, milks and attends the horses by himself and manages the farm. Although he is intellectually slow, he is a born farmer who is successful due to his instinct and intuition. His physical strength and masculinity are reiterated:

> He sat down heavily, to take off his boots and gaiters. ... His shoulders were rather sloping than broad, and he reached for his boot-laces with ruddy, large, shapely hands, in which the full veins stood out. His limbs were heavy, his thighs and knees seemed massive. And when he stood up his neck and face were surcharged with blood, veins stood out even on his forehead.
>
> (*VicG* 182)

This characterisation of the blind farmer is revealing when analysed in terms of the ideology of degeneration and the Great War as a purifier. As we have seen in Chapters 1 and 2, according to the theory of race degeneration, a healthy farmer is a typical image of wholesome stock, the opposite of degraded folks living in urban areas. This blind man is portrayed as a virile farmer, full of vigour and vitality, and uncontaminated by the degenerative elements inherent in urban life. He has lost his sight and become a typical Lawrentian hero:

> He was very acute in his hearing and touch, ... he seemed even to *feel* the presence of objects, before he touched them. ... He seemed to move and rock in immediate blood-contact with his surroundings, without the intervention of visual consciousness. And in this state there was a certain rich positivity, bordering sometimes on dark rapture. It was a pleasure to stretch forth the hand and meet the invisible object, and clasp it, darkly possessing darkness. ... He lived in this new way of knowledge, dark blood-contact.
>
> (183; emphasis in original)

Lawrence's celebration of male body and his condemnation of the ruling class could be examined in the context of the theory of race degeneration, which was produced by the fear of the decline of the British Empire.[10] As previous sections have noted, Lawrence uses the war as a prescription for it. In "The Blind Man", the virile farmer has been reborn with mysterious power through the ordeal of battlefield. The Great War is here as a kind of initiation into a new mode of consciousness by which the superhuman possibly leads the degenerated population to resurrection. The widespread discourse of racial degeneration and of the Great War as a purifier thus infiltrates the characterisation of this Lawrentian hero.

This blind man attempts to establish a bond with Bertrand Reid, whose character is depicted in contrast to that of Maurice: "Bertie was a barrister and a man of letters, quick, fine, ironical in his humour. He was very different from her husband" (*VicG* 178). In critical history, it is a cliché to view the two persons representing Lawrentian opposition between darkness and light, blood and mental consciousness.[11] Bertie's intelligence and refinement hinder his emotional and intuitive responses. The example most emphasised in the story is his relationship with women; although he yearns to find and adore his heroine, his obsession with his notion of love makes him virtually impotent to love the opposite sex:

> He longed to be passionately enamoured of a woman, and to marry her. But he was still a bachelor. He had his fixed idea of what his fulfilment should be, just as Isabel had hers. The wonder was that he had never married, out of sheer fixed intention.
>
> (184)

His innate deficiency is symbolised by his ugly legs. His puny limbs make him mentally hesitant and physically inaccessible:

> Isabel always wished he had not got little legs. It was his little, curious legs that kept him forever outside the realm of love. … He, wistful soul, perhaps felt something of this. She looked at him … and his odd little legs.
>
> (184)

Thus, in this text, the polarity between the healthy and the disabled is paradoxically overturned; visually disabled Maurice is presented as a virtually virile farmer, while a successful barrister bears both physical and mental deformities.

This leads to another irony that the essentially healthy male is injured by the war, and those who are supposed to be purified remain intact. In his above-quoted letter to Asquith, Lawrence enumerated those who should be purified: "It is no use adhering to that old 'advanced' crowd—Cambridge, Lowes Dickinson, Bertie Russell, young reformers, socialists, Fabians—they are our disease, not our hope. We want a clean sweep, and a new start" (*3L* 49). Bertrand Reid, who, by his name and character, is apparently an oblique reference to Bertrand Russell,[12] is hence presented as the embodiment of what Lawrence regards as a "disease".

However, we must go beyond this kind of schematic interpretation which, applying the author's idea on the text, concludes that the story criticises the middle classes, who lay too much emphasis on intellect, and instead celebrates instinct, blood consciousness and physical awareness that the author thinks the modern people have lost. This type of reading fails to capture the historical actuality that the text composed in the end of 1918 entails.

The first version of "The Blind Man" alludes to the fact that Isabel is the same type of person as the Scottish barrister. She is an intellectual type of woman with literary talent: she is a reviewer of books for a newspaper, and her infertility is suggested by the fact that she miscarried her first child and fears the birth of her second, in contrast to the published version which emphasises her motherhood. As Bertie's fixed obsession, her idea of love is also an abstract notion of happy home and connubial bliss: "She had one great article of faith, and this was that a woman and a man should be all in all to one another, when they were married and in love with one another" (179). She sticks to Victorian romanticism of idealised matrimony, or what the narrator calls "Isabel's creed of marital happiness" (179). Although she sometimes cannot but feel fear, and at other times despair, of her taciturn husband, her mind tries to suppress her anxiety and persuade herself that she really loves the blind man: "Yet there was an ache and a weariness in her soul as she watched him: an ache and a weariness she could not understand. ... She only reiterated that she loved him" (182).

Moreover, it is suggested that she lives in a different world from that of the blind man. Like Bertie, Isabel is afraid of stepping into darkness, which is her husband's element; instead, she clings rather excessively to the sense of sight to maintain her satisfaction and relief:

> The large, handsome tea-cups and the proud old tea-pot were of a mellow creamy-yellow colour, with a pattern of deep blue and harsh red—there was a spread of fine shape and rare, dauntless colour on the white cloth under the lamp-light. It gave Isabel a feeling of gratification. (180)

Since childhood, Bertrand Reid has been Isabel's old friend; Bertie is to Isabel her "dearest and oldest friend, a man who seemed almost indispensable to her" (177). Unlike the published version in which Isabel disapproves of Bertie's "incurable weakness" (*EME* 58) and is more sympathetic to her blind husband, in the first version the middle-class cousins are almost close allies:

> He [Bertie] was her old friend, a quite distant relative, Scotch as she was. … All her life he had been her friend. … [S]he was deeply, unchangingly fond of him, with almost a blood fondness. … They understood each other naturally, and closely.
>
> (*VicG* 178)

By contrast, the first version emphasises Maurice's feeling of isolation from the kindred:

> He had a curious sense of being outside it all— … a fretful, desolate sense of being excluded from living, the living which he heard in the voices of the two downstairs. He was cut off. … He knew that Bertie's relationship to Isabel was one of true, fond friendship, congenial and natural. Yet he felt outside, like a child outside the fence.
>
> (*VicG* 184)

Thus, ironically, it is not the Scottish barrister, but rather the blind farmer, who is a true intruder in a homogeneous kinship between the middle-class cousins.

At the end of the story, as we have seen, Maurice, alone with the barrister in a dark barn, vehemently insists that they make friends. The working-class ex-soldier's absurd demands for friendship horrify the middle-class man and terribly upset his middle-class wife. This episode illustrates the working-class ex-soldiers' actual situation in post-war Britain. The blind man's abortive attempt allegorically depicts, on the one hand, the isolation of the working-class ex-soldiers, many of whom were disabled, and on the other, the middle-class anxiety towards them as a potential force for social disturbance.

Consequently, "The Blind Man" is a text of multiple facets. In the blind man's characterisation is inscribed the idea of purifying War; writing this story, Lawrence explored the possibility that a superhuman, who was reborn on the battlefield, might sweep off pre-war intellectualism and shallow human relations. The text thus embraces wartime ideology of the Great War as a favourable opportunity for purification and regeneration. However, "The Blind Man" presents only a tentative conclusion, and because of its ironic composition and its ambiguity, it is not a simplistic story that supports and expounds the national ideology of war. The text also divulges crude realities about the returned soldiers' position in the British society at around the time of the armistice—their paradoxical position, both at the centre and the margins: they were hailed as war heroes, but at the same time alienated from non-combatants. "The Blind Man" thus portrays an ex-soldier in a country *un*fit for heroes to live in, unlike Lloyd George's promise, which was given at the time when Lawrence was composing this story.

"Tickets Please": A Story of Immanent Violence in British Society

Comradeship is denied in "The Blind Man", but in "Tickets Please", its female version is actualised in a rather perverted form. Annie Stone, a woman tram conductor, takes revenge along with other tram girls on a handsome inspector, significantly named John Thomas Raynor, who flirts with her but who ultimately breaks off the relationship. The girls punish this womaniser who violates norms such as faithfulness and connubial bliss, ideologies long nurtured in Victorian society. "Tickets Please" remains ironic about the Victorianism throughout the text, from the consciously elaborate mock-Victorian literary style at the beginning[13] to the last scene, in which in the cosy waiting room serving as a mock-Victorian home, the girls are seized by mass hysteria, a typical symptom in Victorian women:

> At that moment they were rather horrifying to him, as they stood in their short uniforms. He was distinctly afraid.
> "Come on, John Thomas! Come on! Choose!" said Annie.
> "What are you after? Open the door," he said.
> "We sha'n't—not till you've chosen," said Muriel.
> "Chosen what?" he said.
> "Chosen the one you're going to marry," she replied.
> (*EME* 42)

The girls do not allow the boy to carry on flirtations with them. Sticking to the principle of monogamy, they are possessed by the obsession that men should desire women, or rather, that women must be desired by men. With the shortage of men during the war, except for those who the narrator terms "unfit" (34) cripples and hunchbacks, these odd women craved healthy, suitable husbands. The perverted courtship in the waiting room reveals their ignominious social position, in which the females do not choose, but rather are chosen, by the privileged male, much like marketable commodities.[14]

This story has been interpreted, for example, as a dramatised version of "castration anxiety" developed in the author's childhood experience (Wheeler 244), or that of women's "reverse rape", in which appears Lawrence's misogynist abhorrence to newly unleashed women (Gilbert 291). It is true that we cannot ignore these sexual- and gender-oriented implications involved in the story, but to focus solely on biographical or feminist issues would obscure another dimension of the tale. For example, during World War I, British women were urged by wartime propaganda to give white feathers, a visual symbol of the public accusation of cowardice, to young Englishmen dressed in civilian clothes, who seemed fit to enlist but stayed at home because of pacifist principles or other reasons. In this context, the episode in "Tickets Please" can be seen as an allegory of wartime England: young ladies punish a young man who enjoys romances with women conductors without sharing the burden of war. "Tickets Please" depicts a climate of mistrust and fear among the citizens during the late-war period.[15]

Despite its mock-Victorian beginning, allusions to the war are abundant in the text. The tram drivers and conductors are presented as something analogous to the military. The girl conductors are likened to experienced soldiers: "In their ugly blue uniforms, skirts up to their knees, shapeless old peaked caps on their heads, they have all the *sang froid* of an old non-commissioned officer" (*EME* 35). The drivers are described as "unfit", the word applied to physically or mentally disabled soldiers, as well as those incapable of military service.[16] What bonds them together is the spirit of comradeship, which was the central part of war discourse: "There is very good feeling between the girls and the drivers. Are they not companions in peril, shipmates aboard this careering vessel of a tram-car, for ever rocking on the waves of a stormy land" (36). Thus, in the frenzy of war, the women and the physically disabled, both of whom are essentially the opposite of the military, metamorphosed into quasi-military forces, from which is alienated John Thomas, who is "young", "the right age" and "also good-looking" (36). The text portrays the brutality this pseudo-military body possesses, which suddenly erupts at a provocation.[17]

The horrors of war are everywhere on the home front; even the annual Statutes Fair, where John Thomas and Annie have a first date, is now infiltrated by mass-technology, strongly suggestive of the machines widely deployed on the front:

> *The roundabouts* were veering round and grinding out their music, the side shows were making as much *commotion* as possible. In the cocoa-nut shies there were no cocoa-nuts, but artificial *war-time substitutes*, which the lads declared were fastened into the *irons*. There was a sad decline in brilliance and luxury. None the less, the ground was *muddy as ever*, there was the same *crush*, the press of faces *lighted up by the flares and the electric lights*, the same smell of *naphtha* and [of new-] fried potatoes, and of *electricity*.
>
> (37; my emphasis)

A large throng of crowd, flashes of electric lights, muddy ground and unpleasant smell of oil—the annual fair where the new technologies have been introduced is thrown into turmoil like trench warfare where machine guns, tanks and poison gasses were newly mobilised.[18] Also, as we have seen in Chapter 6, in the author's imagination the roundabouts are associated with war frenzy through Mark Gertler's painting *Merry-Go-Round*; he saw in the paining a madness of war heightened by the mechanical device. Here the boundary between the playground's commotion and the battlefield's tumult has almost blurred.

Now, the waiting room seems the only peaceful space, the girls sitting "round the fire and [having] a cup of tea. Outside was the darkness and lawlessness of war-time" (40). Violent madness, however, dominates even inside of this mock-image of a traditional haven for a male master of a household. Enlisted to support revenge by Annie, who is described as "a tartar" (36), a squad of girls attack the inspector. Carried away beyond themselves, the Bacchic girls are infuriated and, at the same time, enjoy devouring the captured as if they are actually savage barbarians:

> But at Annie's signal they all flew at him, slapping him, pinching him, pulling his hair, though more in fun than in spite or anger. …
>
> She had taken off her belt, and swinging it, she fetched him a sharp blow over the head, with the buckle end. He sprang and seized her. But immediately the other girls rushed upon him, pulling and tearing and beating him. Their blood was now thoroughly up. He was their sport now. They were going to have their own back, out of him. Strange, wild creatures, they hung on him and rushed at him to bear him down. … Nora had hold at the back of his collar, and was actually strangling him. … He struggled in a wild frenzy of fury and terror, almost mad terror. … The girls rushed at him, clenched their hands on him and pulled at him: or they rushed at him and pushed him, butted him with all their might: or they struck him wild blows. He ducked and cringed and struck sideways. They became more intense.
>
> (42–43)

The way in which Annie and the rest of the girls attack John Thomas is indeed cruel and ferocious, as the word "tartar" invokes. This term does not simply indicate Annie's barbarism and savagery; it was a favourite simile applied to German soldiers during the Great War. As Chapter 5 has previously noted, the term "Tartar" was associated with the "Hun", unmistakably evoking images of the "savage" German soldiers in the minds of contemporary readers, along with the other words and phrases used to describe the girls in the story: "Strange, wild creatures" (43), "unnatural strength and power" (43), "supernatural strength" (43), "gleaming eyes" (43), "a terrifying lust" (44) and "devilishly" (44). These expressions are reminiscent of the Huns portrayed in *Movements in European History* as cruel, futile destroyers. Mindless violence that the "tartar" does in "Tickets Please" thus synchronises with the ruthless destruction by the warlike nomadic tribe of the fifth century. The tragedy caused by the women in the story are literally futile because they have destroyed the only "healthy" man when the other "healthy" males have gone to the battlefields. The women on the home front are apparently the opposite of male-dominated military—the non-combatants of the opposite sex. The female bandits, however, share similar characteristics of savagery and volatility displayed by patriarchal, male militarism, and the bullying scene depicts the excessive violence and brutality that surged on the home front, as well as the battlefields, during the war.

Thus, the lynching scene portrays people afflicted with cruelty and madness kindled and fuelled by the Great War. Furthermore, the anti-Victorianism in the text represents the contemporary scepticism towards the Victorian values. At the later stage of the war, British people—especially the young generations—began to feel sceptical about "Victorian Old Men" and to entertain a belief, as Samuel Hynes demonstrates, that "the stupidities and follies of the Victorian past had caused the war" (*War Imagined* 248). Hence, *Eminent Victorians*, a satirical portrait of the four celebrated Victorians by Lytton Strachey published in 1918, acquired a wide readership. "Tickets Please" thus reveals the ethos of late-war British society: the epidemic of violence spread even on the home front; the gulf was created between the belligerent citizens and those who were reluctant to contribute to war activities, and between the old generations who decided to launch the war but deemed to have sacrificed nothing and the younger generations who were forced to sacrifice everything for the nation.

As demonstrated, Lawrence's writings of the late-war period bear traces of national ideologies in the characterisation of Lawrentian heroes and in the use of circulated terms infused with contemporary wartime connotations. These texts are, however, by no means a volume of simple propaganda. They disclose the dark side of British society, which was overshadowed by the brave and belligerent nationalism: the disintegration of society and the alienation of people that appear as conflicts between the classes, the two sexes, the generations and combatants versus non-combatants. These wartime stories articulate the essential isolation of people during the Great War, despite the widespread praise of comradeship and the often-quoted phrase of constructing "a fit country for heroes to live in". Thus, Lawrence's ambivalent texts of the late-war period occasionally show traces of national ideologies, but, simultaneously, they subvert the war discourses, divulging the crude realities of British society possessed by an epidemic insanity called the Great War.

Notes

1 One of the proponents in this vein of analysis is Sarah Cole. In *Modernism, Male Friendship, and the First World War*, she examines extensively how elements of modernism intersect with the contemporary discourse of comradeship, a concept that attained prominence during the First World War. Cole argues that Lawrence's works are ingrained with the combined effects of longing for male friendship and its subsequent failure. See Cole 185–251. She mainly focuses on Lawrence's novels such as *Aaron's Rod* and *Kangaroo*, merely making a few cursory remarks on Lawrence's short stories. However, Cole's analysis and her exploration of the historical and cultural contexts of wartime and post-war Britain offer valuable information and insights for Chapters 7 and 8 of this book. Trudi Tate also offers an intriguing comment on Lawrence's ex-soldiers. Tate asserts that Lawrence's portrayal of returned soldiers differs from the typical depictions of war-injured men in the writings of other authors in the two subsequent decades: the wounded veterans in Lawrence's texts appear serene rather than traumatised. See Tate 115–23. Santanu Das is another noteworthy critic even though his remarks on Lawrence are succinct. He discerns echoes of discourses on male intimacy and touch during the First World War in reference to the final scene of the published version of "The Blind Man". See Das 234. Das' theory that the experience of the "sensuous" world of trenches and war hospitals is fundamental to the comprehension of the literature and art of the First World War is also applicable to Lawrence's works.

2 The First World War encouraged the habit of reading, particularly among women and war workers, both in the trenches and on the home front. Escapist fiction was especially sought by the lower-middle and working classes. See Jane Potter 89, McAleer 71–99 and Maunder xxxiii–liii.

3 Jane Potter argues that wartime romance novels "were, in effect, vehicles for the dissemination of patriotic ideals and models of appropriate wartime behaviour" (91). For her analysis of "The Infant-in Arms", see 103–07. Sharon Ouditt, analysing *The Land Girl's Love Story* by Ruck, summarises the essence of Ruck's works: "the trajectory of the love story is supported by the detail of government propaganda to produce some lively escapism in which true love and war work are securely housed within the walls of patriarchy, patriotism and conventional femininity" (Ouditt 64).

4 Maria Casado Villanueva examines the story in relation to Western fairy tales such as "Sleeping Beauty" and "Beauty and the Beast" and argues that "The Thimble" can be interpreted as both assimilating and subverting plotlines and imagery reminiscent of these fairy tales. She concludes that "For Lawrence, fairy tales provide underlying archetypal plots which endow his realistic rendering of modern experience with a universal dimension" (60).

5 Laurence Steven maintains that the disfigurement helps Daphne relinquish her idea of romantic love, arguing that the "destroyed face becomes a useful symbol—one which informs the theme of superficiality running through the story" (Steven 247).

6 See Harrison, "Men No More Than the Subjective Material of the Machine" 77.

7 Casualty figures are notoriously difficult to specify. See Winter, *Great War* 65–99, *World War I* 206 and Cole 188.

8 It is no coincidence that in "The Waste Land", T. S. Eliot, after alluding to "The Fox" by Lawrence, refers to "rats' alley", the soldiers' slang for the trenches on the Western Front. See Southam 161. All quotations from "The Fox" are from the holograph manuscript version of 1918, printed in *A D. H. Lawrence Miscellany*, ed. Harry T. Moore (Carbondale: Southern Illinois UP) 28–48.

9 Mark Kinkead-Weekes argues that the first version "gains a positive vision", and that by the mutual touch Maurice and Bertie attain to "a new sense of being, a new kind of knowing and the blood-brotherhood, the total commitment to lasting relation, that Lawrence had always wanted with another man" (*TE* 480). This interpretation seems to me to be an overly optimistic reading.

10 In Lawrence's celebration of masculinity reverberates an underlying fear of physical degeneration, which was prevalent among the British at the turn of the century:

> And why is the English race neutral, indifferent, like a thing that eschews life, save that it has said so insistently: "I am this spirit. This body, it is not me, it is unworthy." The body at last begins to wilt and become corrupt. But before it submits, half the life of the English race must be a lie. The life of the body, denied by the professed adherence to the spirit, must be something disowned, corrupt, ugly.
>
> (*STH* 81)

11 Kingsley Widmer, for instance, argues that "the blind man duels … with a pale, cerebral figure from the 'light' world of society, success, and rationalized intellect" (Widmer 44). Conversely, Nils Clausson points out their resemblance in his deconstructive reading: "despite Lawrence's overt intention to portray the two men as thematic opposites, the language of the text regularly undermines that intention by suggesting their similarities" (Clausson 121).

12 Michael L. Ross identifies Russell as Reid's model, arguing that the "situation depicted in 'The Blind Man' recalls … one of the most bizarre episodes in Lawrence's personal history: his friendship of 1915–16 with the philosopher Bertrand Russell" (Ross, *Mythology* 287). Kinkead-Weekes insists that only Bertie's "name could suggest (but probably does not) any hint of Bertie Russell" (*TE* 479). However, considering his first name, "Bertrand" in the first version, which was later altered into "Bertram" in the published version, as well as Lawrence's vituperation on Russell's intellectualism and their relationship, which irretrievably broken down during the war, it is likely that Russell contributed to a certain degree to the characterisation of Bertrand Reid. For another view, see Paul Delany and John Bayley, who argue for the possibility of J. M. Barrie as Bertie's model (Delany, "Who Was 'The Blind Man'?" 92–99, Bayley 126–27).

13 Discussing the beginning of this story, Lionel Trilling points to Victorianism in the text:

> Prose of this kind, with its avowed intention of charming the reader and making him warm and comfortable, was common enough in the fiction of the Victorian period. ... At the beginning of the story Annie seems ready to be the satisfactory heroine of a Victorian novel.
>
> (Trilling 123–24)

14 Kiernan Ryan in his Marxist reading interprets the last scene as revealing women's status as "market commodities" and John Thomas as a transgressor of "the basic code of the sexual market by sampling and soiling all the wares then refusing to buy, to pay the price of marriage" (216).

15 A few critics have analysed this story in its social and historical contexts. For example, Andrew Harrison succinctly elucidates the link between the violence in the story and the warfare on the home front. See Harrison, "Men No More Than the Subjective Material of the Machine" 80–82. Jarica Watts analyses how Lawrence employed mythographic narratives to demonstrate that during the Great War, when the notion of heroic manliness was under threat, both male soldiers and male citizens were sacrificial victims. See Watts 64–84.

16 Since the last decades of the previous century, the word "unfit" had been frequently used in the context of social Darwinism; however, the word acquired wider connotations at the onset of the Great War. It was applied to those deemed unsuitable for military service because of innate physical weakness and to physically or mentally disabled ex-soldiers. See Cole 193.

17 A sudden eruption of destructive forces triggered by minor provocations is a recurring feature of Lawrence's wartime fiction. In *Women in Love*, one might easily recall Hermione's attack on Birkin with a ball of lapis lazuli. In *Touch and Go*, a play composed just before the armistice, Mrs Barlow, while quarrelling with her son Gerald, abruptly strikes him fiercely on the head with her large fan, while the mine owner becomes infuriated by Job Arthur Freer's criticism and repeatedly kicks him. In "Samson and Delilah", a returned miner from the US is battered by his wife and her protectors. Even in "The Rex", a short piece based on the author's childhood life, the eponymous puppy, whose name could be seen as an oblique reference to the "Kaiser", suddenly transforms into a savage dog due to tail-docking.

18 John Hargrave's description in *The Great War Brings It Home* (1919) illustrates the perception of the war as a highly mechanised campaign:

> Never before had science been applied to such an extent for destructive purposes. The nations used poison-gas, thousands of shells per day, huge heavy howitzers, trench-mortars, long-range artillery on rails, hand-grenades, bombs and bomb-catapults, machine-guns and Lewis guns, airships and aeroplanes.
>
> Every kind of scientific warfare was applied—and the result was a deadlock for four years.
>
> (49)

8 Class Conflicts in Ambivalence from "Daughters of the Vicar" and "Hadrian" to *Lady Chatterley's Lover*

In the first few decades of the twentieth century, writers from the working class began to write stories set in colliery districts. James C. Welsh's *The Underworld* (1920) and Ellen Wilkinson's *Clash* (1929) were published during Lawrence's lifetime, and the 1930s witnessed the rapid emergence of other working-class writers from mining backgrounds including Harold Heslop, a miner in Durham, Walter Brierley from Derbyshire and Lewis Jones from South Wales.[1] However, the class conflicts these writers depicted are markedly different from those by Lawrence. They portrayed the exploited miners' point of view and recorded their devastating living and working conditions, which made their themes straightforwardly political. On the other hand, Lawrence rarely depicted class conflict as a pure political struggle between capital and labour, except in his play *Touch and Go*. In *Women in Love*, for example, the class struggle is ironically sublimated into a leader worship by the masses. In his other works, the conflict between the classes is cultural rather than political, such as inter-class relationships in courtship and marriage, as can be seen from his early works like *The White Peacock* and *Sons and Lovers* to his last novel *Lady Chatterley's Lover*. However, there is one thing in common between Lawrence and other working-class writers: their texts often openly declare their antagonism towards the ruling classes.

Lawrence was always class-conscious and never forgot that he was a miner's son. When analysing his texts, however, critics tend to pay more attention to sexual matters than to class issues. For example, when analysing "Daughters of the Vicar", Janice Hubbard Harris lays emphasis on "sexual ambivalence" and maintains that "Lawrence tends eventually to dismiss class as the central concern, focusing instead on conflicts more deeply embedded in his characters' psyches" (Harris 46, 55). Likewise, when analysing "Hadrian", Judith Ruderman focuses on Lawrence's fundamental problems with the "devouring mother" and argues that the story is of a "pre-oedipal concerns" in which the author attempts to take

DOI: 10.4324/9781032675671-9

his revenge upon Magna Mater (Ruderman 83). I would not deny that sexual issues are significant themes in Lawrence's stories and that these analyses do offer a psychologically convincing explanation to them, but these approaches tend to obscure another dimension that Lawrence's texts hold within them. In this chapter, I analyse how the middle-class ideologies permeate Lawrence's apparently anti-bourgeois texts over three stages of his life. The first text to be analysed is "Daughters of the Vicar", composed before the outbreak of the First World War (the first draft in 1911, rewritten in 1913 and revised in the following year). The second is "Hadrian", published as "You Touched Me", written and revised after the armistice. Finally, Lawrence's last novel *Lady Chatterley's Lover*, composed from 1926 to 1928. Along with the last novel, I will provide a brief discussion of *Touch and Go* as a supplementary perspective.

The plots of these three stories display the same pattern. Each stories centres on the relationship between a ruling-class lady, who is either virtually or symbolically virgin, and a working-class man who intrudes into and disrupts the lives of a secluded ruling-class family in a mining community, from which every couple eventually plans to emigrate to Canada. These texts are ostensibly a critique of an outdated and inflexible bourgeois and aristocratic society. The first two stories present lifeless and insensitive middle-class characters, who as heirs of the Victorian reformers reach out to the working class, but their supposedly philanthropic acts disrupt their relationships. *Lady Chatterley's Lover* can also be read as Lawrence's condemnation of the upper class and admiration of a virile working-class man; a stifled upper-class lady finds solace and true love in her affair with a gamekeeper. These texts are, however, by no means unequivocally opposed to the governing classes if analysed from the viewpoint of the social and political contexts of the times when they were composed. The period from the late Victorian era to the first decades of the twentieth century witnessed the decline of the bourgeois hegemony and the rise of the working class, and Lawrence's texts record the transition of middle-class views concerning the rising lower classes.

Middle-Class Anxiety and Its Solution in "Daughters of the Vicar"

"Daughters of the Vicar" focuses on the relationship between the middle and working classes in a mining district in the author's countryside. The eponymous heroines Mary and Louisa live in the desolate vicarage of Mr Lindley, who moved from his curacy in Suffolk with his newly wed wife and brought up their daughters in the last phase of the Victorian era. The vicar is class-conscious and believes in the essential differences between the classes. When Lindley contracts an illness, the family welcome Edward Massey, a young clergyman of good family and private means, who becomes Mary's husband. However, Massey is a somewhat physically and emotionally deformed specimen and Louisa cannot forgive her sister for marrying this insensitive man. At that time, she begins seeing Alfred Durant, who has returned from military service to be a coal miner, and, who is, for Louisa, the complete opposite to her brother-in-law. Confined to her bed with illness, Alfred's mother asks Louisa to wash her son's back. When she washes Alfred, who is bathing after supper, his body overwhelms her; this is a moment of epiphany for her:

> The water in which his arms were plunged was quite black, the soap-froth was darkish. She could scarcely conceive him as human. ... Then he remained rigid and submissive, his two arms thrust straight in the panchion, supporting the weight of his shoulders. His skin was beautifully white and unblemished, of an opaque, solid whiteness. Gradually Louisa saw it: this also was what he was. It fascinated her. ... Her heart ran hot. She had reached some goal in this beautiful, clear, male body. She loved him in a white, impersonal heat. ... Now her soul was going to open, she was going to see another. She felt strange and pregnant.
>
> (*PO* 72–73)

Louisa is awakened by the sight of the male body, which she has never experienced in her sheltered bourgeois life, and she eventually leaves her family for the love of the miner. Through this depiction of the contrasting lives of the vicar's two daughters, the plot ostensibly criticises the lethargic and obsolescent middle class in favour of an admiration for the vibrant working class. This text, however, discloses another dimension if analysed in terms of the political and social context of the class struggle at the time the story was composed—just before the First World War.

The beginning of the story suggests class tensions when the narrator describes the building of the new church at Aldecross as follows:

> To suit the convenience of these new collier-inhabitants, a church must be built at Aldecross. There was not too much money. And so the little building crouched like a humped stone-and-mortar mouse. ... It had an uncertain, timid look about it. And so they planted big-leaved ivy, to hide its shrinking newness. So that now the little church stands buried in its greenery, stranded and sleeping among the fields, while the brick houses elbow nearer and nearer, threatening to crush it down. It is already obsolete.
>
> (40)

Here, the miners' red brick dwellings are multiplying and threaten to demolish the "little church" that stands dormant, covered in ivy. This passage illustrates the situation in which the newly emerging working classes threaten the obsolete middle classes, who no longer possess wealth or social prestige to dominate the district. The vicar actually experiences the working-class subversion of the status quo:

> ... Mr Lindley had considered himself as belonging indisputably to the upper or ordering classes. He had to be humble to the county families, but still, he was of their kind, whilst the common people were something different. He had no doubt of himself.
>
> He found, however, that the collier population refused to accept this arrangement. They had no use for him in their lives, and they told him so, callously. ... The men ... were cheerfully contemptuous of him, with a preconceived contempt he was powerless against.
>
> (40–41)

His wife, Mrs Lindley, tries to dominate the locals, but her desire to impress them is met with scornful ridicule. She eventually confines herself indoors to produce the couple's heirs: "Children were born one every year; almost mechanically, she continued to perform her maternal duty, which was forced upon her" (41). It is ironic that this privileged woman plays the part of the proletariat according to its original definition: those who only serve the state by producing offspring.[2]

In this situation, where the working class begins to threaten the ruling class, the Lindleys retreat to the tradition of the Victorian middle class and stick to one of the most cherished mid- and late-Victorian ideals: philanthropy. True to their beliefs, the parents educate their daughters at home to inculcate the values of the class they belong to:

> Their father and mother educated them at home, made them very proud and very genteel, put them definitely and cruelly in the upper classes, apart from the vulgar around them. ... Gradually Mr and Mrs Lindley ... [were] bitterly repressing and pruning their children into gentility, urging them to ambition, weighting them with duty.
>
> (41–42)

As a result of this education, the daughters follow the middle-class tradition of social reform. Despite the fact that Mary and Louisa apparently choose contrasting ways of life—one marrying a clergyman, the other a coal miner—their behaviour can be regarded as two forms of the philanthropic practice of "saving" the lower classes.

Mary adopts this tradition by marrying Massey, a clergyman, who is the epitome of Victorian philanthropy. He is

> perfect in his sense of duty: as far as he could conceive Christianity, he was a perfect Christian. Nothing that he realised he could do for anyone did he leave undone. ... Now he attended assiduously to the sick man, investigated all the affairs of the parish or the church which Mr Lindley had in control, straightened out accounts, made lists of the sick and needy, padded round with help and to see what he could do.
>
> (49)

Being inculcated in middle-class values, Mary believes it is her duty to admire and attend her future husband: "Seeing his acts, Miss Mary must respect and honour him. In consequence she must serve him" (50). Mary, who always escorts Massey on his visits of parish duty, honours and serves him faithfully and thus fulfils her role as a minister's wife to practice philanthropy.

On the other hand, like the late Victorian middle-class reformers who delved into "Unknown England", Louisa, stirred by curiosity about the exotic and unknown, ventures into working-class life. Her adventure is described from her point of view with such adjectives as "foreign", "strange and exciting" and "curious" (71, 73). There she discovers Alfred Durant, who seems the opposite of the cerebral and benumbed middle class. Through her eyes, Alfred is described as a man of strong physique: "*Miss Louisa saw* the fine outline of his breast, under the blue sailor's blouse, as his chest began to heave" (52; my emphasis). With a mixture of curiosity, admiration and patronage, Louisa peeps into an exotic alien world as a middle-class observer. At the same time, she regards her brother-in-law and her sister as degenerated: "*In Louisa's eyes*, Mary was degraded, married to Mr Massey. She could not bear to think of her lofty, spiritual sister degraded in the body like this" (59; my emphasis). Mary's view synchronises with the growing worry about the physical decline of the British race, which was widely entertained by the contemporary British. Hence, from the point of view of the ruling class like Louisa, Alfred can be seen as a typical example of an idealised labourer, who has a strong physique and is fit for service.

The text therefore reveals middle-class ambivalence towards the lower classes. The masculine labourers possess physical vitality that is necessary for race regeneration, but at the same time, as the opening passage of this story illustrates, they are an object of fear who threaten bourgeois hegemony. This conflicting sentiment is inscribed in the text, and the rest of the story serves to alleviate middle-class anxiety by invalidating the binary opposition between frail middle class and virile working class, and also by evicting the working class to the colonies.

While Louisa projects a romanticised image onto Alfred, the text reveals the miner's intrinsic impotence: although he is physically strong, he is emotionally immature. He returns home as an ex-serviceman, but is "naïve and inexperienced as a boy" and "quite chaste" (67). Although he is comfortable with the idea of women and enjoys lewd talk with men, he recoils from real women: "But when the ready woman presented herself, the very fact that she was a palpable woman made it impossible for him to *touch* her. And this incapacity was like a core of rottenness in him" (67; my emphasis). Like Massey, his natural impulses are blocked and Alfred is aware and ashamed of this fact.

It is Louisa who rescues Alfred. One reason of his immaturity is that he is dominated by his mother: "Without knowing it, he had been centralised, polarised in his mother. It was she who had kept him" (78). After his mother's death, Louisa, who has *touched* him when she washed his body, visits him again. The miner is leaving for a pub but she says she wants to be with him and boldly asks "Don't you want me?" (82). Although hesitant and uncertain, Alfred finally responds with a passionate embrace. Recovering from a deep swoon, he feels himself revitalised:

> Then, gradually, as he held her gripped, and his brain reeled round, and he felt himself falling, falling from himself, and ... a moment of utter darkness came over him, and they began to wake up again as if from a long sleep. He was himself.
>
> (82)

After this initiation, Alfred is sexually matured enough to accept a woman as his own:

> His eyes were strange and glowing, with a tiny black pupil. Strange, they were, and powerful over her. And his mouth came to hers, and slowly her eyelids closed, as his mouth sought hers closer and closer, and took possession of her.
>
> (82–83)

As a form of middle-class salvation, Louisa gives her hand to a miner who could not fulfil himself as a male.

Ironically enough, however, Alfred cannot overcome his mental inability and remains passive. After the "long, hurting kisses", he "felt as if his heart were hurt ... and he scarcely dared look at her. ... There was something he wanted to say, that he dared not" (83). He meekly obeys her request to ask her father's permission for their marriage, which again reveals his passive attitude:

> "Miss Louisa—Louisa—promised to marry me—" [said Alfred.]

"You asked Miss Louisa if she would marry you—yes—," corrected the vicar.

(84)

Louisa is irritated by his unmanly behaviour—"Miss Louisa was angry to see him standing there, obedient and acquiescent. He ought to show himself a man" (86)—but Alfred readily accepts the vicar's demand that he and Louisa move to Canada. He remains passive and never challenges the authority.

The story's ending would reassure a bourgeois readership. As Chapter 1 has noted, emigration policy at the turn of the century had the political intention of evicting the lower classes of society. In "Daughters of the Vicar", the working class ex-soldier is ultimately sent to the colony, suggesting that the social menace implied at the beginning of the story could be eliminated. Thus, "Daughters of the Vicar" is ambivalent. The text apparently denounces the lethargic and benumbed middle classes for their rigid attitudes and stifling lives, contrasting them with an ex-soldier with a massive physique. Simultaneously, however, the text records conflicting sentiments of the middle class towards the working class—as both an object of admiration and fear. Eventually, the text alleviates their anxiety concerning proletarian subversion by expelling the working-class character from the country.

Returned Soldier and Working-Class Threat in "Hadrian"

Set in a traditional bourgeois household, "Hadrian" also presents a critique of middle-class philanthropy where the adoption of an orphan and a "touch" by a lady have ironic consequences. Like the description of the vicarage in "Daughters of the Vicar", the description of the Pottery House in "Hadrian" also symbolises the decline of the middle classes:

> The Pottery House was a square, ugly, brick house girt in by the wall that enclosed the whole grounds of the pottery itself. To be sure, a privet hedge partly masked the house and its grounds from the pottery-yard and works: but only partly. Through the hedge could be seen the desolate yard, and the many-windowed, factory-like pottery, over the hedge could be seen the chimneys and the out-houses. But inside the hedge, a pleasant garden and lawn sloped down to a willow pool, which had once supplied the works.
>
> The pottery itself was now closed, the great doors of the yard permanently shut. No more the great crates, with yellow straw showing through, stood in stacks by the packing shed. No more the drays drawn by great horses rolled down the hill with a high load. No more

> the pottery-lasses in their clay-coloured overalls, their faces and hair splashed with grey fine mud, shrieked and larked with the men. All that was over.
>
> (*EME* 92)

A hedge on the estate separates the Pottery House and the pottery. The pottery ceased its activity long ago and is now desolate. The ex-manager's dwelling place is "ugly" and the pastoral setting as "a pleasant garden and lawn" merely discloses middle-class vanity and ostentation and enhances the estate's forlorn atmosphere. The Pottery House is a relic of the Victorian era when the thriving middle classes employed workmen under a system of philanthropic paternalism.

This ossified middle-class household is now surrounded by energetic working-class inhabitants: "Outside in the street there was a continual racket of the colliers and their dogs and children. But inside the pottery wall was a deserted quiet" (93). Furthermore, in this setting, the gulf between the two classes is unbridgeable; the hollow pride of the middle class prevents them from mingling with the lower. This is why the Rockley girls of the Pottery House, Matilda and Emmie, could not marry:

> Matilda and Emmie were already old maids. In a thorough industrial district, it is not easy for the girls who have expectations above the common to find husbands. The ugly industrial town was full of men, young men who were ready to marry. But they were all colliers or pottery-hands, mere workmen. The Rockley girls would have about ten thousand pounds each when their father died. … [They] refrained from sneezing away such a fortune on any mere member of the proletariat.
>
> (92–93)

Ted Rockley, the head of the pottery, "was an intelligent man who had had some education, but preferred to remain as if he were one with the rest of the working people" (93). He represents the paternalistic bourgeois managers of the previous generation, as depicted by Thomas Crich in *Women in Love*, who sympathised with his workmen, and, unlike the next generation who regard their labourers as a means to make profit, cooperated with them to create harmony between the classes. Hence, Rockley's adoption of Hadrian, an orphan from a charity institution, is apparently a practice of outdated middle-class philanthropy. However, it is actually merely parodic; the father adopts a boy because he is fed up with being in a household of women, rather than being motivated by an act of benevolence. This act of perverted paternalism provokes unrest in the family. To the Rockley girls, the charity boy is an alien from a different class:

> Hadrian was just an ordinary boy from a Charity Home, with ordinary brownish hair and ordinary bluish eyes and of ordinary rather cockney speech. The Rockley girls … had resented his being sprung on them. He, with his watchful, charity-institution instinct, knew this at once.
>
> (93)

When Hadrian is 15 years old, he leaves the house for Canada without a word of gratitude, and, when the First World War breaks out, he joins the army and fights in Europe. After the armistice he returns to the Pottery House as an ex-soldier. This rather unexpected return after five years' absence makes the gulf even broader because the Rockley women believe Hadrian seeks an inheritance from their father.

It is here that another parody of philanthropy takes place. One night, Matilda intends to visit her sick father and caresses his head. However, she has forgotten that her father was moved downstairs and Hadrian now occupies that room. Her accidental caress awakens desire in Hadrian:

> But the soft, straying tenderness of her hand on his face startled something out of his soul. He was a charity boy, aloof and more or less at bay. The fragile exquisiteness of her caress startled him most, revealed unknown things to him.
>
> (100)

Here, giving her hand to a lower-class man functions as a caricature of a deformed middle-class benevolence that leads to unexpected and undesirable result for Matilda. Awakened by her touch, Hadrian is suddenly captivated by the idea of marrying her. The motive of his ambition is, however, not romantic, but subversive of the class hierarchy. Hadrian would master her wellborn quality:

> He looked at her curiously. She was not beautiful, her nose was too large, her chin was too small, her neck was too thin. But her skin was clear and fine, she had a high-bred sensitiveness. This queer, brave, high-bred quality she shared with her father. The charity boy could see it in her tapering fingers, which were white and ringed. The same glamour that he knew in the elderly man he now saw in the woman. And he wanted to possess himself of it, he wanted to make himself master of it.
>
> (100)

Here, Hadrian represents the working-class menace, a view shared by the middle class in British society after the armistice. Even before the war, a working-class phobia was growing in the bourgeoisie, as Chapter 6 has demonstrated; it appeared, for example, in C. F. G. Masterman's caricature of the middle-class fear of the working classes, especially their demand for equal rights in politics. Then, the First World War brought about huge structural changes in society. The middle class began to be less certain of their position as the working classes were becoming more confident. In actuality, during the war, British society saw an increase in both organised and spontaneous protests and demonstrations. Eventually, in the last phase of the war, the Representation of the People Act of 1918, which gave the vote to all men over 21 and women over 30 who met a property qualification, was passed, and a growing awareness of democracy was engendered among the working class. In the 1920s, middle-class concerns were amplified as increasingly militant movements, such as public demonstrations and trade union activity, developed and strikes were reported as being associated with anarchism and Bolshevism.

Additionally, after the war, the numbers of working-class veterans flooded the streets from the trenches. To the governing class, they appeared a potent force of social disruption. Their enhanced anxiety was, in the end, confirmed; in Epsom, in June 1919, around the time when "Hadrian" was composed, a large group of Canadian soldiers marched to the police station and demanded the release of two fellow soldiers arrested for drunkenness. They demolished the station and killed a police officer. A series of riots occurred in Luton in the following month, where furious ex-servicemen marched to the town hall and burned it down. These incidents were widely reported by the British press.[3]

Middle-class anxiety prevalent after the armistice is deeply engraved in "Hadrian". Always dressed in khaki, Hadrian embodies the growing threat shared by the governing class after the war. As an uninvited intruder, he comes back to the Pottery House "quite unexpectedly" (95) from the battlefield and his arrival shocks and embarrasses the women. For the Rockley women, this sinister and dangerous "young soldier" (98) is the symbol of the growth of the working-class menace and an imminent threat that might possibly subvert middle-class order. Confronting him,

> Matilda looked a long time at the neat khaki figure. It had something of the charity-boy about it still; but now it was a man's figure, laconic, charged with plebeian energy. She thought of the derisive passion in his voice as he had declaimed against the propertied classes, to her father. (97–98)

Another aspect of his disruption to the household is the dangerous political idea he learned in Canada—democracy. Hadrian argues that "there's too much difference between the men and the employers" (97) in England, and that, in Canada, he could be a master. The Rockley women cannot accept this subversive idea to be applied to England:

> "Is it any different in Canada?" asked Emmie.
> "Oh yes—democratic," replied Matilda. "He thinks they're all on a level over there."
> "Ay, well he's over here now," said Emmie drily, "so he can keep his place."
>
> (97)

Here, the sisters' conversation discloses middle-class fears of post-war egalitarianism.

When Hadrian makes up his mind to marry Matilda, the old man warms to the idea and insists that, unless she consents, he will leave the entire estate to his adopted son. Having failed to persuade their father, the Rockley women beg and threaten Hadrian in vain:

> She [Emmie] went off in search of the solicitor and brought him home with her. There was an interview, and Whittle tried to frighten the youth into withdrawal—but without avail. Then clergyman and relatives were summoned—but Hadrian stared at them and took no notice.
>
> (106)

Law and religion—the two principal apparatuses by which the middle class have governed their world—are powerless against what the narrator calls "the indomitable, dangerous charity boy" (104). Thus, Hadrian represents the imminent danger of the proletariat for the declining bourgeois hegemony.

At the end of the story, Hadrian decides to go to Canada with his new wife and newly acquired wealth. This disappoints all the Rockleys except the patriarch in his dotage. In both "Daughters of the Vicar" and "Hadrian", the working-class characters leave England for Canada. However, unlike the former, in which a threat is dispelled by evicting a dangerous element to the colony, in "Hadrian", the eviction does not solve any problems, and the middle classes are virtually defeated. As the narrator describes, Hadrian "triumphed" (107).

These contrasting endings imply a change in the relationship between the opposing classes before and after the Great War. As an allegory of British society around 1920, "Hadrian" is the story of the middle class' abortive attempt to ward off a working-class intruder into the society they rule. Unlike "Daughters of the Vicar", in "Hadrian", the middle classes can no longer control the growing ambition of the proletariat, and the emigration policy as a means to get rid of social evil no longer works. The dying patriarch symbolises not only the end of the Victorian tradition of philanthropy, but also the collapse of the British Empire. At first, he tells his daughters that he will leave Hadrian only his watch and chain and a hundred pounds, but he suddenly changes his mind when the charity boy presents him with a new idea. For the Rockley women, the moribund father is controlled and manipulated by a rebellious plebeian, and, in this way, the text registers post-war bourgeois anxiety about the collapsing Empire taken over by the proletariat.

As demonstrated, Lawrence's texts are not a simple critique of bourgeois society and an admiration of the working-class life. Descriptions of the inflexibility of the middle class and the vitality of the working class are infused with bourgeois anxiety and discomfort; these stories imply the working class as a potential menace who might subvert bourgeois authority. Thus, Lawrence's stories are inscribed with a fear of the decline of middle-class hegemony and anxiety concerning the rise of the working class that pervaded society before and after the war.

Lady Chatterley's Lover: Temptation to the Bourgeois Myth

> If the country wants anyone it wants a Radical. But I've talked to more people than my mother, and they're weary of us leisured classes coasting round in motor-cars and asking for something to do. All this solemn to and fro between great houses—it's a game without gaiety. You don't find it played outside England.
>
> E. M. Forster, *Maurice*, Part II, Chapter 20

Lawrence's last novel, *Lady Chatterley's Lover*, begins with a statement: "Ours is essentially a tragic age, so we refuse to take it tragically" (*LCL* 5). After his sojourn in the Continent, Australia and America, Lawrence returned to his home country, where he set his last novel. Like his earlier works, the last novel's plot unfolds in a mining countryside in the Midlands, and its central theme is an inter-class love in a stifling society during the "tragic age". The pattern of storyline resembles those of the previous stories analysed in this chapter: a working-class man intrudes into a ruling-class society and gets entangled with a lady, with whom he considers emigrating from England to the colony. In the last novel, Lady Chatterley decides to leave her husband—who was paralysed during the war—for the gamekeeper. The couple contemplates leaving England for Canada but eventually hopes to live on a farm in the English countryside. This plot is certainly radical and provocative, and the chances of the novel to be commercially published were slim in his lifetime. Lawrence managed to publish the novel only privately in Florence and Paris.

There exist two earlier iterations of *Lady Chatterley's Lover*: the first short version is customarily labelled *The First Lady Chatterley* and the second version is titled *John Thomas and Lady Jane*. The three stated versions are similarly plotted but with notable alterations, particularly to the characterisation of the gamekeeper. A critical consensus that the novel transitioned from a realist to a more mythological mode exists apropos the revisions of the drafts. Graham Holderness has contended that the "full historical complexity by the techniques of realism" in the first version is substituted in the final version by "the ritualistic condemnation of a universe of death" (Holderness 224, 226). Likewise, several critics have linked the transfiguration of the gamekeeper's character to myth-making, asserting that the revisions transformed the "realism" or "history" of the earlier *Chatterley* stories into "myth".[4] I take these critical views into account in the sections that follow in attempting to illustrate how and to what extent the draft revisions contributed to myth-making, also considering the significance and implications of such myth-making, specifically in 1920s Britain.

When Lawrence completed the second version *John Thomas and Lady Jane*, a travelogue was published and it became an instant bestseller. First published in 1927, H. V. Morton's *In Search of England* saw its third edition being published in the same year, seventeenth edition in five years and eventually the twenty-ninth edition in 1943. *In Search of England* contributed to establishing a "motoring pastoral genre";[5] in contrast to George Orwell or J. B. Priestley, who explored English suburbia and working-class districts in the 1930s, Morton travelled through the English countryside and small towns by car and documented his admiration of rural landscapes, coupled with various encounters with the local people (see Figure 8.1).

In the travelogue, Morton presents a conventional dualistic view of an industrial town versus countryside, along with the stereotypical idea that the industry had destroyed Merry England:

> Since James Watt invented a new world on Glasgow Green, the town and the country have grown apart. They do not understand one other. Since the so-called Industrial "Revolution" ... English country life has declined, agriculture has fallen on bad times, and the village has been drained to a great extent of its social vitality.
>
> (Morton ix)

This has become a traditional view since the turn of the century, when the idea of racial degeneration—the idea that, in contrast to "healthy" country inhabitants, people in towns had deteriorated because of the harmful urban life—began to be widely discussed throughout the nation. The underlying motive of Morton's delving into the English bucolic lives was to arrest the deterioration of the English race. The author believes that

Figure 8.1 "A Lane in England" on the opposite side of the title page in H. V. Morton, *In Search of England.*

by returning to the countryside and finding "Englishness" there, degeneration of the English race would be checked:

> The towns should understand the problems of agriculture, because as the life of a country-side declines, as in England to-day, and the city life

> flourishes, the character and physique of a nation deteriorate. … The 'Back to the Land' cry is a perfectly sound instinct of racial survival.
>
> (Morton ix–x)

Morton argues using Lawrentian terms, such as "blood" and "resurrection", that the "healthy" country life is the foundation of the lives of the English people through which the towns' harmful influences can be overcome:

> But granted that a healthy country-side is necessary to a nation, it is then surely the duty of every man to ponder these problems and to enter into them. If those men and women who … are starting out in their thousands to discover rural England will see it … as a living thing, … we may be a step nearer that ideal national life: on one hand the wealthy industrial cities; on the other a happy country-side, ready to give its new *blood* to the towns, guarding the traditions of the race, ready always to open its arms to that third generation from the city in need of *resurrection*.
>
> (Morton x; my emphasis)

This travelogue was well read presumably because, in addition to driving being one of the leisure activities of the middle class, the readers shared the author's concerns about racial degeneration. *Lady Chatterley's Lover* certainly shares some of its main concerns with Morton's book: admiration of the countryside and the vitality it holds for the fear of the deterioration of the human race. Interpreting Lawrence's last novel in terms of the prevailing frame of the mind articulated in Morton's bestselling book reveals *Lady Chatterley's Lover*'s hidden affinity with the dominant ideology to which the novel is opposed. Despite the fact that the novel was hysterically rejected by the middle-class readership, the text's ambivalent nature functions to appease its subversive elements.

Subversion of Dualism

Lady Chatterley's Lover has often been analysed from a dualistic viewpoint.[6] Nevertheless, this conventional approach falls short of fully grasping this text because the dualism is invalidated in this ambivalent text. For instance, in contrast to Lawrence's earlier works analysed in this chapter, where depictions of the upper-class estates suggest adversarial relationships between the upper and lower classes, *Chatterley* presents descriptions of manor houses that suggest a certain level of interconnection between the rulers and the ruled, despite their apparent opposition. This is indicated in the portrayal of Wragby Hall, the Chatterley's estate:

> It stood on an eminence in a rather fine old park of oak trees: but alas, one could see in the near distance the chimney of Tevershall pit with its clouds of steam and smoke, and on the damp, hazy distance of the hill the raw straggle of Tevershall village—*a village which began almost at the park gates, and trailed in utter hopeless ugliness for a long and gruesome mile*: houses, rows of wretched, small begrimed brick houses with black slate roofs for lids, sharp angles and wilful blank dreariness.
> (*LCL* 13; my emphasis)

Unlike the residences of the ruling classes in earlier stories, which are portrayed as being invaded and oppressed by the labourers' dwellings, in *Chatterley*, the English manor house is not under threat from the working-class community. Rather, the mining district starts on the threshold of the park and extends into the surrounding countryside. It is as if the "utter hopeless ugliness" were dispersed from the manor house to the labourers' dwellings. Indeed, the local district has been created by the upper classes. Clifford Chatterley, the owner of Wragby Hall, studied "the technicalities of coal-mining" (10) in Germany and, similar to Gerald in *Women in Love*, launches the coal mining business with passionate enthusiasm. Besides Clifford, other landowners, such as Clifford's godfather Leslie Winter, operate the mining business. The link and interdependence between the upper-class mansions and the mining district are again depicted in the description of Winter's estate, where virtually no border exists between them:

> The park gates, at the back, opened just near the level crossing of the colliery railway; the Shipley colliery itself stood just beyond the trees. The gates stood open, because through the park was a right-of-way that the colliers used. They hung around the park. ... He [Winter] had almost welcomed the colliers in his park.
> (156–57)

Even the Prince of Wales, when he visits Shipley, states, "If there were coal under Sandringham, I would open a mine on the lawns, and think it first-rate landscape gardening" (157). In *Chatterley*, the upper and working classes depend on one another and their complicity helps transform the English countryside.

As it indicates, the relationship between the upper and working classes is not a simple opposition between the ruler and the ruled; rather, the complicity and interdependence between the two classes are recurrently depicted in the text. Clifford and Constance live on "a rather inadequate income" (5), and their livelihood depends on the revenue from mines. It is a working-class nurse who encourages Clifford to go into the mining business: "But under Mrs Bolton's influence, Clifford was tempted to enter this other fight, to capture the bitch-goddess by brute means of industrial production" (107). It is true that Clifford becomes a popular writer and earns 1200 pounds a year. However, this is another example of his dependence on the lower class. Again, Mrs Bolton's stories are a major source of his materials for his writing:

> At first she had not ventured to "talk Tevershall," as she called it, to Clifford. But once started, it went. Clifford was listening for "material," and he found it in plenty. Connie realised that his so-called "genius" was just this: a peculiar talent for perspicuous personal gossip, clever and apparently detached.
>
> (101)

In addition, he owes his creativity to Michaelis, who is from the lower strata of Irish society—"a down-at-heel Dublin street-rat" and "the last word in what was caddish and bounderish" (20). This "hopeless outsider" (21) intrudes into the upper classes, and flirts with Connie and cuckolds her husband, which is ironically the source of Clifford's inspiration:

> And she used all her roused alertness and satisfaction to stimulate Clifford, so that he wrote his best at this time, and was almost happy, in his queer blind way. He really reaped the fruits of the sensual satisfaction she got out of Michaelis' male passivity erect inside her.
>
> (30)

The novel contains abundant examples of master-slave subversion. Clifford is almost entirely controlled by his nurse Mrs Bolton. She satisfies her master's pride by placing "herself absolutely at his service" (100) and is adept at handling the male hysteria. In Connie's eyes, her husband does "sink so horribly into the hands of that woman!" (99). As a result, he is completely tamed by his nurse:

> After this, Clifford became like a child with Mrs Bolton. He would hold her hand, and rest his head on her breast, and when she once lightly kissed him, he said: "Yes! Do kiss me! Do kiss me!" And when she sponged his great blond body, he would say the same: "Do kiss me!" … And he lay with a queer, blank face like a child, with a bit of the wonderment of a child. And he would gaze on her with wide, childish eyes, in a relaxation of Madonna-worship.
>
> (291)

Clifford also depends on Oliver Mellors. This gamekeeper guards the wood against the poaching miners and rears pheasants to be hunted by gentlemen for leisure. The most symbolic episode is the scene wherein the engine of Clifford's bath chair ceases to work and the gamekeeper releases the "prisoner" (189) by pushing the chair back to the mansion. Without the gamekeeper, Clifford is unable to move around his own territory. Furthermore, the gamekeeper's child is the only possible heir to Wragby Hall.[7]

Subversion of dualism is not merely found in the opposition between classes; it also occurs between nature and industry in the mining countryside. It is true that in her room, Connie hears "the rattle-rattle of the screens at the pit, the puff of the winding-engine, the clink-clink of shunting trucks and the hoarse little whistle of the colliery locomotives" and is annoyed with "the stench of this sulphureous combustion of the earth's excrement" (13). Nonetheless, Connie adores a path that is covered with the refuse of the pits; the pathway runs through the park to the gate and changes its colours according to the weather:

> Across the park ran a path to the wood gate, a fine ribbon of pink. Clifford had had it newly gravelled with sifted gravel from the pit-bank. When the rock and refuse of the underworld had burned and given off its sulphur, it turned bright pink, shrimp-coloured on dry days, darker, crab-coloured on wet. Now it was pale shrimp-colour, with a bluish-white hoar of frost. It always pleased Connie, this underfoot of sifted, bright pink.
>
> (41)

The gamekeeper also imagines that the modernised mining activity is destroying his sacred world:

> He went down again, into the darkness and seclusion of the wood. But he knew that the seclusion of the wood was illusory. The industrial noises broke the solitude, the sharp lights, though unseen, mocked it. ... The fault lay there, out there, in those evil electric lights and diabolical rattlings of engines.
>
> (119)

In contrast to the characters' impressions of the woods, the narrator suggests that the mining activity gives the wood its liveliness and vivacity; without the clatter of the shaft, whirr of the engines and whistle of the locomotives, the wood would be lifeless and forlorn:

> The air was soft and dead, as if all the world were slowly dying. Grey and clammy, and silent even of the shuffling of the collieries, for the pits

were working short time, today they were stopped altogether. The end of all things!

In the wood, all was utterly inert and motionless. Only great drops fell from the bare boughs, with a hollow little crash. For the rest, among the old trees was depth within depth of grey hopeless inertia, silence, nothingness.

(65)

Thus, simplistic dichotomies, such as the country park and mining district, upper and lower class and nature and mechanical industry, are repeatedly invalidated in *Lady Chatterley's Lover*. They are not necessarily in opposition but interdependent, and their borders often virtually dissolve.

Representations of the Upper and Lower Classes and Their Crossover

In *Lady Chatterley's Lover*, the upper classes are the target of severe condemnation. They are depicted as narrow-minded profiteers exploiting miners while being virtually reliant on their servants. It is tempting to interpret these representations as Lawrence's criticism of aristocracy, but they cannot be attributed to the author's original findings alone; rather, they generally reflect the conventional views on the upper classes in the early twentieth century.

In 1909, during his People's Budget campaign, David Lloyd George delivered a well-known speech in Limehouse, almost two decades before *Lady Chatterley's Lover* was published. This speech was made famous—or notorious—for its vituperative outburst against the landowning classes. The speech depicted landowners as idle, selfish, arrogant, unfair, exploitative and rapacious:

> The landlord is a gentleman—I have not a word to say about him in his personal capacity—the landlord is a gentleman who does not earn his wealth. He does not even take the trouble to receive his wealth. ... His sole function, his chief pride is stately consumption of wealth produced by others.
>
> (Lloyd George 682)

The strong criticism from the then Chancellor of the Exchequer is directed at the landowners' operation of the coal mining business:

> The landlords are receiving eight millions a year by way of royalties. What for? They never deposited the coal in the earth. It was not they who planted those great granite rocks in Wales. Who laid the foundations of the mountains? Was it the landlord? And yet he, by some divine right,

> demands as his toll—for merely the right for men to risk their lives in hewing those rocks—eight millions a year! ...
>
> If this is an indication of the view taken by these great landlords of their responsibility to the people who, at the risk of life, create their wealth, then I say their day of reckoning is at hand.
>
> (684)

Lloyd George vociferates, pretending to be a hero, "Oh, these dukes, how they harass us!" (683). This oration helped promulgate the stereotypical views on the landowning classes.

This kind of negative image of the upper classes has been circulated since the turn of the century. In his preface to *The Heart of the Empire* (1901), Masterman expressed his views on the upper classes as lavish, idle, ostentatious, impotent and barren:

> At the one end of the scale the lives of a large proportion of the rich are far from satisfactory. Separated from many of the realities of life, they are unable to find natural ways of expending their money, and, in consequence, are driven to indulge in sumptuous living or in vulgar display. ... Tyrannised over by their own conventions, *slaves to their servants*, frequently devoid of any real appreciation of the beautiful, their lives are spent without knowledge of the highest forms of happiness, with disastrous loss of energy and opportunity—a loss that falls on all.
>
> (viii; my emphasis)

If the above passage were added to *Lady Chatterley's Lover*, it would fit quite well. Clifford and his peers live luxurious lives and waste their wealth accumulated by exploiting the miners. Being blind to his spouse's sufferings or the gamekeeper's vitality, Clifford, who is "rather supercilious, and contemptuous of anyone not in his own class" (*LCL* 15), spends every evening gambling with his nurse. One of the typical images of the aristocrats in Masterman's passage is their incompetence, as is indicated by the phrase "slaves to their servants". The portrayals of the ruling class being dependent on the lower classes were widely reproduced since the turn of the century through literary works such as *The Time Machine* (1895) by H. G. Wells and the Jeeves series (1915–74) by P. G. Wodehouse. The master-slave subversion in *Chatterley* follows this trend; Clifford's characterisation is largely based on the traditional views on the upper classes.

Simultaneously, typical representations of the working class are also employed in *Lady Chatterley's Lover*. There are two curiously long and obsessive portrayals of the miners in the text—one is by Connie, who travels through the mining districts by car, and the other by Mrs Bolton, who fluently describes the miners' daily lives to her master. In Chapter 11, on a wet cold day in May, Connie rather abruptly embarks on a car journey across the mining country in the Midlands. As if it were a harsh caricature of the motoring pastoral genre, the car drives through the dreary mining districts and she observes the inhabitants who look like aliens to her eyes. The negative portrayal of the miners in this episode has often been ascribed to the author's own experience when he returned to the Midlands after the General Strike in 1926.[8] However, they are also increasingly influenced by the widespread, conventional conceptions of the working classes. In the novel the miners are portrayed as uncanny creatures of the underground, and with no spontaneous intuition:

> Tevershall! That was Tevershall! Merrie England! Shakespeare's England! No, but the England of today, as Connie had realised since she had come to live in it. It was producing *a new race of mankind.* ... There was something *uncanny* and *underground* about it all. It was an *under-world.*
>
> (153; my emphasis)

As Connie delves into the mining village, her view synchronises with the narrator's voice, revealing the text's fundamental conception of them:

> The world was so complicated and weird and gruesome! The common people were so many, and really, so terrible. So she thought as she was going home, and saw the colliers trailing from the pits, grey-black, distorted, one shoulder higher than the other, slurring their heavy ironshod boots. Underground grey faces, whites of eyes rolling, necks cringing from the pit roof, shoulders out of shape. ... Connie was absolutely afraid of the industrial masses. They seemed so *weird* to her. A life with utterly no beauty in it, no intuition, always "in the pit." ...
>
> Incarnate ugliness, and yet alive! ... They had appeared out of nowhere in their thousands, when the coal had called for them. Perhaps they were only weird fauna of the coal-seams. Creatures of another reality, they were elementals, serving the element of coal. ... Elemental creatures, weird and distorted, of the mineral world!
>
> (159–60; italics in original, my underline)

The miners are portrayed as ugly, mysterious creatures of the underworld. These depictions of the working classes are not necessarily unique to *Chatterley*. Many middle-class social explorers of the late nineteenth century, who delved into the unknown working-class communities, portrayed the working class with curious similarities. They sensationally reported on the devastated lives of those residing in the lower strata of English society, which they referred to as "Unknown England" or "Darkest England', coined after Henry M. Stanley's description of his trip to Africa under the title "Darkest Africa". Hence, Connie's reaction to Mrs Bolton's depiction of the crude realities of the working-class lives is a typical response of the ruling classes: "it sounded really more like a central African jungle than an English village" (102). The social reformers and the middle classes who consumed their sensational reports regarded the labourers as aliens, another race whose wretched living conditions not only horrified them but also aroused their curiosity and satisfied their desire for exoticism and benevolence.[9] A passage from Masterman's *From the Abyss*, reportage of the slums of South London published in 1902, serves as a typical example of the middle-class representations of the working class at the turn of the century. *From the Abyss* and *Chatterley* employ strikingly similar images to depict the inhabitants of the lower strata of society:

> Without warning or observation, a movement and a sound have arisen in those unknown regions surrounding the kindly, familiar London that we know. ... Our streets have suddenly become congested with a weird and uncanny people. They have poured in as dense black masses from the eastern railways; they have streamed across the bridges from the marshes and desolate places beyond the river; they have been hurried up in incredible number through tubes sunk in the bowels of the earth, emerging like rats from a drain, blinking in the sunshine. ... Whence did they all come, these creatures with strange antics and manners, these denizens of another universe of being? They themselves seemed half afraid of their power, awed by unaccustomed daylight and squares and open spaces. ... Only when night fell did their discomfort drop from them. As the darkness drew on they relapsed more and more into bizarre and barbaric revelry.
>
> (*From the Abyss* 2–3; my underline)

Both texts not only share crucial vocabulary, such as "weird", "uncanny", "masses", "black" and "creatures", but also apply curiously similar images to the labourers—they are a crowd of evil creatures that appear from the dark underworld and are unpleasant and threatening to "us" ruling classes. The old class-conception of gentry and peasantry of Merry England had been replaced by the image of an irresponsible rich and a strange, ugly poor. Thus, *Lady Chatterley's Lover* employs the contemporary stereotypical class images and representations to portray both the upper and working classes.

A salient feature in *Lady Chatterley's Lover* is the crossover of class representations; the vocabulary and images of one class are employed to describe the other. For example, typical representations of the upper classes are overlapped with those of the working classes when Mrs Bolton recounts a long tale about the lives of the miners in Tevershall. She discloses the latest gossip in the village, explains the present conditions of the coal mining industry in the Midlands—how much they are mechanised, how much coals each mine produces—and delineates the reckless lives of the young miners in the district:

> They aren't ever serious about anything, except showing off on motor-bikes and dancing at the Palais-de-danse in Sheffield. You can't *make* them serious. The serious ones dress up in evening clothes and go off to the Pally to show off before a lot of girls and dance these new Charlestons and what not. … But I don't see how you're going to get bolshevism, when all the lads want is just money to enjoy themselves, and the girls the same, with fine clothes: and they don't care about another thing. They haven't the brains to be socialists. They haven't enough seriousness to take anything really serious, and they never will have.
>
> (*LCL* 104)

The lives of the landowning classes as described by Masterman are embodied by the miners in Mrs Bolton's endless depiction, who waste their time and money in a vainglorious display of themselves: "Separated from many of the realities of life, they are unable to find natural ways of expending their money, and, in consequence, are driven to indulge in sumptuous living or in vulgar display" (*Heart of the Empire* viii).

Simultaneously, while nursing her master, Mrs Bolton assumes that Clifford is not "so very different from the colliers after all" (*LCL* 83). When describing her husband, who is successful as a writer of well-known novels, Connie employs the same adjectives used to characterise the working classes:

> With his *uncanny*, lame instinct for publicity, he had become, in four or five years, one of the best known of the young "intellectuals." … It was *weird*: and it was nothing. This was the feeling that echoed and re-echoed at the bottom of Connie's soul: it was all nothing, a wonderful display of nothingness. At the same time a display. A display, a display, a display!
>
> (*LCL* 50; my emphasis)

The words "uncanny" and "weird" are frequently used to describe Clifford as if they are the most appropriate adjectives for this landowner. When he completes his boring recitation of Racine, Clifford stares at his wife with "pale, uncanny eyes" (138). He tackles the management of the coal mining industry with "the almost uncanny cleverness" (107) and "an almost uncanny shrewdness" (291), sitting on his bath chair which is described as his "weird wheeled ship" (185). And he gazes at his wife "weirdly" (296) when he discovers her affair with his gamekeeper.

Thus in *Lady Chatterley's Lover*, representations of the upper classes are overlapped with those of the working classes and vice versa. With this crossover of class representations, differences between the classes disappear and the duality between them dissolves. Connie no longer considers the difference between the coal miners in the Midlands and the upper classes in luxurious districts in London: "Connie thought, how extremely like all the rest of the classes the lower classes sounded. Just the same thing over again, Tevershall or Mayfair or Kensington. There was only one class nowadays: moneyboys" (105).

From Touch and Go *to* Lady Chatterley's Lover

It is pertinent at this juncture to briefly consider Lawrence's wartime play *Touch and Go* to offer another perspective on Lawrence's last novel. *Touch and Go* was composed in October 1918, just before the armistice. In other words, this play was written after the opening chapters of *Movements in European History* were composed and before *Women in Love* underwent its final revision the following year. *Touch and Go* and *Women in Love* share a few protagonists, albeit differently named: the industrial magnate in the play is called Gerald Barlow, his artist lover is Anabel Wrath, and Barlow's close friend is renamed Oliver Turton. Ursula does not appear in the play; however, a union representative named Job Arthur Freer is introduced as a new character. As the narratives of the two works revolve around similar characters, *Touch and Go* is frequently discussed in relation to *Women in Love*.[10] Furthermore, as in *Women in Love*, an atmosphere of death and violence pervades the play and the brutality of the First World War is convincingly invoked even though no war erupts in the plot of the play.[11] Thus, the two works display commonalities, and it is indeed relevant to analyse the play in association with *Women in Love*. Nonetheless, I would rather examine hidden affinities between the play and *Lady Chatterley's Lover* in this section.

Touch and Go is set mostly at a marketplace of a mining village in the Midlands and the luxurious drawing room at Lilley Close, the Barlows' home. Gerald Barlow is presented in the play as an exploitative mine owner who, having rejected his father's philanthropic approach to managing the business, places ultimate value on profit maximisation and thus prioritises mechanising the mines. In this respect, Gerald in the play strongly evokes Gerald Crich in *Women in Love*. However, the Gerald in the novel is an ambivalent character endowed with opposing natures of productivity and destructivity who eventually constructs a colossal industrial empire. In contrast, the play's Gerald Barlow enacts an extremely focused role as a mine owner incessantly in conflict with his workers. His management style intensifies discord with the miners, but he never surrenders to the demands of the workers.

No mutual trust exists between the owner and the miners in the play. Barlow calls the mine workers "abominable old limpets" and disparages them, saying "they're just greedy, incompetent, stupid, gloating. ... They're like vicious children, who would like to kill their parents so that they could have the run of the larder" (*Plays* 418). Barlow understands how the miners view him: "They think I'm a sort of criminal who has instigated this new devilish system ..." (418). Job Arthur articulates how the miners really view the mine owner, labelling Barlow a vermin:

> Vermin is what lives on other people's lives, living on their lives and profiting by it. ... I say—that live on the sweat and blood of the people—live on it, and get rich on it—get rich through living on other people's lives, the lives of the working men—living on the bodies of the working men—that's vermin. ... And every parish must destroy its own, every parish must destroy its own vermin.
>
> (421)

Job Arthur incites the crowd of miners at the marketplace, evoking David Lloyd George's denigration of the landowning classes:

> JOB ARTHUR. The obstacle to Labour is Capital.
>
> ...
>
> By Labour we mean us working men; and by Capital we mean those that derive benefit from us, take the cream off us and leave us the skim.
>
> ...
>
> So that if you're going to remove the obstacle, you've got to remove the masters, and all that belongs to them.
>
> (422)

Thus, Job Arthur regards the mine owner as a thief appropriating wealth obtained through the toils and sweat of the miners, a parasite thriving on the labour of common people and a profiteer who ruthlessly exploits the labourers. This stereotypical portrayal of a manager in the coal mining industry is passed on to the owner of Wragby Hall, and the political tension between the upper and lower classes is depicted again in the last novel, mainly in the earlier versions.

In contrast to the play's conventional representation of a mine owner, the miners are dichotomously presented. On the one hand, the miners are not given proper names or individual personalities; they appear only as "Voices" speaking as one. Gerald Barlow describes the anonymous mass of miners as "monsters", and tells Job Arthur that they are "a great swarm of hopelessly little men" (406) lacking wit, courage, real understanding or life intelligence. Barlow's portrayal is reminiscent of the description by Connie in *Lady Chatterley's Lover* as she drives through the dreary mining districts and observes their inhabitants as mysterious creatures of the underworld. In this context, Gerald Barlow and Connie's views overlap, reflecting the ruling class' stereotypical conception of the working class.

Barlow thus views the lower class in conventional terms, but they do discharge a significant role. The "Voices" in the play are not mere witnesses but participants who influence the play's course of events. They are presented on stage as a crowd enacting a role somewhat analogous to the "chorus" in Greek tragedies.[12] The "Voices" do not merely witness the disputes between the protagonists; they also respond with sarcastic comments to the speeches of the main characters or repeat dialogues with derision:

> JOB ARTHUR. Quiet—quiet—quiet a minute, everybody. We give him [Gerald] a minute—we give him a minute to answer—
> VOICES. Give him a minute—a holy minute—say your prayers, Barlow—you've got a minute—tick-tick says the clock—time him—
> JOB ARTHUR. Keep quiet—
> WILLIE. Of all the damned, cowardly—
> VOICES. Sh-h-h! Squeeze him, throttle him. Silence is golden, Houghton. Close the shutters, Willie's dead.—Dry up, wet whiskers—
> JOB ARTHUR. You've fifteen seconds.
> VOICES. There's a long, long trail a-winding—
>
> (426)

The "Voices" comment on events and characters or express moral and social attitudes; they encourage the main characters to speak or interrupt the protagonists; and they sing a popular ballad and a famous First World War song. In so doing, they heighten the atmospheric intensity and control aspects of the plot's development. They represent the multitude demonstrating an antagonistic and creative positivity that can dismantle hierarchies.

Unlike the other main characters in *Touch and Go*, Job Arthur Freer is an original character conceptualised for the play. He is the leader of the miners, the "local secretary for the Miners Federation" (408). He is thus reminiscent of the gamekeeper in the first version of the *Chatterley* stories, in which Oliver Parkin is positioned as the secretary of the communist league. Job Arthur is also described as having a "touch of the artist" (408). He hails from a musical family and plays the violin well. Moreover, he "loves refinement, culture, breeding … and a presence, a fine free manner" (408), evoking Oliver Mellors, the gamekeeper in the final version of *Lady Chatterley's Lover*.

In the play, Job Arthur initially desires to settle the conflicts between capital and labour. He explains that he is not "a red rag Socialist" (374) and argues against the nationalisation of the mines. He is welcomed to the drawing room of the Barlows, and discusses the issues with Barlow. However, he turns into an instigator at the end of the play and supports the striking labourers.[13] The role of conciliator transfers to Barlow's friend Oliver Turton, a Birkin-like figure in the play who shares his first name with the gamekeepers in the *Chatterley* novels. Job Arthur transforms from conciliator to labour movement leader but the gamekeepers of the *Chatterley* stories follow the opposite path.

Which Class Does Mellors Belong to?

Oliver Mellors is a character who embodies the ambivalence that *Lady Chatterley's Lover* entails. His classless nature is symbolised by his unique speaking ability; the gamekeeper speaks Standard English fluently as well as broad dialect, which obscures the social stratum he belongs to: "And talking broad Derbyshire again like the worst, when she, Ivy Bolton, knew he spoke like any gentleman, *really*" (*LCL* 145). He is the son of a miner, but as an exceptionally intelligent boy, he earned a scholarship to attend a grammar school. He spent his adolescent years immersed in books, and in his hut he still has dozens of books on topics that range from politics to science to fiction. During the war, he served in the army and was promoted to officer. Connie's first impression of him—"… he seemed *so* unlike a gamekeeper, so unlike a working-man anyhow. … 'He might almost be a gentleman'" (68)—is confirmed through her relationship with him: "He had a natural distinction, but he had not the cut-to-pattern look of her class. Yet, she saw at once, he could go anywhere. He had a native breeding which was really much nicer than the cut-to-pattern class thing" (274).

Mellors' characterisation as a classless individual stands in stark contrast to his original characterisation in the earlier versions of the novel. The gamekeeper in the first two versions of *Chatterley* stories is originally named "Oliver Parkin" and belongs to the true working class. Unlike Mellors in the final version, Parkin in the first version speaks only in the broad Derbyshire dialect and barely speaks Standard English, which makes his lover feel that he is a complete stranger: "She would never be able to imitate his speech. You couldn't even spell it. ... She gave it up. Culturally, he was *another race*" (*FLC* 65; my emphasis). Connie believes that because Parkin behaves in a genuinely conventional and class-specific manner, the gap between their social classes cannot be bridged:

> He paid the tram-fare for her, pushing his hand in his trousers pocket as the working men do. The tram was crowded, and she felt very strange. These people were as strange to her as if they had been Zulus or Esquimo—nay, more alien, because their form of sophistication was more *weird*.
>
> (171–72; my emphasis)

In reality, class conflict is more intense and class enmity is much fiercer in the first version, which reverberates throughout the text:

> And he [Parkin] spoke, both to her and Clifford, with the broadest accent. He did it deliberately, as many of the local people did nowadays, as an intangible kind of insult to the mincing-mouthed gentry: a defiance, a sort of contempt. He was an excellent keeper because he looked on the wood as his own domain, and because he was practically never interfered with. But he resented even Constance's walking about the woods when the birds were sitting, and he hated Clifford's motor-chair.
>
> (31)

Even after the gamekeeper leaves the wood as a result of the scandal, the hostility recurs in the text: "A strange, quiet, but deadly stream of hatred came out of the ex-gamekeeper. He hated Clifford and the gentry who had shot his pheasants at Wragby. He had felt insulted by them, and he hated them" (169–70). Naturally, Parkin throws himself into the socialist cause, which, as Chapter 1 has previously noted, was the reason for social unrest and disorder from the bourgeois viewpoint. He professes his firm conviction for the communist cause to Duncan Forbes, an artist friend of Connie:

> "That's another thing!" said Parkin, lowering his voice. "I'm secretary for our men, at our works, of the communist league. ..."
>
> . . .
>
> "Really! And you want Soviets, like in Russia?"
>
> "Yes! Workin' men must n't sell their work, it comes to selling your soul, if you have to.—We'll do our share of the work to keep everything alive. But we won't sell our work to make profits for other people."

> "You want to be like Russia? You want to kill off all the upper classes, for example?"
>
> "No! There's no need to kill 'em—except maybe a few."
>
> (206–07)

Consequently, Parkin is characterised as a dangerous element as considered by the ruling class—the cause of the social disturbance.

Through the revisions, however, the gamekeeper becomes less political and aggressive. In the second version, Parkin is not involved in communism, and Connie is pleased with the fact: "I'm so glad you are leaving Sheffield. I was so afraid you were just going to deteriorate into a socialist or a fascist, or something dreary and political" (*FLC* 564). In the final version, Mellors is characterised as a classless individual who no longer engages in the socialist movement. Thus, the gamekeeper becomes declassed and less political, thereby becoming less provocative to the middle-class readership.

In *Lady Chatterley's Lover*, when they decide to live together, the gamekeeper and Connie consider emigrating from England to Canada as one of the possible options. The couples in short stories analysed in the previous sections also choose to emigrate; however, emigration in the 1920s had a different meaning than it did in the years before World War I. Although in *Mrs. Dalloway* (1925) by Virginia Woolf, Lady Bruton, urged by her telescopic philanthropy, argues for "that project for emigrating young people of both sexes born of respectable parents and setting them up with a fair prospect of doing well in Canada" (*Mrs. Dalloway* 97), the influx of immigrants was the centre of debate over eugenics in the Dominion. The argument was led by Charles Kirk Clarke, the most famous Canadian psychiatrist at the time. Clarke and other psychiatrists discovered that a high percentage of immigrant children were "delinquent", "immoral" or "subnormal" and, therefore, they advocated sterilisation and eugenic immigration restriction for the benefit of public health. In 1923, Clarke was invited to London to deliver the Maudsley Lecture, in which he argued, as *The Times* reports, that

> "It is all very well," he said, "for Rudyard Kipling and other enthusiasts to say that what Canada must do is to pump in the population. That is true; but, at the same time, it is necessary to put the suction-pipe in waters not polluted by defect, physical degeneracy, and social failure."
>
> ("Canada's Nordic Needs" 11)

He proceeds to further argue with the help of statistical data that three quarters of "mentally subnormal" children in Canada were those of newly arrived immigrants or of foreign-born citizens and "declares emphatically that the Dominion must take steps to protect itself against the entry of those who are mentally or morally unsound" ("Canada's Nordic Needs" 11, "Immigration and the Unfit" 11).[14] Canada was not the only country that imposed restrictions on immigrants in eugenic terms; the United States, for example, also introduced the Immigration Act termed as the Johnson-Reed Act in 1924.

Hence, in the 1920s, the British emigration policy no longer worked as a method to evict those deemed unfit for society; rather, only those who were eugenically approved could emigrate. The fact that the gamekeeper is eligible to emigrate from England to Canada implies that he is eugenically approved and fit to produce offspring, in contrast to Clifford, who is symbolically and virtually sterilised. It is true that the gamekeeper in the final version can indeed cause social disturbance by eloping with an upper-class lady; yet simultaneously, he embodies an idealised image of the "healthy" English race, in addition to possessing values cherished by the middle class such as intellect, progress and tenderness. In these respects, he is valuable to the nation, and in reality, he decides to stay in England at the end of the novel.

Both couples in the second and third versions do not leave England. However, there is a decisive difference in the endings of these two versions. The alteration of the endings further reveals the ideological complexity of *Lady Chatterley's Lover*. In the last chapter of the second version, Connie and Parkin meet up at Hucknall, "a very dreary, depressing little mining town" (*FLC* 565), to discuss their future. She asks her lover: "Take me somewhere where you can hold me in your arms" (568), and they walk into the wood. Unfortunately, their lovemaking is interrupted by the sudden appearance of a gamekeeper, and Connie and Parkin are expelled from the wood. This scene reveals that the wood is no longer a sanctuary. Since ancient times, woods and trees have been associated with symbolic values such as life, procreation and regeneration. This idea became prevalent since the turn of the century through the works of anthropologists such as James George Frazer, whose *The Golden Bough* (1890–1915) and *Totemism and Exogamy* (1910) had a considerable impact on Lawrence.[15] Nonetheless, this ending implies that love can no longer be consummated even in the wood, and its symbolic values of regeneration and procreation are denied. Their paradise is lost, and the couple plods on through the "dead country-side" (570). This ending divulges the unpalatable fact to the middle classes, who hoped to find a utopia in the English countryside. In this sense, this text presents an opposing vision to that of Morton's *In Search of England*; *John Thomas and Lady Jane* is thoroughly subversive from its title to the ending.

In the final version, again, the wood is no longer the Garden of Eden. The wood is violated by the landowners' egotism. When the war breaks out, the trees are chopped down for trench timber by the landowners who are stirred by patriotic fervour. After the war, trees are replanted in the denuded places to revive "the heart of England" (*LCL* 42). The pheasants are reared, and Connie sheds tears as she feels the warmth of the chick's life in her hands; however, these birds are afterwards to be hunted by the landed gentry. The wood is always watched not only by the gamekeeper but also by his inquisitive ex-wife and a postman. The wood is both literally and symbolically violated by the landowner's motor bath chair and intruded by the working-class poachers. Overrun and disgraced both by the upper and lower classes, the wood is no longer a sacred place for regeneration.

Nonetheless, in *Lady Chatterley's Lover*, the fact that the wood is no longer a paradise is obscured by the new ending. The wood scene in the second version is replaced by Mellors' letter to Connie in the final version. The gamekeeper's epistle narrates that he moved to the countryside and at present works happily on a farm. The couple's final plan is no longer to emigrate but to "have some small farm of their own" (298) after his divorce case is settled. Since the turn of the century, when the idea of racial degeneration was widely circulated among the middle classes, country farmers had been idealised as a "healthy" stock of the English race in contrast to the "degenerated" urban inhabitants—an idea that Morton explicitly propounded in *In Search of England*. Thus, the ending of the final version reflects the bourgeois myth that romanticised the English countryside and idealised country farmers as those uncontaminated by the harmful effects of urban areas.[16] Consequently, Connie's shift from Clifford to Mellors, signifying her leaving the industry and the wood for a country farm, agrees with Morton's " 'Back to the Land' cry"; the ending of the final version serves to reassure the middle-class readership and to reinforce the bourgeois myth that circulated in the first decades of the twentieth century.

Thus, on the one hand, *Lady Chatterley's Lover* invalidates the simplistic dichotomies of the countryside and the mining district, industry and nature, and the ruling and lower classes, revealing interdependence and complicity between them. On the other hand, the text adopts widespread images and beliefs of the early twentieth century. Through revisions, the gamekeeper has been declassed and depoliticised; he is eugenically approved and eventually embellished with an idealised image of a country farmer. This is the ambivalence of *Lady Chatterley's Lover*; the text divulges a crude reality of "a tragic age", subverting the stereotypical dualities of the period when the text was produced. However, the text also endorses the bourgeois myth that admires English bucolic life and its inhabitants, which allays middle-class fears of racial degeneration. Therefore, although *Lady Chatterley's Lover* deals with an apparently controversial theme of an antisocial, illicit love affair, portraying a couple who must challenge the rigid conventions of a narrow-minded, oppressive society in order to pursue true love, the text integrates into itself the frame of reference and dominant discourses of the period, thereby making the novel less subversive and more acceptable to the middle-class readership.

Notes

1 Ian Haywood notes that, like the 1950s and 1960s, in the 1930s, "working-class fiction achieves a cult status and popular mystique in British culture" (36).

2 "Roman citizen of the lowest class, person who served the state not with his property but only with his offspring" (*OED*: "proletary", etymology).

3 See Marwick 108–16, 229–50, 297–314, Ayers 99–135, Cole 202–11 and Hynes, *War Imagined* 281. Cole argues that the working-class ex-soldier was regarded "as a potential force for destruction, a man who paradoxically threatens the very society he was trained to protect" (203).

4 See, for instance, Gill 347–64 and Martin, " 'History' and 'Myth' " 63–74. Tony Pinkney also acknowledges this general outline but questions the over-simplified dichotomy between pure realism and pure myth. He argues that the sophisticated earlier versions encompassed varied elements of myths and narrative modes but was transformed in the final version into a somewhat impoverished monologic text. See Pinkney 134–47. Conversely, Charles Ferrall and Dougal McNeill disagree with the consensus, contending that "the revisions of the novel intensify both the 'sex' and the 'politics' " (84). See Ferrall and McNeill 83–103.

5 See Matless 64–67.

6 Examples are numerous. See, for example, Stephen Gill, who argues that the

> novel rests on an opposition of two kinds of life, represented by two contrasted men in opposed settings. Lady Chatterley moves between Clifford entrenched in his property and Mellors deep in his sacred wood. The difficulty of the pattern, though, is quite simply that the literal facts of the setting … take on a symbolic weight because of Lawrence's determination to align every element of his imagined world on one side or the other.
>
> (Gill 358)

Scott Sanders presents five types of the "scheme of oppositions" that structure the novel: nature/culture, forest/Wragby, working class/ruling class, body/mind and silence/language (Sanders 191). Graham Martin also argues that "in *Lady Chatterley's Lover* … we find a substantial extrapolation of the 'life'/'ideas' opposition in terms of social class" ("D. H. Lawrence and Class" 44).

7 Courtney Pina Miller, employing Bakhtin's theory of the carnival, argues that Connie's roleplaying—she serves tea to Mellors—and their exchange of dialect function to upend class-based hierarchies. See Miller 11–21.

8 For example, Sanders argues that "Connie Chatterley retraces Lawrence's drive through the colliery district" (175). Likewise, referring to Lawrence's essay "Return to Bestwood", Martin argues that

> Details like a car-drive through the district are the seed of key passages in the [*Chatterley*] novels. … The climate of incipient industrial unrest, of the miners' class feeling about mine-owner families like the Chatterleys, has its roots in Lawrence's observations.
>
> ("'History' and 'Myth'" 66)

In recent criticism, Ferrall and McNeill argue that

> Lawrence's visit to England during the lockout provoked his interest in class politics, [and] his apocalyptic combination of this despair and radicalism was, at least in part, the consequence of the miners' defeat. It intensified as Lawrence brooded on the hopeless condition of the working class and industrial civilisation. … [T]he defeat of General Strike sharpened and intensified a number of themes … that run through his work.
>
> (85)

9 Samuel Hynes argues that to the middle classes, the working classes "were no longer simple, dependent inferiors to be dealt with in a district-visitor manner; they were a mysterious and frightening new force" (*Edwardian Turn of Mind* 63).

10 Paul Delany asserts that "*Touch and Go* can also be seen as a sequel to *Women in Love* …" (*Nightmare* 381). Likewise, Holderness argues that the play "rewrote" the "central element of the novel [*Women in Love*]" (Holderness 211). However, their evaluations of the play are totally opposite. See Delany, *Nightmare* 381–83 and Holderness 211–14.

11 Moran perceives the war in the background of the play and interprets the last scene as Lawrence's call for a retreat from the excessive violence of war. See Moran 73–74, 120–21.

12 For the function of the chorus in Greek tragedies, see Abrams 51–52.

13 Sylvia Sklar rather unfairly labels him: "a potential turncoat who represents the conventional go-between in the disputes of management and men, yet a human being with sensitive, if spoiled, potential" (Sklar 190).

14 For the debate over eugenics in Canada and its immigration policy from 1890 to 1940, along with the role played by psychiatrists, see Dowbiggin 133–78. For a historical context of British migration to Australia, see Game 102–06.

15 Citing abundant examples in Europe, Frazer argues in his monumental work *The Golden Bough* that

> In the religious history of the Aryan race in Europe the worship of trees has played an important part. …
>
> From an examination of the Teutonic words for "temple" Grimm has made it probable that amongst the Germans the oldest sanctuaries were natural woods. However this may be, tree-worship is well attested for all the great European families of the Aryan stock. Amongst the Celts the oak-worship of the Druids is familiar to every one, and their old word for a sanctuary seems to be identical in origin and meaning with the Latin *nemus*,

> a grove or woodland glade, which still survives in the name of Nemi. Sacred groves were common among the ancient Germans, and tree-worship is hardly extinct amongst their descendants at the present day.
>
> (Frazer 7–9)

Critics have been lured to this image of the "sacred wood" when interpreting *Lady Chatterley's Lover*. For example, Gill argues that "Mellors's wood does become a sacred and sensitive wood in which the lovers can find fulfilment and escape from the encircling world which seems to be as wholly antagonistic as the wood is friendly" (Gill 358). Comparing the wood to the Garden of Eden, Sanders argues that in "Sherwood Forest, last remnant of the virgin world, the lovers recover that state of primal oneness between man, woman and nature which had been dissolved by consciousness, and by mind's chilling instrument—language" (Sanders 201).

16 David Bradshaw also points to a reactionary vision *Lady Chatterley's Lover* offers, focusing on the "scarlet trousers" that Mellors advocates in his letter to Connie. Bradshaw argues for the possibility of John Hargrave's direct or indirect influence on the final version of *Lady Chatterley's Lover*. Hargrave published *The Confession of the Kibbo Kift* in 1927 and Lawrence acquired a copy in January 1928. Bradshaw concludes that

> Addressing their readers from the dissident margins of English cultural life, both books offer a backward-looking vision of a reborn nation, and the programme Mellors puts forward has a great deal in common with that outlined by Hargrave in his stridently revivalist *Confession*. ... Mellors is a Kinsman in all but name and this, more than anything else, helps to explain his thoughts on economic matters and his singular taste in trousers.
>
> ("Red Trousers" 369–70)

Epilogue

Which Class Do Lawrence's Texts Belong To?

Lady Chatterley's Lover was privately published in Florence in July 1928. Next year, before another private publication in Paris in May, Lawrence's autobiographical essay titled "Myself Revealed" appeared in print in February and then a nostalgic article titled "Nottingham and the Mining Countryside" was composed in September. The coal miners in these pieces provide a striking contrast to those portrayed in his last novel. In these essays, Lawrence expresses his empathy with the miners. They are no longer uncanny, weird creatures. On the contrary, they are either an object of pure admiration or that of compassion. Living in a homosocial male space that is the opposite of the modern world of rationality and capitalism, miners are idealised with such words as "vital vibration", "old blood-affinity" and the "dark intimacy" (*LEA* 180, 181, 290). In "Nottingham and the Mining Countryside", for example, Lawrence celebrates the instinctive and intimate harmony of miners with a nostalgic evocation:

> Under the butty system, the miners worked underground as a sort of intimate community, they knew each other practically naked, and with curious close intimacy, and the darkness and the underground remoteness of the pit "stall", and the continual presence of danger, made the physical, instinctive and intuitional contact between men very highly developed, a contact almost as close as touch, very real and very powerful. This physical awareness and intimate *togetherness* was at its strongest down pit.
>
> (*LEA* 289; emphasis in original)

Both women and ruling-class men are expelled from this Lawrentian community. In the late essays, the middle classes are severely condemned, and at the same time women are criticised as the embodiment of the bourgeois possessive instinct. In "Enslaved by Civilisation", composed a few

DOI: 10.4324/9781032675671-10

months after the first private publication of *Lady Chatterley's Lover*, Lawrence argues that women and the middle classes, who control education and capitalism, are accomplices in destroying the warmth, togetherness and vitality of working men in England:

> The last time I was back in the Midlands was during the great coal strike. The men of my age, the men just over forty, were there, standing derelict, pale, silent, with nothing to say, nothing to do, nothing to feel. . . . The men of my generation were broken in: they'll stay on the lines and rust there. For wives, schoolmasters, and employers of labour it is perhaps very nice to have men well broken in. But for a nation, for England, it is a disaster.
>
> (*LEA* 159)

Thus, in the late essays, Lawrence's deep empathy for the miners is captured in a twofold representation: they are both heroes and victims.

It appears that Lawrence counterbalances the negative portrayals of the miners in *Lady Chatterley's Lover* by idealising them in the last essays composed after its publication. What is intriguing here is, however, that Lawrence's rendition of the miners has much in common with the depiction of the miners that followed in the next decade. In keeping with the attitudes of the Victorian philanthropists who preceded them, middle-class authors and filmmakers of the 1930s explored "Unknown England" and began to document the lives of working-class men. In 1934, J. B. Priestley published *English Journey: Being a rambling but truthful account of what one man saw and heard and felt and thought during a journey through England during the autumn of the year 1933*. Traveling from Southampton through Birmingham, Nottingham and Manchester to Newcastle, Priestley visited various districts in economic distress and recorded the lives of people living in a slump. One of the most impressive and shocking chapters to the contemporary readers in this travelogue was "To East Durham and the Tees", in which he portrayed the lives of the miners living in "mean ugliness" (Priestley 327). Priestley's portrayal of the poor and bleak lives of labourers inspired George Orwell, who explored the conditions of a mining town in northern England in *The Road to Wigan Pier* (1937). This is a vivid account of the lives of miners, who, in the lowest class of society, faced unemployment, bad housing and social injustice. Simultaneously, the film industry produced documentaries concerning industrial Britain and its labourers. One of the influential films of this genre is *Coal Face* (1935), produced by John Grierson in collaboration with W. H. Auden and Benjamin Britten. In this 12-minute film, the director Alberto Cavalcanti captured Welsh miners working underground.[1]

These bourgeois documentarians depicted labourers as victims of social injustice inherent in the capitalist system. Stirred by their conscience that their class was the cause of suffering, middle-class writers became ashamed of their life of ease. For example, when mingling with working-class people, Priestley expresses self-disgust: "they made me feel like a fat rich man" (Priestley 333). Instead, he admires their masculine world and argues for their dignity and worth.[2] Likewise, Orwell, who thought that labourers suffered from social injustice although they were his betters, casts an envious gaze towards the male body of working-class men in *The Road to Wigan Pier*:

> It is impossible to watch the "fillers" at work without feeling a pang of envy for their toughness. . . . It is only when you see miners down the mine and naked that you realise what splendid men they are. Most of them are small . . . but nearly all of them have the most noble bodies; wide shoulders tapering to slender supple waists, and small pronounced buttocks and sinewy thighs, with not an ounce of waste flesh anywhere. (Orwell 19–20)[3]

Grierson's films also emphasise the worker's masculinity by a succession of close-ups of males working in dark pits.[4] Thus, in the documentaries of the 1930s, miners were represented as the victims and heroes in an exclusively male world, and the middle-class creators of reportage multiplied romanticised images of labourers. This imagery evokes the depiction of miners in Lawrence's late essays.[5] Admiration for the masculinity of the workers and aversion to the propertied class were not a unique feature of the working-class writer; Lawrence's ardent gaze on the masculine body and male solidarity, as well as his treatment of them as victims of a social system governed by the bourgeoisie, overlap the attitudes of middle-class authors of the succeeding decade.

The age of modernity is characterised by the emergence of mechanical civilisations, the rise and domination of capitalism and divisions between the rulers and the ruled based on social classes, sexes and races. These developments enabled the large-scale exploitation of the oppressed as well as natural resources by those in power. However, from the turn of the century, Britain began experiencing the decline of bourgeois hegemony and the rise of the working classes in tandem with the diminishing sway of the British Empire. Coal mining industry typified this historical shift, as it characterised the use of industrial technology via the capitalist principle to manipulate nature and exploit the oppressed classes, ultimately evolving into a locus of intense conflict. Lawrence grew up in a mining countryside in the Midlands and his texts were written during the period when discords and contradictions were generated and intensified, climaxing into the First World War.

I would like to conclude this book by expressing a rather audacious assertion; I would contend that Lawrence's ambivalent texts encapsulate the discords and contradictions inherent in the age of modernity. Michael Hardt and Antonio Negri argue that modernity did not denote a uniform movement; rather, it was created through continual strife: "Europe and modernity are neither unitary nor pacific constructions, but . . . were characterized by struggle, conflict, and crisis" (*Empire* 70). Hardt and Negri identify the conflict as the clash between two modes: the revolutionary forces represented by the multitude on the plane of immanence and the reactionary forces attempting to reappropriate the power of the multitude, posing order against desire: "*Modernity itself is defined by crisis*, a crisis that is born of the uninterrupted conflict between the immanent, constructive, creative forces and the transcendent power aimed at restoring order. This conflict is the key to the concept of modernity . . ." (*Empire* 76; emphasis in original).

Thus, the textual ambivalence evident in Lawrence's works could be construed to embody the internal struggles of the opposing forces that shaped modernity. Revolutionary and reactionary elements are both intricately entwined in the narrative structure of Lawrence's texts. The subversion of dualism recurrently noted in his texts could denote a form of resistance against the dominant discourse, which, according to Hardt and Negri, seeks to impose control and discipline "through the construction and mediation of dualisms" (*Empire* 140). Lawrence has often been viewed as an author whose philosophy and works are radical and subversive: his texts criticise the ruling classes that deployed people for mass production and destruction and censure the society that negated the singularity of individuals and suppressed their true feelings. Lawrence's texts are certainly subversive and expose deceptions to annihilate such reactionary forces. However, Lawrence's texts are not monologic; they are ambivalent. His texts incorporate reactionary components, including national ideologies, bourgeois principles and the predominant structure of feeling. Thus, competing voices are heard in his ambivalent and multilayered texts. The revolutionary and reactionary elements are intricately intertwined in his characters, plots and settings. Consequently, Lawrence's texts are inscribed with the dynamism of conflicting power struggles. Some of his apparently apolitical texts embed reactionary ruling class ideologies and wartime propaganda. Some texts are intended to serve as scathing critiques of their times but also bear discernible traces of the contemporary rationales and frames of reference that they intend to subvert. Some of Lawrence's works tackle radical and controversial themes but simultaneously endorse dominant discourses, making them less subversive and more acceptable to the ruling classes. Lawrence's texts thus encompass ambivalent, often conflicting, strata and hence become even more intense and profound, enabling prolific potential readings. Rereading Lawrence, then, is an attempt to understand the unresolved conflicts that have formed the age of modernity and, perhaps, an exploration of a prospective altermodernity.

Notes

1 Marsha Bryant argues that like "London's male urban explorers of the late-Victorian period, documentary observers of the 1930s transgressed class lines to establish contact with the working classes" (Bryant 106). See also Colls and Dodd 21–26, in which they analyse the British documentary films in terms of the "national-collectivist myth".

2 For a more detailed analysis of the social and historical context of the publication of Priestley's travelogue, see Baxendale and Pawling 61–70.

3 Orwell's rendition of the coal miners also incorporates myth-making. In his autobiography, a Yorkshire communist activist Ernie Benson severely criticises Orwell for his arbitrary choice of the material and, as a result, for contributing to the distribution of a false image of miners in Wigan:

> One of the local Party members, Jim Grady, told me that when Orwell was gathering material for the book, he asked Jim's brother to take him round the slummiest areas of Wigan and district. . . . [B]ut . . . the slum areas would contain a great number of workers homes whose grimey [sic] exteriors belied the cleanliness to be found inside. This wasn't that kind of house, however, that Orwell wanted to portray. He was interested in picking on the scruffy, lumpen ignorant workers, and whether he intended it or not, projected their image as being typical of Wigan as a whole. How little people with such ideas know about us of the working class.
>
> (Benson 159)

4 Bryant argues that "Documentary's most sustained homoerotic looking at coal miners occurred within the British documentary film movement" (Bryant 116). See also Baxendale and Pawling 17–45.

5 Beatrix Campbell, a writer, playwright and feminist, points out the similarities of the miners portrayed by Lawrence and Orwell. She argues that the miners

> are men's love object. They bring together all the necessary elements of romance. . . . That makes them victim and hero at the same time, which makes them irresistible—they command both protection and admiration. They are represented as beautiful, statuesque, shaded men.
>
> (Campbell 97)

Bibliography

Primary Sources

Asquith, Cynthia. *Diaries: 1915–1918*. Knopf, 1969.

Barclay, Florence Louisa. *My Heart's Right There*. Putnam's, 1914.

Barrie, James Matthew. *Peter and Wendy*. 1911. Hodder and Stoughton, 1913.

Booth, William. *In Darkest England and the Way Out*. International Headquarters of the Salvation Army, 1890.

Bottomley, Horatio. "Now for the Vendetta!" *John Bull*, 15 May 1915, pp. 6–7.

"Canada's Nordic Needs." *Times*, 25 May 1923, p. 11.

Cavalcanti, Alberto. "Coal Face." GPO Film Unit, 1935.

Chambers, Jessie. *D. H. Lawrence: A Personal Record*. Jonathan Cape, 1935.

Chesterton, Gilbert Keith. *A Short History of England*. Chatto & Windus, 1917.

Eliot, Thomas Stearns. *The Complete Poems & Plays of T. S. Eliot*. Faber and Faber, 1969.

Ellis, Havelock. *The Problem of Race-Regeneration*. Cassell, 1911.

———. *The Task of Social Hygiene*. Constable, 1912.

Frazer, James George. *The Golden Bough: A Study in Magic and Religion: Part I the Magic Art and the Evolution of Kings, Vol. II*. 3rd ed., Macmillan, 1911.

Galton, Francis. *Essays in Eugenics*. Eugenics Education Society, 1909.

———. *Hereditary Genius: An Inquiry into Its Laws and Consequences*. Macmillan, 1869.

Gibbon, Edward. *The Decline and Fall of the Roman Empire*. 1776. Edited by Oliphant Smeaton, vol. 1, Dent, 1910.

———. *The Decline and Fall of the Roman Empire*. 1781. Edited by Oliphant Smeaton, vol. 3, Dent, 1910.

Gilpin, William. *Three Essays: On Picturesque Beauty; on Picturesque Travel; and on Sketching Landscape; with a Poem, on Landscape Painting; to These Are Now Added Two Essays*. 1792. 3rd ed., T. Cadell and W. Davies, Strand, 1808.

Grant, Arthur James. *A History of Europe*. Longmans, Green, 1913.

Gray, Herbert Branston. *The Public Schools and the Empire*. Williams & Norgate, 1913.

Green, John Richard. *A Short History of the English People*. 1874. Macmillan, 1889.

Groß, Hans. "Degeneration und Deportation." *Politisch-Anthropologische Revue*, vol. 4, 1905/06, pp. 281–86.

Haggard, Henry Rider. *Rural England: Being an Account of Agricultural and Social Researches Carried out in the Years 1901 and 1902*. Longmans, Green, 1902.
Hansard's Parliamentary Debates, vol. 178, 1865.
Hargrave, John. *The Great War Brings It Home: The Natural Reconstruction of an Unnatural Existence*. Constable, 1919.
Hay, Ian. *The First Hundred Thousand: Being the Unofficial Chronicle of a Unit of "K(I)"*. William Blackwood, 1915.
Hobhouse, Leonard Trelawny. *Democracy and Reaction*. T. Fisher Unwin, 1904.
———. "Government by the People." *Liberalism and Other Writings*. Edited by James Meadowcroft, Cambridge UP, 1994, pp. 123–35.
Hudson, William Henry. *Nature in Downland*. Longmans, Green, 1900.
Huxley, Thomas Henry. *Evolution and Ethics and Other Essays*. Macmillan, 1895.
"Immigration and the Unfit." *Times*, 26 May 1923, p. 11.
Jefferies, Richard. *The Open Air*. 1885. Chatto & Windus, 1909.
Jones, Paul. *War Letters of a Public-School Boy*. Cassell, 1918.
Keynes, John Maynard. *The Economic Consequences of the Peace*. Macmillan, 1920.
Kipling, Rudyard and Charles Robert Leslie Fletcher. *A School History of England*. Clarendon, 1911.
Kitchin, George William. *A History of France: Down to the Year 1453*. Clarendon, 1873.
Lawrence, David Herbert. *England, My England and Other Stories*. Edited by Bruce Steele, Cambridge UP, 1990.
———. *The First and Second Lady Chatterley Novels*. Edited by Dieter Mehl and Christa Jansohn, Cambridge UP, 1999.
———. "The Fox." *A D. H. Lawrence Miscellany*. Edited by Harry T. Moore, Southern Illinois UP, 1959, pp. 28–48.
———. "The Germans, Goths, and Vandals." c. 1918, Manuscripts and Special Collections, University of Nottingham, Nottingham. Manuscript La L 19.
———. *Lady Chatterley's Lover and A Propos of "Lady Chatterley's Lover"*. Edited by Michael Squires, Cambridge UP, 1993.
———. *Late Essays and Articles*. Edited by James T. Boulton, Cambridge UP, 2004.
———. *The Letters of D. H. Lawrence*. Edited by James T. Boulton, vol. 1, Cambridge UP, 1979.
———. *The Letters of D. H. Lawrence*. Edited by George J. Zytaruk and James T. Boulton, vol. 2, Cambridge UP, 1981.
———. *The Letters of D. H. Lawrence*. Edited by James T. Boulton and Andrew Robertson, vol. 3, Cambridge UP, 1984.
———. *Movements in European History*. Edited by Philip Crumpton, Cambridge UP, 1989.
———. *Paul Morel*. Edited by Helen Baron, Cambridge UP, 2003.
———. *The Plays*. Edited by Hans-Wilhelm Schwarze and John Worthen, Cambridge UP, 1999.
———. *The Poems*. Edited by Christopher Pollnitz, Cambridge UP, 2013–18.
———. *The Prussian Officer and Other Stories*. Edited by John Worthen, Cambridge UP, 1983.
———. *The Rainbow*. Edited by Mark Kinkead-Weekes, Cambridge UP, 1989.

———. *Reflections on the Death of a Porcupine and Other Essays*. Edited by Michael Herbert, Cambridge UP, 1988.
———. *Sons and Lovers*. Edited by Helen Baron and Carl Baron, Cambridge UP, 1992.
———. *Studies in Classic American Literature*. Edited by Ezra Greenspan, Lindeth Vasey and John Worthen, Cambridge UP, 2003.
———. *Study of Thomas Hardy and Other Essays*. Edited by Bruce Steele, Cambridge UP, 1985.
———. *The Vicar's Garden and Other Stories*. Edited by Neil H. Reeve, Cambridge UP, 2009.
———. *The White Peacock*. Edited by Andrew Robertson, Cambridge UP, 1983.
———. *Women in Love*. Edited by David Farmer, Lindeth Vasey and John Worthen, Cambridge UP, 1987.
Lloyd George, David. "The Land and the People. Limehouse, July 30, 1909." *Life of David Lloyd George*. Edited by Herbert Du Parcq, vol. IV: Speeches, Caxton, 1912, pp. 678–85.
Machen, Arthur. *War and the Christian Faith*. Skeffington, 1918.
Mais, Stuart Petre Brodie. "The Public Schools in War-Time." *Fortnightly Review*, vol. 98, 1915, pp. 142–52.
"Manifesto on Public Morals by the National Council of Public Morals." *Times*, 31 May 1911, p. 5.
"The March of the Huns." *Times*, 29 Aug. 1914, p. 9.
Masterman, Charles Frederick Gurney. *The Condition of England*. Methuen, 1909.
———. *From the Abyss: Of Its Inhabitants by One of Them*. R. B. Johnson, 1902.
———. *The Heart of the Empire: Discussions of Problems of Modern City Life in England, with an Essay on Imperialism*. 1901. 2nd ed., T. Fisher Unwin, 1907.
Moore, George. *Esther Waters*. Edited by David Skilton, Oxford UP, 1999.
Morgan, John Hartman. *German Atrocities: An Official Investigation*. 2nd ed., T. Fisher Unwin, 1916.
Morrell, Ottoline. *Ottoline: The Early Memoirs of Lady Ottoline Morrell*. Edited by Robert Gathorne-Hardy, Faber and Faber, 1963.
Morton, Henry Vollam. *In Search of England*. Methuen, 1927.
Murry, John Middleton. "The True Internationalism." *The Athenaeum: A Journal of Literature, Science and the Arts*, no. 4716, 17 Sept. 1920, p. 365.
Nordau, Max. *Degeneration*. D. Appleton, 1895.
Orwell, George. *The Road to Wigan Pier*. Edited by Peter Davison, Secker, 1986.
Pound, Ezra. "Provincialism the Enemy." *Selected Prose 1909–1965*. Edited by William Cookson, New Directions, 1973, pp. 189–203.
Priestley, John Boynton. *English Journey: Being a Rambling but Truthful Account of What One Man Saw and Heard and Felt and Thought during a Journey through England during the Autumn of the Year 1933*. Heinemann, 1934.
Prior, James. *Forest Folk*. T. Nelson & Sons, 1907.
Report of the Committee on Alleged German Outrages Appointed by His Britannic Majesty's Government and Presided over by the Right Hon. Viscount Bryce. HMSO, 1915.
"The Retreat of the New Attila." *Times*, 14 Sept. 1914, p. 9.

Ruck, Berta. *Khaki and Kisses*. Hutchinson, 1915.
Ruskin, John. *The Works of John Ruskin*. Edited by Edward T. Cook and Alexander Wedderburn, vol. 18, Allen, 1905.
Schopenhauer, Arthur. *Essays of Schopenhauer*. Translated by Mrs. Rudolf Dircks, Walter Scott, 1897.
Schreiner, Olive. *Woman and Labour*. T. Fisher Unwin, 1911.
Spencer, Herbert. *The Man Versus the State*. Williams & Norgate, 1902.
———. "The Social Organism." *Essays: Scientific, Political, & Speculative*. Vol. I, Williams and Norgate, 1891, pp. 265–307.
Sullivan, Edmund Joseph. *The Kaiser's Garland*. Heinemann, 1915.
"The Two Germanies." *Punch, or the London Charivari*, vol. 147, no. 3818, 1914, p. 213.
Webb, W. H. "History, Patriotism, and the Child: A Plea for the Fuller Teaching of British History in Elementary Schools." *History*, vol. 2, no. 1, 1913, pp. 53–54.
Wells, Herbert George. *Experiment in Autobiography: Discoveries and Conclusions of a Very Ordinary Brain (since 1866)*. 1934. Faber and Faber, 1984.
———. *The New Machiavelli*. Edited by Simon J. James, Penguin, 2005.
———. *The Outline of History: Being a Plain History of Life and Mankind*. George Newnes, 1920.
———. *The Time Machine: An Invention: A Critical Text of the 1895 London First Edition, with an Introduction and Appendices*. Edited by Leon Stover, McFarland, 1996.
———.*Tono-Bungay*. Edited by Patrick Parrinder, Penguin, 2005.
Woolf, Virginia. *Mrs. Dalloway*. Edited by Anne E. Fernald, Cambridge UP, 2015.

Secondary Sources

Abrams, Meyer Howard and Geoffrey Galt Harpham. *A Glossary of Literary Terms*. 11th ed., Cengage Learning, 2015.
Adburgham, Alison. *Liberty's: A Biography of a Shop*. Allen & Unwin, 1975.
Alldritt, Keith. *The Visual Imagination of D. H. Lawrence*. Edward Arnold, 1971.
Althusser, Louis. "Ideology and Ideological State Apparatuses." *Lenin and Philosophy*. translated by Ben Brewster, Monthly Review Press, 1971, pp. 127–86.
Arai, Hidenaga. *Literature Along the Lines of Flight: D. H. Lawrence's Later Novels and Critical Theory*. Rodopi, 2014.
Ayers, David. *English Literature of the 1920s*. Edinburgh UP, 1999.
Baron, Helen. "Lawrence's *Sons and Lovers* Versus Garnett's." *Essays in Criticism*, vol. 42, no. 4, 1992, pp. 265–78.
Baxendale, John and Christopher Pawling. *Narrating the Thirties: A Decade in the Making: 1930 to the Present*. Macmillan, 1996.
Bayley, John. *The Short Story: Henry James to Elizabeth Bowen*. Harvester, 1988.
Bell, Michael. *D. H. Lawrence: Language and Being*. Cambridge UP, 1992.
Bennett, Nick. "Apocalyptic Ambiguities: D. H. Lawrence, Mythology, and the Meaning of the Great War." *D. H. Lawrence Review*, vol. 42, no. 1–2, 2017, pp. 6–28.

Benson, Ernie. *To Struggle Is to Live: A Working Class Autobiography*. Vol. 2: Starve or Rebel, People's Publications, 1980.
Bermingham, Ann. *Landscape and Ideology: The English Rustic Tradition 1740–1860*. U of California P, 1986.
Bishop, Paul. "Schopenhauer's Impact on European Literature." *A Companion to Schopenhauer*. Edited by Bart Vandenabeele, Blackwell, 2012, pp. 333–48.
Black, Michael. *D. H. Lawrence: Sons and Lovers*. Cambridge UP, 1992.
Booth, Howard John. "*The Rainbow*, British Marxist Criticism of the 1930s and Colonialism." *New D. H. Lawrence*. Edited by Howard J. Booth, Manchester UP, 2009, pp. 34–58.
Boulton, James Thompson. "D. H. Lawrence's *Odour of Chrysanthemums*: An Early Version." *Renaissance and Modern Studies*, vol. 13, 1969, pp. 4–48.
Bouttier, Sarah. "War and Continuity in D. H. Lawrence's Works." *Études Lawrenciennes*, vol. 46, 2015. https://doi.org/10.4000/lawrence.231.
Bowler, Peter John. *Evolution: The History of an Idea*. U of California P, 1989.
Bradshaw, David. "Introduction." *Women in Love*, by D. H. Lawrence, edited by David Bradshaw, Oxford UP, 1998, pp. vii–xxxviii.
———. "Red Trousers: *Lady Chatterley's Lover* and John Hargrave." *Essays in Criticism*, vol. 55, no. 4, 2005, pp. 352–73.
Breen, Judith Punchner. "D. H. Lawrence, World War I and the Battle between the Sexes: A Reading of 'The Blind Man' and 'Tickets, Please'." *Women's Studies*, vol. 13, 1986, pp. 63–74.
Brooker, Peter and Peter Widdowson. "A Literature for England." *Englishness: Politics and Culture 1880–1920*. Edited by Robert Colls and Philip Dodd, 2nd ed., Bloomsbury, 2014, pp. 141–87.
Brunsdale, Mitzi M. "The Effect of Mrs. Rudolf Dircks' Translation of Schopenhauer's 'The Metaphysics of Love' on D. H. Lawrence's Early Fiction." *Rocky Mountain Review of Language and Literature*, vol. 32, no. 2, Spring 1978, pp. 120–29.
Bryant, Marsha. "W. H. Auden and the Homoerotics of the 1930s Documentary." *Caverns of Night: Coal Mines in Art, Literature, and Film*. Edited by William B. Thesing, U of South Carolina P, 2000, pp. 104–25.
Bullen, J. Barrie. "D. H. Lawrence and Sculpture in 'Women in Love'." *The Burlington Magazine*, vol. 145, no. 1209, 2003, pp. 841–46.
Cain, Peter J. *Hobson and Imperialism: Radicalism, New Liberalism, and Finance 1887–1938*. Oxford UP, 2002.
Campbell, Beatrix. *Wigan Pier Revisited: Poverty and Politics in the 80s*. Virago, 1984.
Ceadel, Martin. *Pacifism in Britain 1914–1945: The Defining of a Faith*. Clarendon, 1980.
Clark, L. D. *The Minoan Distance: The Symbolism of Travel in D. H. Lawrence*. U of Arizona P, 1980.
Clausson, Nils. "Practicing Deconstruction, Again: Blindness, Insight and the Lovely Treachery of Words in D. H. Lawrence's 'The Blind Man'." *College Literature*, vol. 34, no. 1, 2007, pp. 106–28.

Cole, Sarah. *Modernism, Male Friendship, and the First World War*. Cambridge UP, 2003.

Collini, Stefan. *Liberalism and Sociology: L. T. Hobhouse and Political Argument in England 1880–1914*. Cambridge UP, 1979.

Colls, Robert and Philip Dodd. "Representing the Nation: British Documentary Film, 1930–45." *Screen*, vol. 26, no. 1, 1985, pp. 21–33.

Crumpton, Paul I. "D. H. Lawrence and the Sources of *Movements in European History*." *Renaissance and Modern Studies*, vol. 29, 1985, pp. 50–65.

Daleski, Hillel Matthew. *The Forked Flame: A Study of D. H. Lawrence*. 1965. U of Wisconsin P, 1987.

Das, Santanu. *Touch and Intimacy in First World War Literature*. Cambridge UP, 2006.

Delany, Paul. *D. H. Lawrence's Nightmare: The Writer and His Circle in the Years of the Great War*. Harvester Press, 1979.

———. "Who Was 'The Blind Man'?" *English Studies in Canada*, vol. 9, no. 1, 1983, pp. 92–99.

Dowbiggin, Ian Robert. *Keeping America Sane: Psychiatry and Eugenics in the United States and Canada, 1880–1940*. Cornell UP, 1997.

Eagleton, Terry. *Exiles and Émigrés: Studies in Modern Literature*. Chatto & Windus, 1970.

Ebbatson, Roger. *Lawrence and the Nature Tradition: A Theme in English Fiction 1859–1914*. Harvester, 1980.

Ehlert, Anne Odenbring. *"There's a bad time coming": Ecological Vision in the Fiction of D. H. Lawrence*. Uppsala University, 2001.

Endo, Fuhito. "Singular Universality: D. H. Lawrence and Marxism." *D. H. Lawrence Studies*, vol. 20, no. 1, 2016, pp. 93–109.

Fawcett, Edmund. *Liberalism: The Life of an Idea*. Princeton UP, 2014.

Fernihough, Anne. *D. H. Lawrence: Aesthetics and Ideology*. Clarendon Press, 1993.

Ferrall, Charles and Dougal McNeill. *Writing the 1926 General Strike: Literature, Culture, Politics*. Cambridge UP, 2015.

Freeden, Michael. *The New Liberalism: An Ideology of Social Reform*. Oxford UP, 1978.

Game, David. *D. H. Lawrence's Australia: Anxiety at the Edge of Empire*. Routledge, 2015.

Gilbert, Sandra M. and Susan Gubar. *No Man's Land: The Place of the Woman Writer in the Twentieth Century*. Vol. 2: Sexchanges, Yale UP, 1989.

Gill, Stephen. "The Composite World: Two Versions of Lady Chatterley's Lover." *Essays in Criticism*, vol. 21, no. 4, 1971, pp. 347–64.

Gorman, Daniel. "Liberal Internationalism, the League of Nations Union, and the Mandates System." *Canadian Journal of History*, vol. 40, no. 3, 2005, pp. 449–77.

Granofsky, Ronald. *D. H. Lawrence and Survival: Darwinism in the Fiction of the Transitional Period*. McGill-Queen's UP, 2003.

Green, Eleanor H. "Lawrence, Schopenhauer, and the Dual Nature of the Universe." *South Atlantic Bulletin*, vol. 42, no. 4, Nov. 1977, pp. 84–92.

Greenslade, William. *Degeneration, Culture and the Novel 1880–1940*. Cambridge UP, 1994.

Hardt, Michael and Antonio Negri. *Empire*. Harvard UP, 2000.

———. *Multitude: War and Democracy in the Age of Empire*. Penguin, 2005.

Harris, Janice Hubbard. *The Short Fiction of D. H. Lawrence*. Rutgers UP, 1984.

Harrison, Andrew. *D. H. Lawrence and Italian Futurism: A Study of Influence*. Rodopi, 2003.

———. "'Men No More Than the Subjective Material of the Machine': Lawrence, Machinery, and War-Time Psychology." *D. H. Lawrence, Technology, and Modernity*. Edited by Indrek Männiste, Bloomsbury Academic, 2019, pp. 73–84.

Haywood, Ian. *Working-Class Fiction: From Chartism to Trainspotting*. Northcote House, 1997.

Holderness, Graham. *D. H. Lawrence: History, Ideology, and Fiction*. Gill and Macmillan, 1982.

Hollington, Michael. "Boundaries, Frontiers, and Cross-Pollination in *Movements in European History*." *"Terra Incognita": D. H. Lawrence at the Frontiers*. Edited by Virginia Hyde and Earl G. Ingersoll, Fairleigh Dickinson UP, 2010, pp. 26–36.

Hough, Graham. *The Dark Sun: A Study of D. H. Lawrence*. Duckworth, 1956.

Howkins, Alun. "The Discovery of Rural England." *Englishness: Politics and Culture 1880–1920*. Edited by Robert Colls and Philip Dodd, 2nd ed., Bloomsbury, 2014, pp. 85–111.

Hughes, Meirion and Robert Stradling. *The English Musical Renaissance 1840–1940: Constructing a National Music*. 2nd ed., Manchester UP, 2001.

Humphries, Andrew F. *D. H. Lawrence, Transport and Cultural Transition: 'A Great Sense of Journeying'*. Palgrave Macmillan, 2017.

Hynes, Samuel. *The Edwardian Turn of Mind*. Princeton UP, 1968.

———. *A War Imagined: The First World War and English Culture*. Atheneum, 1991.

Jones, Greta. *Social Hygiene in Twentieth Century Britain*. Croom Helm, 1986.

Keating, Peter. *Kipling the Poet*. Secker & Warburg, 1994.

Kennedy, Paul Michael. *The Rise of the Anglo-German Antagonism 1860–1914*. G. Allen, 1980.

Kevles, Daniel J. *In the Name of Eugenics: Genetics and the Uses of Human Heredity*. Harvard UP, 1995.

Kinkead-Weekes, Mark. *D. H. Lawrence: Triumph to Exile 1912–1922*. Cambridge UP, 1996.

Knapp, James F. *Literary Modernism and the Transformation of Work*. Northwestern UP, 1988.

Krockel, Carl. *D. H. Lawrence and Germany: The Politics of Influence*. Rodopi, 2007.

———. *War Trauma and English Modernism: T. S. Eliot and D. H. Lawrence*. Palgrave Macmillan, 2011.

Kushigian, Nancy. *Pictures and Fictions: Visual Modernism and the Pre-War Novels of D. H. Lawrence*. Peter Lang, 1990.

Kuttner, Alfred Booth. " 'Sons and Lovers': A Freudian Appreciation." *The Psychoanalytic Review*, vol. 3, no. 3, 1916, pp. 295–317.
Leavis, Frank Raymond. *D. H. Lawrence: Novelist*. Chatto & Windus, 1955.
Ledger, Sally. "In Darkest England: The Terror of Degeneration in *Fin-De-Siècle* Britain." *Literature and History*, vol. 4, no. 2, 1995, pp. 71–86.
Littlewood, J. C. F. "Son and Lover." *The Cambridge Quarterly*, vol. 4, no. 4, 1969–70, pp. 323–61.
MacDougall, Hugh A. *Racial Myth in English History: Trojans, Teutons, and Anglo-Saxons*. Harvest House, 1982.
Martin, Graham. "D. H. Lawrence and Class." *D. H. Lawrence*. Edited by Peter Widdowson, Longman, 1992, pp. 35–48.
———. " 'History' and 'Myth' in D. H. Lawrence's Chatterley Novels." *The British Working-Class Novel in the Twentieth Century*. Edited by Jeremy Hawthorn, Edward Arnold, 1984, pp. 63–74.
Martz, Louis Lohr. "Portrait of Miriam." *Imagined Worlds: Essays on Some English Novels and Novelists in Honour of John Butt*. Edited by Maynard Mack and Ian Gregor, Methuen, 1968, pp. 343–69.
Marwick, Arthur. *The Deluge: British Society and the First World War*. 2nd ed., Palgrave, 2006.
Matless, David. *Landscape and Englishness*. Reaktion, 1998.
Maunder, Andrew. "Introduction." *British Literature of World War I*. Edited by Andrew Maunder, vol. 1, Pickering, 2011, pp. xxxiii–lxiii.
McAleer, Joseph. *Popular Reading and Publishing in Britain 1914–1950*. Clarendon, 1992.
Meyers, Jeffrey. *Painting and the Novel*. Manchester UP, 1975.
Michelucci, Stefania. *Space and Place in the Works of D. H. Lawrence*. Translated by Jill Franks, McFarland, 2002.
Miller, Courtney Pina. "Erotic Class Masquerade: Sex and Working-Class Dialect in D. H. Lawrence's *Lady Chatterley's Lover*." *Open Library of Humanities*, vol. 6, no. 1, 2020, pp. 1–26.
Mitchell, Brian R. *British Historical Statistics*. Cambridge UP, 1988.
Moorman, Mary. *George Macaulay Trevelyan*. Hamish Hamilton, 1980.
Moran, James. *The Theatre of D. H. Lawrence: Dramatic Modernist and Theatrical Innovator*. Bloomsbury, 2015.
Mosse, George Lachmann. "Introduction." *Degeneration*, by Max Nordau, U of Nebraska P, 1993, pp. xiii–xxxvi.
Moynahan, Julian. *The Deed of Life: The Novels and Tales of D. H. Lawrence*. Princeton UP, 1963.
Nehls, Edward, editor. *D. H. Lawrence: A Composite Biography*, vol. 1. U of Wisconsin P, 1957.
"New Novel: 'The Rainbow'." *The Westminster Gazette*, 9 Oct. 1915, p. 3.
O'Malley, Seamus. " 'The final aim is the flower': Wild and Domestic Nature in *Sons and Lovers*." *D. H. Lawrence Review*, vol. 39, no. 2, 2014, pp. 25–45.
Ouditt, Sharon. *Fighting Forces, Writing Women: Identity and Ideology in the First World War*. Routledge, 1994.

Pick, Daniel. *Faces of Degeneration: A European Disorder, c. 1848–c. 1918*. Cambridge UP, 1989.

Pinkney, Tony. *D. H. Lawrence and Modernism*. U of Iowa P, 1990.

Potter, Jane. *Boys in Khaki, Girls in Print: Women's Literary Responses to the Great War 1914–1918*. Oxford UP, 2005.

Potter, Rachel. *Modernism and Democracy: Literary Culture 1900–1930*. Oxford UP, 2006.

Richardson, Angelique. "The Life Sciences: 'Everybody Nowadays Talks About Evolution'." *A Concise Companion to Modernism*. Edited by David Bradshaw, Blackwell, 2003, pp. 6–33.

Rieber, Marie-Therese. *Liberty: The History*. Welbeck, 2021.

Robbins, Keith. *History, Religion and Identity in Modern Britain*. Hambledon, 1993.

Ross, J. J. "An English History: Kipling's Joint Authorship, with C. R. L. Fletcher, of *A School History of England* (1911)." *Kipling Journal*, vol. 60, no. 240, Dec. 1986, pp. 31–42.

Ross, Michael L. "The Mythology of Friendship: D. H. Lawrence, Bertrand Russell, and 'The Blind Man'." *English Literature and British Philosophy: A Collection of Essays*. Edited by S. P. Rosenbaum, U of Chicago P, 1971, pp. 285–315.

Ruderman, Judith. *D. H. Lawrence and the Devouring Mother: The Search for a Patriarchal Ideal of Leadership*. Duke UP, 1984.

Ryan, Kiernan. "The Revenge of the Women: Lawrence's 'Tickets Please'." *Literature and History*, vol. 7, no. 2, 1981, pp. 210–22.

Rylance, Rick. "Ideas, Histories, Generations and Beliefs: The Early Novels to *Sons and Lovers*." *The Cambridge Companion to D. H. Lawrence*. Edited by Anne Fernihough, Cambridge UP, 2001, pp. 15–31.

Sanders, Scott. *D. H. Lawrence: The World of the Five Major Novels*. Viking, 1974.

Schneider, Daniel J. *D. H. Lawrence: The Artist as Psychologist*. UP of Kansas, 1984.

Schorer, Mark. "Technique as Discovery." *The Hudson Review*, vol. 1, no. 1, 1948, pp. 67–78.

Scott, James F. "'Continental': The Germanic Dimension of *Women in Love*." *Literatur in Wissenschaft und Unterricht*, vol. 12, 1979, pp. 117–34.

Searle, Geoffrey Russell. *A New England? Peace and War 1886–1918*. Clarendon, 2004.

Sklar, Sylvia. *The Plays of D. H. Lawrence: A Biographical and Critical Study*. Vision, 1975.

Smith, Andrew. "Vampirism, Masculinity and Degeneracy: D. H. Lawrence's Modernist Gothic." *Gothic Modernisms*. Edited by Andrew Smith and Jeff Wallace, Palgrave, 2001, pp. 150–66.

Soloway, Richard A. *Demography and Degeneration: Eugenics and the Declining Birthrate in Twentieth-Century Britain*. U of North Carolina P, 1990.

Southam, Brian Charles. *A Student's Guide to the Selected Poems of T. S. Eliot*. 6th ed., Faber and Faber, 1994.

Sproles, Karen Z. "D. H. Lawrence and the Pre-Raphaelites: Love among the Ruins." *D. H. Lawrence Review*, vol. 22, no. 3, 1990, pp. 299–305.

Squires, Michael. *The Pastoral Novel: Studies in George Eliot, Thomas Hardy, and D. H. Lawrence*. UP of Virginia, 1974.

Steven, Laurence. "From Thimble to Ladybird: D. H. Lawrence's Widening Vision?" *D. H. Lawrence Review*, vol. 18, no. 2–3, 1985–86, pp. 239–53.

Stevens, Hugh. "*Women in Love*, Psychoanalysis and War." *New D. H. Lawrence*. Edited by Howard J. Booth, Manchester UP, 2009, pp. 80–97.

Stewart, Jack. "Landscape Painting and Pre-Raphaelitism in *The White Peacock*." *D. H. Lawrence Review*, vol. 27, no. 1, 1997 and 1998, pp. 3–25.

———. *The Vital Art of D. H. Lawrence: Vision and Expression*. Southern Illinois UP, 1999.

Storch, Margaret. "Images of Women in *Sons and Lovers*." *D. H. Lawrence's Sons and Lovers: A Casebook*. Edited by John Worthen and Andrew Harrison, Oxford UP, 2005, pp. 139–53.

Storey, Neil R. and Molly Housego. *Women in the First World War*. Shire, 2010.

Sutcliffe, Peter. *The Oxford University Press: An Informal History*. Clarendon, 1978.

Sypher, Wylie. *Rococo to Cubism in Art and Literature*. Random House, 1960.

Tate, Trudi. *Modernism, History and the First World War*. 2nd ed., Humanities-Ebooks, 2013.

Tomalin, Ruth. *W. H. Hudson: A Biography*. Faber and Faber, 1982.

Trilling, Lionel. "*Tickets, Please*: D. H. Lawrence 1885–1930." *Prefaces to the Experience of Literature*. Oxford UP, 1981, pp. 123–27.

Trotter, David. *The English Novel in History 1895–1920*. Routledge, 1993.

Valverde, Mariana. "'Slavery from Within': The Invention of Alcoholism and the Question of Free Will." *Social History*, vol. 22, no. 3, 1997, pp. 251–68.

Villanueva, Maria Casado. "A Reluctant Awakening: Transgression and the Sleeping Beauty Motif in D. H. Lawrence's 'The Thimble'." *Journal of the Short Story in English*, vol. 68, Spring 2017, pp. 52–64.

Waites, Bernard. *A Class Society at War: England 1914–18*. Berg, 1987.

Wallace, Jeff. *D. H. Lawrence, Science and the Posthuman*. Palgrave Macmillan, 2005.

———. "Science and Technology." *D. H. Lawrence in Context*. Edited by Andrew Harrison, Cambridge UP, 2018, pp. 232–41.

Watts, Jarica. " 'Show Yourself a Man': Ritualistic Sacrifice and the Crisis of Masculinity in D. H. Lawrence's 'Tickets Please'." *D. H. Lawrence Review*, vol. 44, no. 1, 2019, pp. 64–84.

Weiss, Daniel A. *Oedipus in Nottingham: D. H. Lawrence*. U of Washington P, 1962.

Wheeler, Richard P. " 'Cunning in his overthrow': Give and Take in 'Tickets, Please'." *D. H. Lawrence Review*, vol. 10, no. 3, 1977, pp. 242–50.

Widmer, Kingsley. *The Art of Perversity: D. H. Lawrence's Shorter Fictions*. U of Washington P, 1962.

Williams, Linda Ruth. *Sex in the Head: Visions of Femininity and Film in D. H. Lawrence*. Harvester, 1993.

Williams, Raymond. *The Country and the City*. Oxford UP, 1973.

Winter, Jan Murray. *The Great War and the British People*. Macmillan, 2003.

———. *World War I: The Experience*. Angus, 2006.

Worthen, John. *D. H. Lawrence: The Early Years 1885–1912*. Cambridge UP, 1991.

———. "Introduction." *The White Peacock*, by D. H. Lawrence, edited by Alan Newton, Penguin, 1987, pp. 11–33.

Zapf, Hurbert. "Taylorism in D. H. Lawrence's *Women in Love*." *The D. H. Lawrence Review*, vol. 15, no. 1–2, 1982, pp. 129–39.

Zoll, Allan R. "Vitalism and the Metaphysics of Love: D. H. Lawrence and Schopenhauer." *D. H. Lawrence Review*, vol. 11, no. 1, 1978, pp. 1–20.

Index

Note: Page numbers in *italics* indicate illustrations. Endnotes are indicated by the page number followed by "n" and the note number e.g., 193n12 refers to note 12 on page 193.